FIGHTERS
OVER THE
FALKLANDS

FIGHTERS
OVER THE
FALKLANDS

DEFENDING THE ISLANDERS' WAY OF LIFE

DAVID GLEDHILL

FONTHILL

Fonthill Media Limited
Fonthill Media LLC
www.fonthillmedia.com
office@fonthillmedia.com

First published in the United Kingdom 2013

British Library Cataloguing in Publication Data:
A catalogue record for this book is available from the British Library

ISBN 978-1-78155-222-3

Typeset in 10.5pt on 13pt Sabon.
Printed and bound in England

Contents

Foreword

By Air Commodore Ian R. W. Stewart, CBE BSc, FRAeS, RAF

Fast Jet aircraft have been policing the skies over the Falkland Islands since May 1982 and hundreds of aircrews have journeyed to the South Atlantic to protect the integrity of the Islands. Despised this prolonged campaign by the Royal Air Force, contemporary accounts by fast jet aircrew operating so far from home are rare. I am delighted that Dave Gledhill has decided to put together this detailed account of life in the Falkland Islands from an aircrew perspective. This book will bring back memories for those who were lucky enough to fly from Port Stanley or Mount Pleasant, but for others it will give an insight to a world that has been hidden from public view for too long.

Dave and I served together on the Tornado F3 Operational Conversion Unit at Royal Air Force Coningsby in the mid-1990s and having heard his accounts many times, it gave me great pleasure to read his book. Dave was a gifted navigator who has portrayed an aspect of his work in his fascinating account. It is hard to imagine the extraordinary life that aircrew lead in the Falkland Islands, many thousands of miles from home, but Dave has managed to capture his unique experiences, allowing others to read about and enjoy the wild world of the fighter aircrew.

Deploying fast jet aircraft to the other side of the world and then operating them continuously for decades is a mammoth achievement and the Royal Air Force can be rightly proud of the women and men who have supported and operated these aircraft in the South Atlantic. The sense of adventure and achievement is always heightened on operations and Dave has captured the enormity of this protracted but very necessary military activity. Nobody can guess what might have happened had we not built up a protection force on the Falkland Islands, history does not reveal its alternatives, but we do know that the past few decades have been largely peaceful.

Dave Gledhill is a member of a prestigious group of aviators who made their name as navigators following a long tradition that dates back to the origins of flight. Being lost in an aircraft is an uncomfortable feeling and hence navigation is an essential skill. Nevertheless, the term navigator hides a multitude of activities carried out by aircrew who undertook their profession in the back seats of the Royal Air Force's fast jet aircraft. Dave commanded 1435 Flight in the Falkland Islands and he now takes us on an exciting journey to the South Atlantic. Dave is an accomplished aviation author who also uses his skills to raise awareness and money for some important charities. If you enjoy his book, you will also be rewarded by knowing you have supported his worthy causes.

I commend the charity supported by this book. Military service and charity often go hand in hand and so I wholeheartedly encourage people to buy this book to further the work of 'Hounds For Heroes' who provide assistance dogs for injured service personnel.

Author's Note

As I looked at adding my own contribution to the Falklands story I avoided recounting the war in detail, although I felt a short summary was vital to set my own experiences in context. Being an aviator, I have tended to dwell on the air aspects of the joint operation which is not to belittle the contribution from the other Services but reflects my own part of the subsequent operations. Commentators and analysts will say it was a naval operation. Single service experts will draw out their own service's contribution and try to justify individual budgets. The reality is that it was, arguably, the first truly joint operation since the Second World War. The contributions from each Service including the Royal Marines and the Special Forces were absolutely vital to the outcome.

During the conflict, in the air, the Sea Harrier pilots from both the Fleet Air Arm and the Royal Air Force were magnificent. They operated their aircraft in the most arduous conditions and acquitted themselves with distinction. The crews of the RAF Harriers, the Vulcans, the transport aircraft and the maritime patrol aircraft were also tested to the limits and passed. At sea, ships companies adapted to the sudden crisis with skill and courage, with sometimes limited equipment optimised for a Cold War fight. On shore, the soldiers engaged in hand to hand combat with battles as fierce as those fought by their predecessors during Second World War. Although many of their enemies were conscripts, they also fought skilled professionals on the Argentinian side who fought equally bravely. I should also mention the engineers and logisticians who kept a critical flow of essential items moving to the front line where it was essential to maintain the momentum of operations. Finally, I must mention the doctors and the medics who, literally, saved lives under fire. Inevitably I have missed others who contributed just as much and for that I apologise.

A Falklands detachment was one of those strange tours for RAF personnel. Most of us were dispatched 'kicking and screaming' to this outpost of the United Kingdom. We left behind loved ones and spent months on a remote base in the middle of nowhere. Once there, however, the nature of the operation and the diversity of the local scenery and wildlife was intoxicating. The locals are simply inspiring and I will never forget the words of a grandma from Goose Green who retold her story of being locked away in the village church while Argentinian soldiers used her home as a temporary barracks. If her account of the fate of the Argentinian officer when the village was liberated is true – and I'm convinced it was – I would also have been cowed if set about by this proud old lady wielding her walking stick.

Many of us have recounted endless stories since returning home and more than one of us will have been nominated as a 'penguin bore' as we dined out on our experiences.

I lost two good friends, John Gostick and Jeff Bell, when their Phantom was lost in an accident on Mount Usborne in 1982. They died in the service of their country doing the job they loved. I also mention the other Phantom crew lost on the islands. Although I did not serve on the same squadron as 'C-J' and 'Mongo' I knew them both and their loss was no easier to bear. They made the ultimate sacrifice. I would also like to mention Rob 'Banners' Bannister who was my predecessor as OC1435 Flight. 'Banners' was a navigator and, after he left the Air Force he made the transition to become a commercial pilot. He flew for some years with Eastern Airlines before he passed away at far too young an age of natural causes. 'Banners' was full of life and, when I arrived, he was so enthusiastic about a picture he had taken during his tenure 'Down South' that I have reproduced it in his memory in the colour section.

My thanks also go to a number of friends for their contributions:

Ian Stewart for penning the Foreword.

Steve Clarke at the RAF Air Historic Branch for his usual expert advice.

Dave Middleton, Steve Smyth, David Lewis, Pete McCambridge, Paul Jackson, Ant T and Ted Threapleton for providing photographs to fill in the gaps in my collection, particularly to Midds for the amazing cover photograph.

Paul Courtnage for his recollections of the Ascension Island incident.

Clive Duance for his insights into life at the radar sites.

Anthony Howell for his recollections of the engineering challenges.

Rick Groombridge for his recollections of flying the Mirage.

The Latin American Aviation Historical Society for permission to use the piece "The Electra on the Highway".

I must also thank the 1435 Flight groundcrew and my engineering officer who served during my tenure as OC 1435 Flight. We all had stressful moments but your efforts were never less than 100%. Keeping the jets up and running every day was a true feat of brilliance. I am eternally sorry that I was forced to purloin the QRA gym for a number of months. Hopefully, installation of the new QRA briefing room which I set in train during my time allowed future Bosses to return the gym equipment to its original location. Of course, in retelling some 'secrets' from The Claw I may have overstepped a line but some myths need to be uncovered. If so, I offer my apologies.

As always I must, of course, mention my family Jan, Gemma, Paul and Tim who have suffered the endless discussion as I prepared the book.

As my good friend Ian Stewart has said, I will be donating from my royalties to 'Hounds For Heroes' which is a wonderful charity providing specially trained assistance dogs to injured and disabled men and women of both the UK Armed Forces and Civilian Emergency Services. These dogs do simple tasks such as opening doors but can even operate ATMs giving their owners' mobility and independence which would be impossible without their help.

The final note should be for the heroes who recaptured the islands. Every single member of the Forces, including those who undertook the less glamorous and undoubtedly safer roles in Ascension and the United Kingdom, deserves acknowledgement for their amazing achievement. I returned safely to write a book about the islands but 255 servicemen and a number of civilians paid for the islanders' freedom with their lives.

This book is dedicated to those who lost their lives during the Falklands conflict and in the years since.
'Lest we forget'.

MOD Caveats

CHAPTER 1
The Falklands Conflict

We have maintained the honour of the Crown and the superiority of our influence. Beyond this, what have we acquired? What but a bleak and gloomy solitude, an island thrown aside from human use, stormy in Winter and barren in summer, an island which not even the southern savages have dignified with habitation; where a garrison must be kept in a state that contemplates with envy the exiles of Siberia; of which the expense will be perpetual and the use only occasional.

Dr Samuel Johnson 1771

First impressions are often telling and my lasting memories of the Falkland Islands are of a remote, stunningly beautiful outcrop of rock populated by rural Britons. This latter notion is far from the truth as, despite the fact that the islands are beautiful, the islanders are a keenly independent and hardy race despite their loyalty to the Crown. Even with hindsight, the thought that the islanders would ever wish to come under Argentinian rule seems so unlikely. They live in a remote corner of the former British Empire and are protected as a dependent territory but, colonials they are not. They are self governing under their own Falkland Island Constitution. On a bright day, the beaches and inlets are as striking as any in the world but, with a harsh and unpredictable climate, the only beach goers who brave the cutting winds are the islands original inhabitants, namely the wildlife population. Living on the islands is no easy option.

The day war broke out in the South Atlantic I was mid way through an Armament Practice Camp at the RAF base at Akrotiri in Cyprus. The irony of the comparison was not lost on us in that the Cypriot Government, like the Argentinian Government, is extremely sensitive over the status of the Sovereign Base Areas on the Eastern Mediterranean island. Tensions there have often been high and Nations have also fought to control the territory. Happily, unlike the Turks in 1974, the current Cypriot Government is unlikely to follow a course similar to the Argentinian Junta which decided to stake its claim to the Falkland

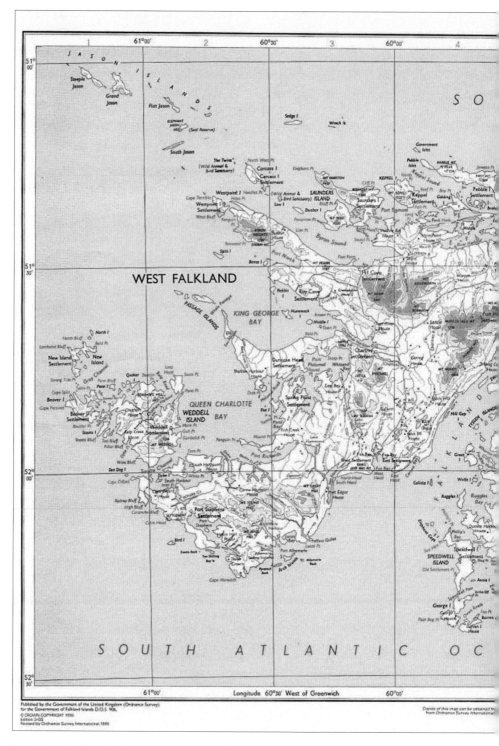

The Falkland Islands. © UK Crown Copyright (1986).

FALKLAND ISLANDS

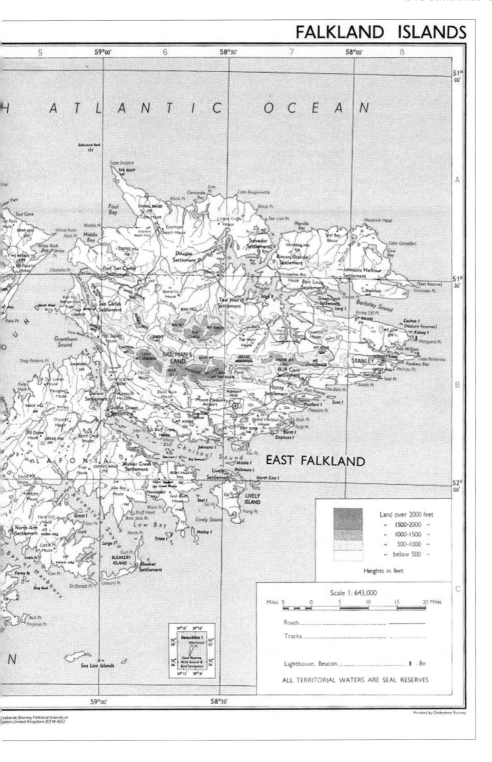

Islands through hostile action in 1982. As the crisis developed, talk of potential operations had us poring over maps attempting to locate the largely forgotten British dependency. Its isolated location at the foot of the South American continent came as a surprise to many. Sitting 400 miles from the Argentinian coastline and 8,000 miles from the UK, the islands are buffeted by the harsh prevailing westerlies or anti-trades. The population is slowly increasing which is an ironic consequence of the conflict and is home to around 3,000 people who make a living mainly through fishing and farming. Although there are only 2 major islands; East and West Falkland, there are over 200 smaller islands dotted around the complex coastline.

The Falklands conflict began, as have so many in the past, with the wrong political signals being sent by London. The Governor, Sir Rex Hunt, had originally been sent down to the islands with a brief from the Foreign Office that, perhaps, the islanders' futures lay with their South American neighbours. At the same time, the British survey ship HMS *Endurance*, which was based in the region, was approaching the end of its service life and the decision had been taken not to replace it. General Galtieri, the Argentinian military ruler, had been making making vocal efforts to persuade the UK Government to yield sovereignty but, in parallel, had been making covert preparations to invade. The decision to retire HMS *Endurance* was taken as a sign that Whitehall had lost interest in the disputed territory. As slowly it became clear to Galtieri that the overt diplomatic route would fail, the agenda changed and the course of events was set.

Initially, the invasion was a strange affair. The 61 Royal Marines stationed at Moody Barracks on the outskirts of Port Stanley had been given advanced warning of the impending attack and had deployed to Government House to protect the Governor, and his staff. The first landings by Argentinian Special Forces at 04:30 on 2 April 1982 at Mullet Creek to the south of the town were followed by further landings to the west and east of the airfield at Port Stanley setting up a pincer attack on the capital. In the face of overwhelming odds, a reluctant Governor ordered the Royal Marines to surrender just after breakfast to avoid inevitable bloodshed. The reluctant Marines were unimpressed as they had already steeled for a fight but, with overwhelming superiority in numbers, the invading troops swiftly took control of key installations and the new Argentinian Military Governor, General Mario Menendez, declared martial law to the dismay of the residents.

In London, a hasty rearguard action was initiated in the corridors of power. Shuttle diplomacy, led by the US Secretary of State Al Haig, began as the Americans tried to act as an intermediary between the two Governments. The Foreign Secretary at the time, Lord Carrington, feeling responsible for the debacle duly resigned. The Defence Secretary John Nott also offered his resignation but was persuaded to remain in post which, with hindsight, probably maintained a vital element of continuity. The diplomatic effort increased as the UN Secretary General, the UN Security Council and the American delegation all sought to negotiate with London and Argentina to solve a problem which, regrettably, seemed to have few amicable solutions. Military planning in the UK began in parallel and the service chiefs prepared options which were presented to Margaret Thatcher, The Prime Minister, outlining ambitious plans to retake the islands. Much to the surprise of many, she accepted the plan and when, as had always seemed likely, diplomacy failed the go ahead was given.

Preparations began to assemble a Task Force and, in a remarkably short time, it sailed on 5 April 1982. The scenes of National unity made the headlines as the carriers, HMS *Invincible* and HMS *Hermes*, sailed from Portsmouth. The scene was repeated around the country over the coming days as other smaller vessels embarked on the long voyage south to join the Task Force. The force comprised a crazy array of ships ranging from large capital warships, through assault ships to ocean liners, the most famous of which was the *Queen Elizabeth 2* which was requisitioned as a troop ship. Given the speed with which the Task Force had been put together, an enforced pause at Gibraltar and again at Ascension Island was needed to allow the logistics tail to catch up. Load plans were hastily re-arranged and, as plans matured, equipment was cross-decked to ensure that all was in the correct place for the planned assault on the Islands. Additional equipment was procured rapidly and flown to Ascension to supplement the force. Contingency plans were dusted off and hastily implemented raising the tempo in the Ministry of Defence to a level not seen in many years. During the lulls, those aboard the ships recorded their feelings reflecting a sense of almost 'phoney war' and there was a naive certainty that the politicians would resolve the problems before conflict became a last option. As the force pressed south through increasingly poor weather, the hoped for political settlement never came. Others, perhaps, more bullish, were seeking an opportunity to convert training to reality. Used to the almost predictable, albeit potentially cataclysmic stand-off of the Cold War, a grim reality was setting in and preparations intensified.

Looking at potential military options led to inevitable conclusions and indeed, the battle plan was to some extent predictable. The Task Force needed a deep water inlet to allow the ships to approach close to shore. A head on assault against Stanley was rejected and was, in fact, the option expected by the occupiers who mined the entrances to Berkley Sound. Although many other options were considered, to be able to retake key settlements yet remain relatively safe from Argentinian counter-attack, left a landing on the western side of East Falkland Island as, perhaps, the only viable option. The airfield at Goose Green was a vital base to the invaders yet it was not agreed at that stage of planning that its recapture was essential. Even so, the distances the force would need to move across the harsh terrain in order to retake Stanley meant that, once ashore, helicopters would be needed to move vital equipment and personnel forward. For that reason a bridgehead was vital where a logistics base could be established. In the event, the Task Force Commander, Rear Admiral Sandy Woodward, agreed a plan with the Land Commander, Major General Jeremy Moore, which began with an amphibious landing in San Carlos Water. Once beachheads had been established, ground troops would strike out across country along 3 axes of attack. The infantry units of 3 Para and 42 Commando Brigade would take a northerly route, 2 Para and 5 Brigade would mount attacks along a southern axis via Goose Green with elements of 42 Commando being airlifted forward by helicopter through a central corridor. The elements would come together to the west of Mount Kent, just 20 miles short of Port Stanley for a final assault on the Capital. In the rear, Royal Navy ships would mount a defensive barrier to guard against Argentinian air attack. Although air support would be provided by the carriers, the risk of losing even one carrier was unacceptable and they would be forced to operate well to the east of the islands for much of the time leading to extended transit sorties and reduced time on task for the fixed wing aircraft. For the Harrier pilots this would shape the conflict.

In the rear area at Ascension Island, the most complex fleet of combat and support aircraft the UK had ever deployed was being assembled. At times, the small isolated airfield in the middle of the ocean was the busiest piece of concrete in the world yet ill prepared for the influx. An array of tankers, fighters, bombers and transport aircraft of all types, slowly filled every available piece of tarmac as supplies continued to arrive, overloading already stretched facilities. Taxy patterns on the cramped airfield were difficult and accommodation was at a premium. Every unit in the Armed Forces was keen to contribute but stories of non-essential personnel being returned to UK became prevalent as facilities were stretched to capacity. From the air perspective not only was Ascension a stepping off point, but the airfield was to play a crucial role on one of the opening gambits of the campaign providing a base for the RAF's most ambitious contribution; that of the Operation Black Buck raids by the Vulcans of 44 (Rhodesia) Squadron.

As the preparations continued, back on the islands the islanders were learning how unpleasant life could be under Argentinian military rule. The residents of Stanley found themselves swamped by the occupying force and some decamped to the settlements in an effort to avoid the worst excesses but even they were not safe. The residents of Goose Green were rounded up and held in the village church for weeks whilst the occupying soldiers requisitioned their homes and took their food. One fact kept them focussed. The Task Force was sailing towards them and Mrs Thatcher was intent on retaking the islands.

The conflict began with the retaking of South Georgia on 25 April 1982 which was an amazing feat involving heroism of the highest order yet went almost unreported. It started badly when a small force of SAS soldiers which had been inserted covertly to carry out a reconnaissance were caught out by the extreme weather and the decision was taken to extract them. Attempts were thwarted as the rescue helicopter crashed in appalling weather, as did a second and it was only the third helicopter which finally returned the small force to HMS *Antrim*, albeit crash landing on the deck in truly appalling conditions. Fighting proper began shortly afterwards when a small force of Royal Marines and Special Forces were put ashore. In the meantime, a Lynx from HMS *Brilliant*, using rockets and guns, caught the Argentinian submarine Santa Fe on the surface and attacked rendering it inoperative. After a short barrage of naval gunfire and under threat of attack from the Marines, the garrison promptly surrendered.

Events were overtaken rapidly by the first major casualties of the war. Within days, each side lost one of its major capital ships The sinking of the Belgrano by the nuclear submarine HMS *Conqueror* on 2 May 1982 brought a grim reality to the operation which was by then known in the press by its codeword Operation CORPORATE. Part of an Argentinian maritime force, it had been manoeuvring close to the southern edge of the Total Exclusion Zone which had been declared by Britain. It could, undoubtedly, have threatened the carriers with just a minor change of heading and it led to the first key political decision from The Prime Minister. She decided, without hesitation, to give the order to engage and its sinking with the loss of 368 lives was the first signal that the operation would not be casualty free. Somewhat jingoistic celebrations in the National Press were short lived as it was followed by a loss of our own. Within two days HMS *Sheffield*, a Type 42 destroyer, was sunk by an Exocet missile fired from an Argentinian Super Etendard operating from the air base at Rio Gallegos. In yet another irony, the ship was sunk by a French supplied missile launched from a French supplied aircraft. One of our close allies was proving to be the supplier of some of the most effective weaponry ranged against the Task Force. That said, the fact that the Argentinians operated equipment supplied by our own defence industry was not lost on the combatants. Indeed, Argentina operated Type 42 destroyers similar to those providing air defence coverage for the Task Force. In a further irony, preparatory exercises between the enemy Type 42s and the Argentinian combat air forces resulted in all the attacking aircraft being engaged and simulated destroyed by the Argentinian Navy. The outcome caused consternation at the highest levels of command in Argentina and raised the spectre of serious losses.

Sitting about 70 miles south east of Stanley and 18 miles west of the main force on an air defence picket line, HMS *Sheffield*, one of our own Type 42s, was one of three Type 42s in the defensive screen. Along with HMS *Glasgow*, it was one of the closest vessels to the attacking Argentinian forces and appeared first on the attacking aircraft's radar becoming a natural target. The Etendards were detected as far away as 40 miles by HMS *Glasgow*'s Type 965 radar but were not engaged by either ship and successfully launched 2 missiles. As both missiles guided towards the Sheffield there were procedural errors such as the crew transmitting on the satellite communications equipment which blinded the ship's radar warning equipment. In the absence of counter fire and without the use of defensive chaff, a strike was likely. One missile struck amidships on the right hand side between the galley and the forward engine room and, even though the warhead failed to explode, the unspent fuel ignited causing a massive fire. A second missile missed, ditching short in the sea. The fire quickly raged out of control and burned fiercely for some days at which stage the Captain ordered his crew to abandon ship. Despite efforts to take her in tow, deteriorating weather caused the ship to take on water through the damaged hull and the ship developed a list and sank on 10 May 1982.

The engagement might have been survivable but subsequent analysis of the tactical situation and deficiencies in the construction of the vessel highlighted problems which meant the ship's loss was inevitable. A peacetime Navy rapidly learned the lessons of survival, although many more ships were to be lost before victory could be claimed. The crews learned lessons about where their equipment would fail them but, more importantly, they quickly learned where their strengths lay.

I felt the loss deeply as my own Squadron had maintained close contacts with HMS *Sheffield* and we had carried out air defence exercises with the crew only a few years before she sailed to war. In a joint maritime exercise, our Phantoms had provided combat air patrols in defence of the exercise task force, ironically intercepting Buccaneers carrying out anti ship strikes from RAF Lossiemouth in Northern Scotland. Sadly, for whatever reason, those training events had not equipped the crew fully for what was to unfold. After the exercise I had received a signed picture of the ship as a thank you for planning the exercise. Given those close links, the loss weighed heavily.

As the Task Force approached within range, Sea Harriers were joined by RAF Harrier GR3s which had been deployed aboard the ill fated Atlantic Conveyor. The RAF aircraft and pilots immediately began operating from the carriers alongside the Sea Harriers against targets on the islands. In parallel, a major combat mission by an RAF aircraft was launched on 1 May 1982. The task was simple. All that was needed was for a single Vulcan to drop its load of twenty-one 1,000-lb bombs onto the runway at Stanley in order to interdict the strip and render it unusable by the Argentinian Air Force. A simple mission statement but

HMS *Sheffield* in calmer waters. © UK Crown Copyright (1981).

the preparation for the raid was mind-blowingly complex. The sheer distances involved required a complex refuelling plan which guaranteed that it would be one of the most complicated bombing missions ever undertaken. I could not hope to summarise the mission in a few paragraphs but Rowland White's outstanding summary in *Vulcan 607*, should be at the top of the reading list for anyone with even a passing interest in military operations in the Falklands. Preparation was intense. The Vulcan had to be reconverted to the conventional bombing role from its most recent role of nuclear strike and the crews had to be trained in air-to-air refuelling techniques by day and night. The Vulcan's antiquated H2S bombing system was updated to accept inertial navigation inputs from a Carousel inertial navigation system. Tactics and electronic countermeasures were improved to give the crew a chance of surviving the sophisticated Argentinian defences. The defensive aids were improved by adding an AN/ALQ 101-10 jamming pod on a hastily installed wing pylon. Unlike the Vulcan's own aging jammers, the responsive pod was programmed against the hostile anti-aircraft systems deployed on the islands. Operating from Ascension Island, the Vulcan would need seventeen refuelling brackets from fifteen Victor tankers to transfer enough fuel to give the crew the chance of returning to the forward operating

Vulcan XM607 which flew the Black Buck raid.

base at Wideawake. Even then, margins would be incredibly tight. The raid was planned to hit Stanley airfield at 0700 Greenwich Mean Time on 1 May 1982 and was given the codeword Operation Black Buck. It proved to be the longest operational bombing mission in history to date and dumped thousands of pounds of high explosive ordnance onto an unsuspecting enemy. Although pundits have since questioned the effectiveness of the mission, in that the only bomb which landed on the concrete runway failed to stop flight operations, the psychological effect of the raid must have been truly stunning. The Argentinian garrison could no longer feel safe from attack. There was also an implied threat to bases on the mainland. With the runway length reduced, the raid put an end to fast jet operations from Stanley even though the runway remained in use for transport aircraft and the Pucara close support aircraft which had been deployed to the islands. XM607, the Vulcan which flew the bombing mission was preserved and retains pride of place on show at RAF Waddington, its home base for so many years and home to 44 Squadron. It still sports the hastily added wing pylons which carried shrike anti radiation missiles in addition to the AN/ALQ 101-10 jamming pods during the crisis.

There was a gap between the early operations and the date of the actual landing. Diplomatic efforts finally failed on 18 May 82 leaving little chance of an alternative solution. At 1125 on 20 May 1982, Brigadier Julian Thomas finally received orders to attack. After a feint at Stanley Harbour, the amphibious landing force sailed onwards into Falkland Sound from the South and into the sheltered inlet of San Carlos Water. Poor weather which might have protected the force from attack broke and, by nightfall, the sea was calm and the skies clear. The landing was largely unopposed, although an Argentinian observation post on Fanning Head, stubbornly refused to surrender. Another small force which had withdrawn began harassing the landing zone and shot down two Gazelle helicopters with small arms fire. The first task was to secure the beachhead and artillery guns and Rapier air defence missiles were hastily positioned on the surrounding hillsides before troops began to dig in. These missiles should have guaranteed protection from air attack but the RAF and Army gunners had not deployed into such an environment before and lessons on positioning Rapiers were quickly learned. The coming days were to see the worst losses inflicted on the Royal Navy since the Second World War as the Argentinians counter attacked using air power. During the coming five days, four vessels, HMS *Ardent*, *Antelope*, *Coventry* and the civilian vessel *Atlantic Conveyor* were sunk and a further seven, HMS *Argonaut*, *Antrim*, *Brilliant*, *Broadsword*, *Glasgow*, *Sir Galahad* and *Sir Lancelot* were damaged. Luckily, it was subsequently learned that the Argentinian pilots were flying extremely low to avoid the defences such that their bombs were failing to arm properly and were not exploding. Newsreel at the time captured the exploits of the attacking pilots who pressed attacks home using mostly 'dumb' bombs against heavily armed ships crewed by highly professional seamen who were amongst the best in NATO. It also captured the final moments of a number of those Skyhawks and Daggers whose pilots would never return to the mainland. In the first incident of unintended consequences, the fact that the bombs were failing to fuse was announced by an unwary politician in the House of Commons providing valuable intelligence to the enemy. People were learning forgotten lessons that 'Loose Lips' do indeed sink ships.

There followed a few days of surprising indecision in London. Goose Green housed not only the airfield operating Pucara light bombers but was also garrisoned by the Argentinian 12th Regiment which was a strategic reserve and reaction force. Failure to negate the threat would have left both the beachhead and the flank open to counter attack. Approval to attack was eventually given on 26 May 1982 and 2 Para marched south towards the settlements of Darwin and Goose Green. Both settlements sit on a narrow strip of land linking the two halves of East Falkland and the Argentinian defensive positions were well sited and equally well prepared. The Paras met stiff resistance and, under shelling

The Memorial to Lieutenant Colonel 'H' Jones.

from the defenders, the attacking force became bogged down around the southern edge of Darwin. Only fierce hand-to-hand combat broke the defensive line and allowed them to close on Goose Green itself. During the battle, the commander, Lieutenant Colonel 'H' Jones died attacking a defensive position earning a Victoria Cross for his leadership and bravery. I later walked the ground where Colonel Jones fell and can only marvel at the bravery he exhibited that night. As the British forces closed, in a stunning piece of psychological warfare, the Commander of the Paras sent a note in the hand of a POW to the Argentinian Commander offering him the option to surrender. His other option was to await bombardment. Shortly after dawn the Argentinian garrison surrendered to the smaller British force which took 983 Argentinian troops as prisoners of war. One of the most iconic images that emerged from the engagement was the sight of Argentinian helmets and weapons lying abandoned on the village green. It was the first demonstration of British intent. When the village was liberated paratroopers released 114 villagers from their makeshift prison in the Village Hall where they had been since the start of the invasion. I was to hear their stories first hand some years later.

One of the key capabilities on which the British commanders relied was the helicopter. Its use was intrinsic yet, with the loss of the Atlantic Conveyor, only one heavy lift Chinook helicopter had survived; the famous 'Bravo November'

Goose Green Settlement.

as three of the RAFs newest helicopters went down with the container ship along with six Wessex and a Lynx. The Navy had a number of helicopter types such as the Sea King, Wessex and Gazelle light helicopter but the loss of the heavy lift Chinooks was a serious blow. To press the attack on Port Stanley, the land forces had little option but to cover the rough terrain on foot, past the natural line of hills which ringed the town to the West and on into the capital. Not only troops had to be moved but also tons of supplies, food, water and ammunition had to follow the same route. The helicopters provided the means to do this as the roads were simply not fit. In the absence of helicopters, troops simply walked to Stanley across unyielding terrain. Some of the images captured during this phase, which earned the nickname of 'yomping' or 'tabbing', became iconic. Who would ever forget the picture of the Royal Marine in full battle gear with a radio pack bearing the Union Flag walking across the desolate scrubland?

In the meantime, 3 Para and 42 Commando pushed forward along a northerly route via Douglas settlement and Teal Inlet to approach Mount Kent from the northwest. No. 42 Commando pushed along the central ground supported, where possible, by helicopters to keep up the momentum. After their successes in Goose Green, 2 Para and 5 Brigade pushed along the lower ground to the south aiming for Fitzroy settlement. It was this force which was to suffer the worst losses of the campaign. In an effort to maintain tempo, The Welsh Guards were moved forward, initially in the assault ship HMS *Fearless* and finally by the landing ships *Sir Galahad* and *Sir Tristram*. The aim was to put them ashore in Bluff Cove which was to the southwest of their goal, an ideal position from which to begin the push for Stanley. As they lay at anchor in Bluff Cove both ships were hit by bombs from a pair of Skyhawks which attacked at low level, closely followed by a further pair of Mirages. Both ships were seriously damaged and explosions wracked the vessels. A disorganised evacuation followed and the Welsh Guards were effectively neutralised as a fighting unit through heavy casualties and by the loss of most of their equipment. There was much debate whether the losses could have been reduced by providing major warships as air defence cover, or whether earlier disembarkation could have prevented the losses completely. Either way, the attack left fifty-three dead and forty-six injured, many suffering shocking burns. It was a low point in the campaign.

The air battle was typified by heroism on both sides. Despite being on opposing sides I remember feeling admiration for the attacking Argentinian pilots who demonstrated skill and determination, attacking heavily armed naval warships with free fall bombs. There can be no doubt that their low flying skills were equal to the task as they were caught by the cameras, often under heavy fire and, in one classic shot, pursued by surface-to-air missiles. On the defensive force, the Sea Harriers of the Naval Air Squadrons were flown by pilots both from the Fleet Air Arm and the RAF. Their contribution was simply superb. The Sea Harrier FRS1 had been under-developed in true British style. Already short of legs, the Sea Harrier pilots often had to operate from positions well to the east of the islands to ensure that the carriers stayed out of range of the attackers. This meant that fuel in the combat area was precious and it added to their already challenging task. The pilots acquitted themselves with distinction claiming twenty enemy kills at the expense of only a single loss to ground fire. Undefeated in air-to-air combat, the Harriers were one of the key assets which assured victory. Although the Sea Harrier radar was rudimentary at that time, it was perfectly capable in the medium level environment and only suffered when operating against low level targets. The key was that the 'Shar', as it was known, was upgraded with the latest versions of the Sidewinder infra-red guided air-to-air missile. The AIM-9L version was introduced rapidly into service giving an all-aspect capability which their opponents lacked. Although the Argentinians were also equipped with Sidewinders, they fielded the earlier AIM-9B stern-aspect missile which placed them at a disadvantage. The uncooled AIM-9B could not be fired in a high 'G' turn and target evasion could defeat the missile. Additionally, it was a point of debate whether the Argentinians were equipped with defensive aids such as radar warning receivers and countermeasures dispensers. There were concerns over the capability of the AIM-9L to defend against infra-red flares in its original form and the vulnerability took some years to overcome. It transpired that the Argentinians had, probably, not carried the appropriate dispensers and, certainly, there was no evidence of the use of flares in combat.

The lessons learned in the conflict led directly to upgrades which were later introduced into the Sea Harrier FA2 in 1993 which transformed the aircraft's capability. The addition of a Blue Vixen pulse Doppler radar and AMRAAM gave the aircraft a true look down shoot down capability which would have totally changed the outcome of the air battle had it been available in 1982. The 'Shar' continued to give sterling service until the type was retired in 2006.

The twenty-eight Sea Harriers supplemented by fourteen Harrier GR3s of the RAF were to prove critical in the campaign. Unprepared as the Task Force sailed, the RAF Harriers were adapted to operate from a carrier and the crews trained in onboard procedures. They followed on, shipped south aboard the container vessel *Atlantic Conveyor*. In one of the major strokes of luck, the Harriers flew off the ill-fated vessel shortly before it was attacked by an Exocet-armed Super Etendard. The ship was sunk but they survived. Had they been lost, the delay in providing replacements would have had a crucially detrimental effect on the campaign. Although dual role, the Sea Harrier lacked the flexibility and diversity of ground attack weapons which the RAF equivalent enjoyed, particularly in the shape of laser guided munitions. It would also have diverted the Sea Harrier from the vital defensive counter air role giving attacking Argentinian fast jets more leeway.

The final push on Port Stanley saw some of the bloodiest hand-to-hand fighting of the war. Argentinian forces were dug in on the mountains outside the capital. The exhausted British troops, who had suffered diabolical weather conditions, had struggled through rough and boggy terrain, arriving at the foothills which were to become household names in the UK as the battles raged. Mount Kent, Mount Longdon, Two Sisters, Wireless Ridge and Mount Tumbledown provided a natural barrier between the British forces and their goal. After a short pause to regroup, the final battles began with the British troops attacking the stark hillsides which were sown with mines and protected by well dug in defenders armed with mortars and machine guns. Supported by covering fire from HMS *Avenger* which fell remarkably close to their own positions they finished the operation with bayonets. The attack on Mount Tumbledown was the last battle of the war. Technology had been employed in a modern campaign yet the tactics employed by the infantry at that phase of the battle were more akin to the fiercest campaigns of the Second World War. The heroism of those involved can never be questioned. A period of heavy psychological pressure on the enemy ensued as the Task Force prepared for a final assault.

The British troops now held the hills surrounding the capital and the Argentinian forces had retreated into the town and troops filled the streets. Cold

Headquarters, Land Forces
Falkland Islands

INSTRUMENT OF SURRENDER

I, the undersigned, Commander of all the Argentine land, sea and air forces in the Falkland Islands ~~approximately~~ surrender to Major General J. J. MOORE CB OBE MC* as representative of Her Brittanic Majesty's Government.

Under the terms of this surrender all Argentinian personnel in the Falkland Islands are to muster at assembly points which will be nominated by General Moore and hand over their arms, ammunition, and all other weapons and warlike equipment as directed by General Moore or appropriate British officers acting on his behalf.

Following the surrender all personnel of the Argentinian Forces will be treated with honour in accordance with the conditions set out in the Geneva Convention of 1949. They will obey any directions concerning movement and in connection with accommodation.

This surrender is to be effective from *2359* hours ZULU on *14* June (*2059* hours local) and includes those Argentine Forces presently deployed in and around Port Stanley, those others on East Falkland, ~~~~ West Falkland and all the outlying islands.

.... Commander Argentine Forces

.... J. J. MOORE
Major General

.... Witness

........*2359*........ hours *14* June 1982

The Instrument of Surrender.

and hungry after the heavy fighting of the previous days, there was a good deal of resentment at the amount of food stockpiled in the logistics centres which had not been sent forward and unrest was rife among the invaders, particularly the conscripts. With the British preparing for more hand-to-hand fighting which would have been costly in lives on both sides, it was clear to the Argentinian commander that he had few options left.

The surrender came at dawn on 14 June 1982 and was broadcast to the UK immediately afterwards avoiding further inevitable bloodshed. The second-in-command of the Ghurkhas coined the iconic phrase, 'Gentlemen, a white flag has been seen flying over Port Stanley'. After the cheers subsided, it was his heartfelt rejoinder which said most: 'Bloody marvellous!' At 9 p.m. the Argentinian commander surrendered to Major General Jeremy Moore ending the conflict. Liberation was sweet and 2 Para were the first unit to march into Stanley to the rapturous cheers of the islanders. The question was whether life could return to any semblance of normality.

The surrender was reported in Parliament by a jubilant Prime Minister and the victory was placed on record in Hansard.

> Early this morning in Port Stanley, seventy-four days after the Falkland Islands were invaded, General Moore accepted from General Menendez the surrender of all the Argentinian forces in East and West Falkland together with their arms and equipment. In a message to the Commander-in-Chief Fleet, General Moore reported: 'The Falkland Islands are once more under the Government desired by their inhabitants. God Save The Queen. General Menendez has surrendered some 11,000 men in Port Stanley and some 2,000 in West Falkland. In addition we had already captured and were holding elsewhere on the island 1,800 prisoners, making in all some 15,000 prisoners of war now in our hands.

Baroness Young in a statement to the House of Lords reflected on the losses:

> Mr. Speaker, the House will join me in expressing our deep sense of loss over those who have died, and our sorrow for their families. The final details will not become clear for a few days yet, but we know that some 250 British servicemen and civilians have been killed. They died that others may live in freedom and justice. The Battle of the Falklands was a remarkable military operation, boldly planned, bravely executed, and brilliantly accomplished. We owe an enormous debt to the British forces and to the Merchant Marine. We honour them all. They have been supported by a people united in defence of our way of life and of our sovereign territory.

It was against this backdrop that I was acquainted with the Falkland Islands.

CHAPTER 2
The First Phantom Detachment

Military options were included in the original operational plans to allow Phantoms to be deployed to the Falkland Islands to enhance the air defence coverage. At an early stage during the build up, we were warned on 92 (East India) Squadron to prepare for a possible deployment, although it never developed beyond initial planning and at a very early stage the commitment was given to 29 (Fighter) Squadron.

Admiral Woodward, the Task Force Commander, considered establishing a beachhead on West Falkland where a landing strip could be built to allow Harriers to operate. Had this been possible, the ability to mount combat air patrols to the west of the islands and engage the Argentinian combat aircraft before they reached the British forces would have changed the whole nature of the conflict, albeit at the cost of adding another high value installation to be protected. A temporary runway of AM2 matting, which would have provided an operating strip, was lost when the Atlantic Conveyor was sunk. Had it been installed following the landings it would have been possible to fit arrestor cables, as was eventually achieved, to allow Phantoms to operate. Admittedly, the Harrier was much more adaptable in such austere conditions as this type of operation was the concept for the aircraft from its inception. Unfortunately, it was more lightly armed in the fighter role and lacked air intercept radar. For that reason, air planners were keen to deploy a dedicated air defence fighter as soon as possible. Had the plan for the airstrip come to fruition, one can only imagine how difficult it would have been for the sappers to build an airstrip under fire. As the campaign developed, the lack of a runway consigned the Phantom to a backstop role and it was much later before the enhanced capability arrived on the islands.

On 25 May 1982 a detachment of three Phantoms XV466, XV468 and XV484, led by the Commanding Officer of 29 (Fighter) Squadron Wing Commander Ian McFaddyen, arrived on the remote outcrop at Ascension Island. Their mission was urgent as tension was high. It was not beyond possibility that the Argentinians would mount a surprise attack on the busy airhead which their military planners knew was absolutely vital as a logistics bridgehead. The runways and taxiways were packed with aircraft of all varieties and would have offered a lucrative target for an ambitious 'targeteer'. The congested traffic patterns on the airfield meant that even minor damage would cripple the air effort. Tales that emerged after the conflict described complex chess matches to get the right aircraft to the runway threshold in the correct order at the correct time. The ability to do that proved to be, literally, a case of life or death when the Black Buck raids were mounted. If the reserve Victor tankers had been blocked on the ground, the Vulcan would have run out of fuel well short of its home base. Had that occurred, the strong message the raid had sent to the Argentinians would have been diluted. The Argentinians certainly had the theoretical capability to hit Ascension using the Skyhawk or Super Etendard which were both able to refuel in the air from the C130 tanker. There was also the risk of tactical transports carrying special forces being tasked to raid key installations. In the event, the Argentinian tankers were heavily tasked to support attacks against the British aircraft carriers so interdiction against the supply chain in the rear area around Ascension or in the sea lanes never materialised. The lethal attack against Atlantic Conveyor, however, proved how vulnerable the Task Force could be when attacks were pressed home closer to the Falklands even with effective air defence coverage. As the conflict unfolded, the Phantoms took on the less glamorous but still vital role of policing the northerly air corridors into the operational area around the airhead.

I was not involved with the operational detachment as by then I had returned to the UK from RAF Germany and was working through instructor training on the Phantom Operational Conversion Unit. Despite the role, morale stayed high among the Phantom crews and friends told stories of high jinks which broke the monotony of an air defence mission without the daily threat facing the Task Force. As the 29 (F) Sqn crews rotated through Ascension, the returnees related their experiences. Clearly frustrated at being unable to contribute as much as their Harrier colleagues, they consoled themselves in the knowledge that the task, although not as glamorous as their counterparts, was essential nonetheless. Throughout the deployment, crews had to remain alert to the risk of attack but there were instances where our own forces were at risk of engagement if air defence procedures broke down. A colleague told a cautionary tale after Phantom crews had met a British warship returning from the South Atlantic. It shows, graphically, the problems of identification facing the air defence crews.

It all seemed like a good idea at the time, but in retrospect I had to speculate at the wisdom of carrying out an unannounced 'attack' on 2,800 tonnes of warship, armed to the teeth and recently engaged in a war where assault from the air was a real and terrifying threat. Indeed, some nights later, the tables were turned in an incident that almost cost the helicopter pilot from one of our ships his life. He had, apparently, decided to visit the Island for the night, so he flew his 'cab' towards Wideawake airfield. He too was unannounced and the first anyone knew about it was when the radar site atop Green Mountain detected an unidentified contact heading for the Island. The fighter controller on duty reacted accordingly and alerted my navigator and I who were on QRA that night. Receiving an authentic codeword and an instruction to scramble to engage and destroy an inbound target, we raced into the dark, suddenly unfriendly, air in a haze of adrenaline and apprehension. My nav fired up the radar and I armed and tuned our missiles. We turned north and started to search for our quarry. It rapidly became apparent that whatever we were chasing was at low level and lights out - neither fact adding to the perceived friendliness of our quarry.

Something, however, was not quite right. The target was quite a slow mover that made it either a helicopter or a transport aircraft. The latter could well have been an Argentinian transport bringing armed troops to Ascension. As I mentioned, this was the key link in our logistics chain and Argentina would have done well to disrupt it in just this way. On the other hand, if this was a helo, where had it come from and what was it doing? Ascension Island is, after all, 1,000 miles from nearest land. As we had the time to investigate before the target would reach the Island, we set about a thorough search of the area. Before long we found a large surface contact. Cautiously approaching closer, we were able to identify it as a British Naval vessel by using our newly delivered night vision goggles. Turning back to our target, we were eventually able to find and identify it as a wayward RN Lynx helicopter. I never did meet the pilot concerned and I still wonder if he ever knew how close he had come to a watery grave that night. He had been looking down the wrong end of a Sparrow air-to-air missile with my finger on the trigger. Only a 'feeling in the bones' had saved him. I wonder if someone aboard an RN frigate had similarly targeted a four-ship of F4 Phantoms a few mornings before?
(© Paul Courtnage)

It is reassuring that RAF crews were trained to analyse their targets before engaging. The crew had been instructed to engage and would have been fully justified in pulling the trigger. Happily common sense prevailed.

As the conflict ended, the first British troops reoccupied Stanley airfield and found a scene of devastation. For some time, the defeated Argentinian forces had camped out on the airfield after a riot in the capital had forced the British forces to contain them more effectively. Temporary accommodation more reminiscent of a shantytown sprung up and anything which could be put into use as a shelter was earmarked by the restless troops. Some even chose the discomfort of the cockpits of wrecked aircraft as a respite from the harsh climate. This situation

A wrecked Pucara on the airfield. Ropes have been draped over the airframe to build a makeshift tent. Temporary shelters built by the POWs from tin and ammunition boxes dot the landscape. © Steve Smyth.

dragged on for some months before the defeated troops were repatriated to Argentina. The airfield had been attacked extensively, both by the Black Buck Vulcans and by Sea Harriers and Harrier GR3s from the carriers. Inevitably, the explosive ordnance personnel were the first to tackle the mayhem as unexploded ordnance lay everywhere. The Argentinians had dumped Russian made SA-7 man portable air defence missiles, American built Mk82 500-lb bombs, French Exocet anti ship missiles and our own British made Tigercat surface-to-air missiles all over the airfield. The Harrier attacks had left the scars from BL755 cluster bombs. The weapon was based on the original 1,000-lb bomb with a central skeleton configured with fourteen sub-munitions bays. The 147 small bomblets were discharged into the airflow laying down an elliptical pattern on the ground. Designed against armour, a shaped charge would pierce a considerable thickness of steel plate but an ancillary effect was anti-personnel. Thousands of small fragments were released on detonation and were lethal to anyone who happened to be in the vicinity. In any attack using this weapon, some bomblets failed to explode and these, ironically, still littered the operational areas hampering movement. Our own weapons were causing a risk to life. To make matters worse, the combat aircraft which the Argentinians had abandoned had been booby trapped and had to be made safe to prevent further loss of life. Official records show that it took four days before the airfield was considered safe to use.

With the Phantoms still based in Ascension Island, the immediate air defence task fell to the pilots of the RAF Harrier squadrons. For the first few months after the conflict, it was a case of making do with what was available. The RAF ground attack Harriers aboard HMS *Hermes* were immediately flown ashore. They began to operate in the unfamiliar role initially from a temporary strip at Kelly's Garden before moving to the newly named RAF Stanley where they used the short 4,000-foot strip. The Harriers of 'Hardet' had been modified to carry the latest version of the American Sidewinder missile and two of these were carried on underwing pylons. Although many of the pilots who had been involved in combat and acquitted themselves so well had already returned to the UK, their replacements were also skilled in air combat manoeuvring and trained regularly in this discipline during training sorties in UK. The Harrier GR3 was not equipped with onboard radar but fighter controllers based in the control and reporting centres in the rapidly deployed air defence ground units could direct the pilots into an attack using their ground based radars. As always, the Harrier's main limitation was its lack of fuel. The often quoted radius of action for its bombing role had little relevance in air defence where combat persistence was king. It was, however, an extremely agile aircraft with a good thrust to weight ratio and still offered a significant stop-gap capability with its AIM 9L missiles. Those early years were not, however, without incident and the risks of the rapid modifications to the weapons systems were demonstrated graphically. A Harrier launched from the main runway at RAF Stanley for a mission and, as the wheels left the ground, the Sidewinders left the aircraft. On most combat aircraft including the Phantom, the Sidewinders were jettisoned by firing the missiles forward off the rails, albeit unarmed. Unfortunately, a Sidewinder required only a simple voltage to operate its release circuit and a stray voltage could wreak havoc. As they jettisoned, they struck the ground and tragically injured a number of personnel working alongside the runway. The details of the incident are captured starkly in Air Chief Marshal Sir Peter Squire's diary who was commanding the squadron at the time:

The No 1 (Fighter) Squadron Operation Corporate Diary for the period Monday, 12th to Sunday, 18th July 1985 by Wing Commander Peter Squire.
The weather remains cold with frequent snow showers. On 13 July, members of the Welsh Guards are clearing snow from the runway when we scramble a GR3. The Sidewinder AAMs jettison on take-off causing serious injuries to eleven soldiers. I watch it from the hill beside the ops wagon and race down to be of assistance. A SAS NCO,

Harrier GR3s at 'Hardet'. © Steve Smyth.

waiting for the C-130, sets up communications with HQ BFFI in Stanley to summons additional medical assistance. There will be a Board of Inquiry in due course but I secure permission for the pilot to remain flying. (© UK Crown Copyright 2012)

A harsh reality.

The most important task was to begin an airbridge to resupply the garrison with essential supplies to supplement supplies delivered by sea. After Stanley was liberated the limitations of the short runway meant it was still impossible to land large jet aircraft so the immediate task fell to the venerable C130 Hercules and its crews operating from the UK via Ascension Island. Even the Hercules lacked the range to operate unrefueled so complex tanker plans were needed to bridge the distance with the transport aircraft taking on fuel from Victor tankers *en route*. During the conflict, Hercules crews had operated 'out and back' from Ascension, airdropping loads to deployed forces and ships with sortie durations approaching twenty-four hours being common. With a base established on the islands, they could land and disembark supplies and passengers in a more ordered fashion and, more importantly, refuel for the return trip. For many months, the Hercules was the only transport aeroplane able to cope with the short strip. The priority was to upgrade the airfield at the renamed RAF Stanley to allow larger aircraft to operate. One of the fascinating stories which only emerged some years later was how we bought the essential materials which would be the core of the upgrade.

Air Vice Marshal Ron Dick was the Air Attaché at the British Embassy in Washington in 1982 and recounted the story to the RAF Historical Society some years later (published in the RAFHS Journal 30 in 2003). He recounted stories of his many visits to J3 (Operations) in the Pentagon with details of his increasingly outrageous demands on behalf of his Government. On this occasion he asked to buy an airfield which was greeted with some scepticism by his US colleagues. On his shopping list was a 7,000-foot runway, a parallel taxiway and arrester gear. Amazingly, the US military owned such contingency facilities but they were allocated as war stocks for the US Marines and held in reserve on the east coast of the USA. Despite the, apparently, outrageous nature of the request, and showing the strength of the special relationship, the AM2 matting which was used for building temporary runways was released and shortly afterwards shipped to the Falklands from Baltimore. Its journey south proved more predictable than its predecessor and it arrived safely on the islands where work began to install it.

Normally providing facilities for the inter-settlement air service, the original 4,000-foot runway at Stanley had to be extended to cope with the extra and larger aeroplanes and this was done by reinforcing the overrun area to the west of the airfield. Matting was laid over the original concrete runway and a newly reinforced extension by Army engineers. An AM2 runway consists of, literally, hundreds of sections of interlocked metal planks which have a load carrying capability able to take the weight of a Phantom or a C130 Hercules. Although the Air Attaché had secured a 7,000-foot runway which may have been enough to allow routine Phantom operations, geography constrained the extension and only 6,000 feet of useable surfaces could be installed. This was still barely adequate for a high performance aircraft such as the Phantom so radical thinking was needed. Hydraulic arresting systems, or RHAGs, were installed providing three cables; one at each end of the airfield and one at the midpoint of the runway. Using the cables on a daily basis turning Stanley into what was effectively a static aircraft carrier, would be how the Phantom squadron would operate. More AM2 planks would provide operating surfaces and dispersals.

With the airfield upgrade complete, a small detachment of Phantoms, still under the command of Ian McFaddyen, headed south arriving in The Falkland Islands on 17 October 1982. XV469 was the first Phantom to land at Stanley after its 3,750-mile trip during which it took fuel from Victor tankers *en route*. They were followed by a further eight aircraft from the squadron during the following week. Arriving at RAF Stanley, the Phantoms immediately began providing QRA taking over from the Sidewinder-armed, ground attack Harriers which had been operating as a makeshift reaction force. Despite squadron status, the detachment was initially nicknamed 'Phandet', and operated from the small aircraft servicing platform in front of the control tower until the new dispersals were ready to take

USAF Combat engineers lay an AM2 matting runway in the Middle East.© United States Air Force.

the full squadron. For a short period, the two types operated together before eventually, it was considered that the risk of rogue attacks had receded and the Harriers were relieved and flew home to UK. There could be no doubt about the importance of the contribution this unique aircraft and its pilots, both RAF and Royal Navy, had made to the campaign. It was fitting that a few photographs captured the unique joint formations which were mounted at that time.

Although the rotary hydraulic arrestor gear or RHAGs were similar to those installed at UK airfields they were considerably more powerful and were more like the units installed on aircraft carriers. With only a 600-foot run-out these cables brought the Phantoms to rest in half the usual distance. RHAGs were normally used to stop the Phantom in an emergency but with only 6,000 feet of runway available at Stanley they were brought into action on a routine basis and all missions would end in the approach end cable. From its approach speed of 145 knots, a Phantom was brought to rest in about 14 seconds. One of the aircraft's original design features now allowed it to operate in an unfamiliar environment. A feature of operating from Stanley would be that, until the new airfield at Mount Pleasant could be built, diversions in the event of bad weather or the runway being blocked, were not available. With bases in Argentina denied,

Next pages: Stanley airfield seen from a Phantom in the overhead. © David Lewis.

A formation of Phantoms and Harriers escort two C130 tankers. © David Lewis.

the only realistic alternatives were in Chile and this assumed that the Chilean Government remained supportive. Such a diversion was not without risk as the aircraft would have to pass close to Argentinian airspace *en route*, probably in formation with a vulnerable Hercules tanker. For that reason, Phantoms landing back at RAF Stanley carried extra fuel needed to hold off in the event of bad weather. As much as 4,000 lbs of fuel could remain in the tanks, more typical of the reserve held when bad weather was affecting the home base in UK. This was enough to give a good loiter time in the overhead but insufficient to reach a mainland diversion without air-to-air refuelling or AAR. Add to that the fact that Phantom crews at home operated from longer runways and, normally, without the extra weight of the missile load and the gun, this meant that the operating challenges for the newly deployed crews were significant. Operational aggression had to be tempered with caution.

The new dispersals were laid at the eastern end of the airfield on both sides of the runway and, slowly, small rubber hangars, nicknamed 'rubs', were erected to provide shelter from the harsh climate giving a semblance of permanence. This meant that the aircraft could be serviced in dry conditions making life significantly more bearable for the engineering personnel who worked in the extreme conditions. It also meant that the aircraft were protected from the weather. Surprisingly, until it was pressurised, the Phantom leaked like a sieve. If left outside without cockpit covers, water would find its way into the cockpit and play havoc with electronic systems. An aircraft which had been left outside would frequently suffer from problems on start up and the radios were particularly badly affected. At this time, ex RAF Germany crews were familiar with operating in hardened shelters unlike their UK colleagues, so procedures were quickly introduced based on RAF Germany standard operating procedures. The aircraft began to operate from the 'rubs' for normal training sorties, although the QRA aircraft still parked alongside the squadron buildings and had to be protected from the more extreme weather with cockpit covers.

Life was harsh for the early detachments and not only for the squadrons but all the personnel at Stanley. Initially living in tents, air and ground crew were soon accommodated aboard a requisitioned passenger ferry named the MV *Rangatira* which was moored in Stanley Harbour and adapted rapidly to accommodate additional personnel. Extra berths were squeezed into each of the cabins and the car decks were modified to provide more berths. At its peak, MV *Rangatira* accommodated nearly 1,300 personnel and, although she was nicknamed 'Old Smelly' and austere by most standards, the ship provided far better accommodation than the tented cities which had sprung up around the airfield. In keeping with the heightened tensions, 20mm Oerliken cannons were fitted to the upper deck and a helicopter-landing platform was added giving a constant reminder that Argentina's continued compliance could never be assumed.

Once 29 (Fighter) Squadron had become established, it was responsible for the air defence of the Falkland Islands from its arrival in October 1982 until the end of 1983 when the squadron was rebadged as 23 (Fighter) Squadron which assumed the role, albeit, for the time being, remaining at RAF Stanley. The squadron was manned by personnel from every UK Phantom squadron on a rotational basis serving four month tours on the islands.

The islands still bore the scars of war during those early days following cessation of hostilities. The worst scars were the countless minefields which had been laid by the Argentinians as a line of defence. Many were cleared in the first months by the immensely brave bomb disposal teams. Unfortunately, poor paperwork or inaccurate recording proved a block to completing the task efficiently. If, in the heat of battle, an Argentinian Officer had recorded the number of mines wrongly or mapped the boundaries incorrectly, the BDU teams were unable to verify with certainty that the minefield had been cleared. Just a single mine which could not be accounted for was enough. If there was any doubt, there was no doubt and barbed

Minefields littered the landscape.

wire fences sprung up and remained in place for many years afterwards to prevent the unwary from entering a potential hazardous area. For that reason, I fell across many minefields in the most beautiful locations as I toured the islands. Spotting the red sign with the skull and crossbones became a depressing fact of life.

On a visit to Goose Green, one of the more prominent victims of conflict was the hulk of the Rio Iguazu coastguard patrol vessel which lay abandoned in the inlet near the village for some years. It provided a gaunt reminder of the intensity of battle. As it approached the Argentinian garrison to deliver supplies it was strafed by Sea Harriers of 800 Naval Air Squadron in Choiseul Sound, was badly damaged and the crew ran the vessel aground to prevent it sinking. Still bearing the scars, the only thing that went on board during the years after the war were the seabirds which used the hulk as a nest. Standing on the shore looking at the vessel from close proximity, the swift brutality of modern conflict was dramatically evident. It was only removed some years later.

One of the most important operational locations for the Argentinians had been the airstrip at Goose Green which had been named Air Force Base Condor by the occupiers. Reconnaissance and Attack Group 3 operated 25 Pucara close air support aircraft which rotated between the Goose Green base and Port Stanley. The grass strip had been heavily defended by three 35mm Oerliken anti aircraft guns and a number of Rheinmetall 20mm guns. Point defence by anti aircraft artillery was an effective tactic as the Harrier force found to their cost

The hulk of the Rio Iguazu coastal patrol vessel.

during air attacks on Goose Green as the Army closed in. The Rheinmetall twin 20mm anti aircraft gun had been used in anger against the attacking Harriers during the battle and may even have been responsible for the loss of a Sea Harrier during the attack on 4 May 1982. Although that loss was attributed to the 35mm guns, the smaller calibre weapon was certainly used extensively as the shell cases which still littered the hedgerow proved. There was even speculation that the AAA had been used against troops at the height of the battle and its location would have allowed a clear view over the approaches to the village. With the conflict over, it took some time for the detritus to be cleared but in 1985, although the live rounds had been removed, countless ammunition boxes and spent cases still littered the perimeter of the former airfield. The larger calibre guns were repatriated to UK as spoils of war but a number of the smaller anti aircraft guns had been hastily abandoned as the British troops retook the village and still dotted the perimeter. Their fate is unclear. The hulk of a wrecked Pucara which had been hit during air attacks still lay on the grass airfield, the damage self evident. Investigating the facts after my return, the story was a sad one. The pilot of the Pucara, A-527, had been caught on the ground during an air attack as he began his take off roll along the grass runway. At take off speed, an aircraft has limited manoeuvrability and the pilot was unable to avoid the hundreds of bomblets from a BL755 cluster bomb dropped by a Sea Harrier. The airframe was totally destroyed and he died in his cockpit; one of the early victims of the campaign. The aircraft was disabled on 1 May 82 but the burned out hulk lay abandoned on the airstrip for many years before it was removed.

Most worryingly, the troops who recaptured the airfield found stores of napalm, a mixing facility and discarded napalm tanks. Although by 1985, the hardware was long gone, documents captured after the surrender showed how to fit the napalm tanks to the Pucara and confirmed the chilling reality that napalm could easily have been used against British troops. Sadly, the Argentinians were not alone in leaving discarded military hardware, and I found the tail cone of a BL755 weapon lying just inside a minefield where it fell during an attack on the airfield. The irony was not lost on me. A weapon which had speeded up the fall of the garrison during the war now lay as a piece of junk in a 'no go' area.

Standing looking down on Goose Green from the entrance to the former Argentinian airfield, it was hard to imagine the fighting which had occurred here. If a memory jogger was needed, a short walk into the rolling countryside brought me to the memorial to Colonel 'H' Jones who fell leading his troops into the attack. A simple pedestal and rocks marked the spot where he fell on the upslope of a steep rise in the terrain. Argentinian gun emplacements had been positioned

A Rheinmetall 20 mm anti-aircraft gun abandoned on Goose Green airfield.

The tail cone of a BL755 cluster bomb alongside the minefield marker posts.

The wreck of a Pucara destroyed by Harriers as it attempted to take off.

at the top of the rise on both sides of the steep gulley covering the route into the village with cross fire. He fell as the Paras attacked the positions. I was humbled by his sacrifice in earning the Nation's highest award for bravery and could only stand silently in a mark of respect.

It was also sobering to reflect on what might have transpired but for the decision to recapture the settlement. Had armed Pucaras operated freely from Goose Green against British troops advancing towards Stanley, the outcome of the conflict could have been radically different. Equally, the option to use the 1000 troops of 12th Regiment as a counter attack force would have changed the nature of the 'yomp' across country. As it was, all that remained was the wreckage of war and a few rutted farm tracks leading to the beautiful settlement on the bay.

Back on the airfield at RAF Stanley other Pucaras met their fate at the hands of the Army when they were rendered inoperable as the airfield was captured. Luckily, not all the aircraft were destroyed and a serviceable example was returned to UK for evaluation at the Aircraft and Armament Experimental Establishment at Boscombe Down. After the evaluation was complete, it plied the airshow circuit for a short while before finding its final home in the RAF Museum at Cosford where it still resides. For some time after the war a forlorn line up of Pucaras sat on the airfield awaiting their fate. A few were eventually tipped into a pit on site but the remainder were moved out to Rabbit Range to be used as targets for practice bombing sorties where they were slowly reduced to tiny pieces by the Harrier pilots. A single example survived on the islands and I was to be reacquainted some years later.

Some of the more obvious scars were the bomb craters from the attacks by the Vulcan during the Operation Black Buck raids. Resembling a watering hole, unless you knew the history of the local area it would be easy to mistake the water filled depression for something more natural. Of the twenty-one holes from the first attack only a few were still evident, although close inspection of the aerial view of the airfield shows a clear line across the terrain marking the attack run heading. Much analysis took place to determine the effectiveness of the raid despite the obvious knowledge that the ability to interdict a runway using dumb bombs is limited. Surprisingly, better-informed commentators, who should have known better, were dismissive. Dropping directly along the line of the runway is fraught with risk as a total miss is possible unless the line of attack is absolutely accurate and is precisely along the runway centreline. Equally, dropping the weapons at high crossing angles risks missing the target completely. Bombs have to be released sequentially to prevent them striking each other as they fall from the delivery aircraft. This spacing dictates that they will land some distance apart. The Vulcan crew dropped at an optimum angle, typically 30 degrees, to

A bomb crater made by a 1000 lb bomb dropped by the crew of XM607.

give a better probability that more than one weapon would land on the concrete strip. The remaining weapons would straddle the runway and the attack heading would have been chosen to give a good probability of hitting other high value installations. In any event, the psychological impact of twenty-one bombs landing in close succession at such an early stage of the conflict must have been truly terrifying to the Argentinians many of whom were conscripts with, perhaps, a limited will to defend the remote outpost. The ability to attack an airfield matured significantly over the following years as a series of precision guided munitions replaced the dumb bombs which the Vulcan had delivered during the famous raid. JP233 which carried runway cratering munitions was introduced during The Cold War but to deliver it, Tornado crews had to fly over the target. This weapon was eventually replaced by the Stormshadow cruise missile which allowed the launch aircraft to stand off many miles from its target and launch its attack from well outside the terminal defences. Had the Vulcan crews had this luxury, life would have been much less dangerous.

Once cleared and upgraded, RAF Stanley quickly settled into a routine with the Phantoms providing air defence coverage. Attack from the west was by no means out of the question so crews were wary. Set on the eastern extremities

A 23 (F) Squadron Phantom escorts the Secretary of State for Defence, Michael Heseltine, into RAF Stanley. © Steve Smyth

of East Falklands the airfield was protected to a small extent by the mountain ranges which sat just to the west of the bay. Stunningly pretty in peacetime, set amidst some rugged coastline and golden sandy beaches, it could not throw off the rather depressing air of a war zone which had become a mark during the occupation. The influx of thousands of British military personnel did little to lift that air. In the coming months, as the islands settled back into a strange normality, the first political visitors began to arrive. Naturally, it was the duty of 23 (F) Squadron crews to ensure that there were no shows of force from a disgruntled Argentinian Air Force and the VIPs were seen ashore in an appropriate manner. One of the early visitors was the Secretary of State for Defence who experienced for himself the stresses of an airborne refuelled journey into Stanley. He was escorted by Phantoms for the final leg of his journey.

CHAPTER 3
The Argentinian Air Threat

No one who watched the grainy newsreel showing air attacks against the British Task Force during the Falklands conflict could doubt the low flying skills of the Argentinian pilots. Operating at extreme low level, their error was not inaccurate flying but the fact that they flew their aircraft at such low levels that the fusing mechanism of the bombs they carried had insufficient time to arm properly. To deliver bombs at low level, retard fuses are fitted and fins or small parachutes deploy into the airflow and slow the weapon in flight allowing the delivery aircraft to escape avoiding the blast damage when the bomb detonates. The fuses were set assuming a higher release height so the bombs often passed through the ships before detonating; if at all. Some lodged within the ship lying dormant until defused by a bomb disposal expert. At the limits of range, the pilots faced a formidable opponent in the shape of a determined Royal Navy and, particularly the RN and RAF Harrier pilots flying from the carriers. Ranged against them, was a layered defence consisting of ship-based long-range surface-to-air missiles (SAMs), Rapiers, and short range anti aircraft guns. The extremely capable but at that time newly introduced Sea Wolf surface-to-air missile system was only fitted to a few of the task force ships such as HMS *Broadsword*. The majority of the British warships relied on the longer range but older Sea Dart which was optimised against a medium level threat. Some of the ancillary vessels were armed with little more than machine guns. The Army and RAF Rapiers which were deployed ashore were capable systems but were of an early 'Field Standard' which relied heavily on optical tracking. Designed for a NATO Central Region scenario, the hills and inlets of the Falklands gave Rapier crews a significant challenge in setting up their fire units to counter the low flying Argentinian aircraft. As the fire units were brought ashore, they were set up on the hillsides around San Carlos to give better sight of the surrounding airspace. Ironically, one of the limitations of the system was that the tracker was not easily depressed below level, a requirement not envisaged for the flat plains of Europe. With the fire units on the hills and attacking Mirages and A4s down in the valleys, the Rapier crews had difficulty pointing at the incoming threats and had a much reduced time to lock the missiles onto the target in order to fire. Early estimates suggested that as many as sixteen Argentinian aircraft had been lost to Rapier but these were later reduced to as few as four.

One of the major losses of Argentinian aircraft was to the Sea Harrier and, records show that twenty-two aircraft were lost with 8 being shot down in air-to-air combat with no corresponding losses on the British side. From a defensive point of view, the Argentinian aircraft were ill equipped for the fight. Assessments after the war suggested that they did not have operable radar warning receivers if, indeed, they were even fitted. There was no evidence from the newsreel footage that they were using chaff or flares to defeat missiles aimed against them. With the exception of the Super Etendard which carried the Exocet, the remainder of the fast jets carried only 'dumb' bombs which had to be visually aimed meaning they had to overfly the target leaving them vulnerable to engagement. Unlike their British opponents, they did not use laser guidance heads on these weapons which would have allowed the pilots a limited standoff avoiding the worst of the defensive fire. The combination of factors gave them a potentially lethal challenge so their commitment or bravery could not have been in doubt.

The best estimates of the Argentinian order of battle during the conflict showed that most of the fighters were deployed forward to the bases closest to the Falkland Islands to make best use of their available fuel. Air Force Skyhawks operated from Rio Gallegos and Santa Cruz and their naval equivalents, which were disembarked from the carrier 25 Mayo, operated from Rio Grande. Mirage IIIs operated from Comodoro Rivadavia and Rio Gallegos with the Israeli-built Daggers based at San Julian, Rio Gallegos and Rio Grande. The final combat type, the Super Etendard operated from Rio Grande alongside the Daggers. The only air-to-air refuelling assets were two C130 tankers which operated from Comodoro Rivadavia. It was the lack of refuelling capability which was to shape the conflict and, had more tankers been available, the outcome could have been much different, albeit not all the fast jets were AAR capable. In air combat, fuel is life. The inability to top off the tanks of the attacking fighter bombers prior to them starting their attack runs was to leave them vulnerable to the Sea Harriers. In a Phantom or a Tornado F3, fuel was held as a combat reserve; enough to conduct a supersonic intercept. This was known as 'Tiger Fast'. It would be a brave crew who started an engagement with less than this reserve as, once engaged, it could take time to achieve a firing position for a missile shot or, alternatively, to look for the opportunity to disengage. A mistimed disengagement was invariably lethal as it allowed an opportunity for an opponent to reposition for a missile shot. The more fuel which could be held in reserve, the less likely this would

The main Argentinian Airbases.

occur. The Argentinians had no such luxury and by the time they coasted in over the islands, they were already on fuel minimums if they were to return to their bases on the mainland. Some estimates suggested that the Mirage IIIs had just enough combat fuel for thirty seconds manoeuvring in the area, and certainly unable to use afterburner, giving a huge advantage to the Sea Harrier pilots. This meant that, tactically, the Argentinian pilots were committed to avoiding detection rather than confronting the combat air patrols aggressively.

The Argentinian planners had been able to deploy some tactical aircraft to the islands where they were able to operate for much of the conflict giving better persistence. After the early attacks by the Vulcan and Harriers against Stanley, the fast jets were withdrawn to the mainland. Despite being forward based, the remaining types were much less of a threat consisting of only lightly armed Aermacchi MB339 jets, Beech Turbo Mentors and Pucara light attack aircraft. Although still lethal, these aircraft could not operate from the mainland but had the advantage of being small enough to operate from tactical airstrips on the islands making them a little less vulnerable to attack. None of these types would have given a Harrier pilot much concern in air combat and the odds were firmly in his favour.

One of the benefits of analysing the threat so many years later is the advent of the internet. Former combatants now talk freely online and compare notes about equipment and engagements which occurred many years ago. The discussions offer a fascinating insight into how the individual encounters developed and the, often fatal, outcome. The respect between former enemies is palpable even in the stark environment of cyberspace.

The Argentinians operated two main combat aircraft. In the air-to-air role they received eight single-seater and two two-seater trainer versions of the Mirage III in 1971 directly from France. This initial batch was equipped with the Matra 530 semi-active air-to-air missile and DEFA 30mm cannons for their air-to-air role. A second batch of aircraft was delivered in 1981 which was able to carry the Matra 550 Magic I infra-red air-to-air missile making them much more effective in combat. In addition, a number of Israeli-built Daggers which was a development of the Mirage III/V were delivered in two batches; the first one in 1978 and the second in 1981. Of the thirty-nine aircraft delivered, two were lost during training. Reportedly, the Dagger was able to carry both 1,300 litre and 1,600 litre fuel tanks but carried mainly the latter during combat operations. For air-to-air missions, the Daggers were fitted with 2 Israeli Shafrir Mk-4 infra-red missiles and 2 DEFA 30mm cannons.

For Phantom and Tornado F3 crews defending the islands after the war, the possibility of rogue attacks by Mirages or Skyhawks was not out of the question. For that reason, crews took some time to assess their potential opponents in terms of performance. A good friend, Rick Groombridge, a hugely experienced

A French Air Force Mirage III similar to those operated by the Argentinian Air Force.

fighter pilot and instructor, flew the Mirage III on exchange with the French Air Force in the 1970s and offered an insight into its handling:

> The Mirage III was a contrast after a tour as an instructor on the Lightning. Although it had only one engine its power to weight ratio in the clean wing fit or fitted with its light tanks known as 'Les Supersoniques', was similar to the 'P1' as the French called the Lightning at the time.
>
> Compared to the British aircraft ranged against it during the Falklands campaign, the Mirage was much lighter and quicker than the F4 and its thrust increment in reheat was the same (circa 25%). It also had a rocket fit for high level but this took up fuel space and would not have been carried for the Falklands push. It was very similar to the Tornado except that the pitch response did not fade at high angles of attack as it did not have any spin or stall protection like the Tornado F2/F3. This meant that high AoA [*angle of attack*], handling was benign and the Mirage would not flick into a spin when you maneuvered hard. In fact, in a hard turning environment, the aircraft was a drag master and it 'wallowed'. However, its high thrust to weight ratio meant that you could take advantage of this characteristic at low speed and, without losing any more energy, threaten the opponent. However, once low on energy it was like the F4 and it was not as quick to accelerate as the Tornado, unless you carried the auxiliary rocket.
>
> In a Mirage it was just as easy to pull off the speed in a 'circle of joy' because of its

high pitch response. French pilots used the 'Barn Door' escape manoeuvre, which was similar to 'Viffing' [*vectoring in forward thrust in the Harrier*] which consisted of a rapid yank of the stick at 300kts or below which washed off the speed rapidly causing the attacker to overshoot. If the attacker maintained his energy and the defender was not quick enough to unload, he would lose out. Experienced pilots who trusted their engines down to really slow speeds, say 130kts, would pull this one off regularly! As a basic airframe, the pitch rate was good but in roll it suffered, as all delta wing aircraft do, from an adverse handling characteristic known as roll/yaw coupling. When the pilot rolled the Mirage around its axis, the automatic control inputs corrected the pilot and slowed the roll slightly. The Phantom was slow in roll so, although the Mirage would roll better than the Phantom, it was nowhere near as agile in this regime as the Tornado. It was, however, better in the vertical and, with its high thrust-to-weight ratio and lighter overall weight it out performed both the Phantom and the Tornado F3 in this area. If pilots could employ this tactic it would have been highly successful.

The Mirage had a number of external fuel tanks, the largest of which carried 1600 litres making it very flexible. During the Falklands campaign, the '6 Juliet' tanks, which carried 1300 litres each side, affected performance but, when empty, the limitations were less significant. Post conflict analysis suggests that these tanks were jettisoned in the combat area providing the full performance from the airframe.

Rick mentions one of the often quoted tactics of the Falklands war, namely the Harrier employ 'Viffing' and the Mirage pilot's equivalent the 'barn door' manoeuvre to provide a combat edge. In theory this sounds like a panacea and anyone who has watched Top Gun will have seen the 'Mig' forced out in front by 'Maverick' as his F14 suddenly loses all forward momentum. The Russians flirted with the concept by developing the 'Cobra' manoeuvre a few years ago which achieves a similar effect. Against a wary opponent or in a 'multi bogey' environment this was a dangerous tactic. When used in a one versus one scenario during a basic fighter manoeuvre sortie, the tactic was extremely effective and would leave a less agile or less able Phantom or Tornado pilot struggling to respond. It would have to be used sparingly for real. The 'VIFF' left a defender with little energy to manoeuvre his aircraft and left him totally vulnerable to engagement by another member of the opposing formation. If the fleeting shot opportunity failed, he would need to recover his fighting speed quickly as no fighter pilot wants to be in a combat engagement with absolutely no energy. The manoeuvre would probably be used against a single opponent or as a 'last ditch' manoeuvre to avoid a missile or guns shot. Critically, in the Falklands scenario, such manoeuvres cost a lot of fuel as full power and even reheat was needed to recover. They would have been used sparingly, if at all.

The Mirage was a classic delta wing fighter and whilst I never had the opportunity to fly the aircraft, I did have the chance to fly a representation of an aircraft of this type in the BAE Systems Air Combat Simulator at Warton. The ACS was a twin-domed simulator equipped with a single cockpit in each dome and controlled by a computer. The cockpits had relatively simple instruments which replicated the weapons fit of a generic fighter, albeit quite similar to the Tornado and Typhoon cockpit. Cockpits could be reconfigured by changing instruments to replicate different types. An instructor in a separate control room controlled the training session. The 'world' was projected onto the inside of the dome by a huge projector behind each cockpit giving a realistic representation of the airspace. There was never any attempt to install a two-seat cockpit as the project started life as a company private venture. The two domes could, however, be flown in linked mode allowing a pilot to fly from one cockpit and a navigator to operate in the other. In this mode, the crew fought against the computer. In independent mode, the pilot in each dome fought against each other. During air combat training, we would often put a navigator into the second dome and pit his inferior flying skills against a Tornado F3 flown by a squadron pilot. By giving the navigator a higher performance aircraft, interesting scenarios could be generated giving pilots a different challenge. After the session, computer data could be analysed to determine when each pilot was in a position to launch a missile and how well each pilot had executed his manoeuvres to engage his opponent. The mission could be replayed in the domes to allow individual analysis. Crucially, an alternative model could be loaded into the computer allowing the simulator to fly as a Phantom, Tornado F3 or a Hawk.

The second dome could simulate a number of typical threat aircraft, either controlled by the computer or a pilot. Using the ACS, crews could train in the simulator against the threat they would face 'down south'. As Rick suggests, in a short neutral engagement employing basic fighter manoeuvres a Tornado F3 was well matched against the Mirage and Skyhawk. With better fuel reserves over the islands and employing its superior weapons effectively, a Tornado F3 could hold off a Mirage until it could employ a weapon. The Mirage had much better instantaneous turn performance and excellent nose authority at slow speed and the higher the altitude, the bigger the advantage to the Mirage pilot. With unfettered use of reheat, in a flat fight, the Mirage pilot could employ that advantage arcing the turn and closing for an inevitable missile of guns kill. Whilst the Mirage would generate a very impressive initial turn, this lead to a rapid decay in energy; in other words the Mirage would slow down rapidly. Providing a Tornado crew recognised this and kept their own energy high, they could negate the advantage. The Mirage would look threatening, always able to point at its opponent but in reality the missile faced an impossible task with massive 'undertake' in this scenario. This meant that staying in a turning fight, inevitably, would lead to, at best, a stalemate or at worst a very slow speed fight if the Tornado pilot was naive enough to be suckered in. Once slow, energy could only be regained by using reheat or losing altitude both of which the Mirage pilot would be reluctant to do if on fuel minimums. The advantage in the Falklands was that the Mirage pilots could not afford excessive, if any, use of reheat so the advantage swung back towards the Tornado. A Mirage which stayed 'to play' was lost as his fuel slowly ran out. At best he would have to seek refuge at an RAF base. Using its more effective missiles across the circle gave the Tornado the edge. The ability to lock the weapons onto an opponent was much improved in the Tornado and by the time AMRAAM and ASRAAM had been deployed allied with the Joint Tactical Information Distribution System, or JTIDS, which gave crews superb situation awareness, the advantage was firmly with Tornado F3 crews. Close engagements were unnecessary and a Phantom or Tornado crew would fight a long-range battle. Although the Mirage was able to carry the Matra 530 long-range missile, reportedly, they never carried it on combat sorties over the Falkland Islands, possibly because of the drag penalty. In the UK we had long known that this weapon in the form delivered to Argentina had severe limitations only rectified by the French much later. Discussing the weapon with a French pilot during one squadron exchange, he was extremely dismissive and suggested that it would have been of little use in combat because of system limitations and that the weight penalty was greater than its value. He advocated dumping it in the river on take off to save weight. Discussions among experts after the conflict suggested that the weapon would only have been considered to counter the threat from the long range missions from the Vulcan assuming the Mirage could have been positioned sufficiently far forward to pose a threat. There were few opportunities given the way the conflict developed for the Argentinian pilots to employ the 530 against the Harriers.

The second combat type was the A4 Skyhawk which was in the same category as the Mirage but optimised as a bomber in Argentinian service. The main difference is that it was not fitted with a reheat system but, like the Mirage, it was a low wing loaded delta wing design. Its turning performance was excellent so the TA4 two seat trainer was selected by the US Navy as their aggressor training aircraft replicating Soviet Migs during the Cold War. It had a good thrust to weight ratio and excellent throttle response from its single engine which was essential to allow it to operate from carriers. With these characteristics coupled with excellent slow speed handling and its small size, it was a formidable opponent in the hands of an expert pilot. Reportedly, 130 A4s in total were delivered to Argentina with the first A-4Bs delivered in 1966 and another batch in 1970. In 1976, a further 25 A-4Cs were ordered. The C model had five weapons pylons and could use AIM-9B Sidewinders. The Argentinian

A civilian registered A4N Skyhawk. The earlier Argentinian A4Bs and A4Cs did not have the 'hump back' spine, although the later A4AR did.

Navy also bought Skyhawks in 1971 in the form of 16 A-4Bs plus two airframes for spare parts. These later aircraft were also fitted with five weapon pylons and could carry the AIM-9B. Although the later models had later designations, the Argentinians referred to all their A4s as A4Bs or A4Cs. Whatever the theoretical numbers, come the conflict, only forty-eight Skyhawks were deployed to the southern bases. By then, the fleet was suffering from poor reliability as the effects of an earlier US embargo on spare parts imposed during 'The Dirty War' had made maintenance difficult. Press reports at the time suggested that perhaps only 75% of the aircraft were available at any one time from a potential fleet of eighty airframes.

We also had knowledge of the A4's performance as aircrew who had flown with the US Navy on exchange duties flew the TA4 during their tours. Many RAF test pilots had also flown the aircraft during training. This information was available to crews who operated in the South Atlantic in order to formulate tactics.

The Super Etendard was the enigma and, being used only by the French

Navy in Europe, few of us had the opportunity to fly against it and assess its performance. Not the most manoeuvrable aircraft with its swept wing design, during the conflict it operated in open ocean and was rarely threatened by the Sea Harriers. Facing the Etendard would have held few concerns for a competent Phantom or Tornado crew armed with semi active, head-on capable missiles even though it could carry the Magic I infra-red missile. Sea Harrier pilots would have been equally confident. Its strength was the Exocet missile coupled with air-to-air refuelling which made it an extremely flexible aircraft to employ. Able to stand off from its target, it released its missile at long range allowing the weapon to penetrate the airspace around the Task Force. Reportedly, the Argentinians only received fourteen Exocet missiles with their Super Etendard purchase. Of these, only ten were available during the conflict making those which were available the most precious commodity the Argentinians could call upon. Few could doubt its capability once pictures of the smoking hulk of HMS *Sheffield* were published but in a huge gesture of support to their UK allies, the French refused to supply additional missiles or to provide technical support during the conflict. Recent release of previously classified papers shows that The Prime Minister had to exercise a good deal of robust diplomacy in discussions with the French President to ensure that the flow of assistance stopped. Had her requests been refused, it might have made for interesting discussions in Brussels if France had continued to supply arms for use against a NATO Nation under attack from a non NATO country even if France was not a full member of NATO at that time. As it was, the French were fully supportive.

The concept of operations for Exocet was for the aging P2 Neptune to be used to provide target data to the Etendard pilots to allow the Exocet to be primed before launch. Reportedly, the obsolete maritime patrol aircraft suffered from such poor serviceability that the Argentinians were often forced to rely on Falklands-based ground radars to predict where the task force was operating. Although difficult, by analysing where the Harriers popped up and appeared on radar after launch, a radar operator could guess on the location of the fleet. With foresight and sound operational security procedures, the task force commanders were careful to ensure that the pull up and recovery locations were random making the targeting task much more difficult.

The Skyhawks, Daggers and Super Etendards, were used in the attack role, although there were a few escort missions recorded by the Daggers carrying Shafrir IR missiles. They predominantly flew ground attack missions carrying external fuel tanks, 2 x 1,000-lb or 4 x Mk 82 500-lb bombs on underwing pylons. The Skyhawks, although able to carry Sidewinders were not seen to do so in the bombing role and carried a similar load to the Daggers. The Etendards operated exclusively in the anti shipping role carrying the Exocet missiles and external fuel tanks. The nature of their role meant that it was the one combat type which survived the conflict without loss saying much about the effectiveness of the more clinical attack profiles and weapons fits. The Argentinians operated mostly at low level and this environment poses challenges of its own. Aircraft with a low wing loading, although enjoying better turning performance, suffer from a much harsher ride than aircraft such as the F4 Phantom or Tornado F3. The Mirage and Skyhawk would have been affected at low level and extended periods at extremely low heights would add significantly to the physical stress of a combat mission which would have been extremely high in the first case. I have little doubt that the Argentinian pilots would have been physically drained by the time they pressed any attack over the islands or the task force.

The Mirages, operated by Grupo 8, were optimised for air-to-air role and were never used in the bombing role. In the early stages, they were used in the defensive counter air role against the Sea Harriers but after early losses, it was recognised that they faced severe constraints operating at the limits of range. They were switched to a decoy role trying to tempt the Harriers away from the attack aircraft, albeit with limited success. After those first losses there were no further Mirage casualties. Of significance, on 1 May 1982 a Mirage which engaged in air-to-air combat with a Sea Harrier was damaged after taking a hit from a Sidewinder. With insufficient fuel to return his crippled aircraft to the mainland, the pilot elected to divert to Port Stanley airfield but during the recovery was engaged by his own air defence forces and shot down killing the pilot.

The lack of air-to-air refuelling capability was a severe limitation for the Argentinians. Only the Super Etendards and Skyhawks could refuel in mid air leaving the Mirages and Daggers to work within their fuel constraints and at the limit of combat endurance. In practice, the C130s supported mostly the Super Etendard missions reflecting the operational imperative to destroy the carriers. The anti ship aircraft flew missions approaching four hours in duration which were only possible with AAR support. Towards the end of the conflict there was evidence that the Argentinian Navy and Air Force conducted a coordinated mission on 29 May 1982 to target HMS *Invincible*. Down to a single remaining Exocet, one final set piece was planned using A4 Skyhawks to follow up an Exocet shot and engage with 'dumb' 500-lb bombs. Operating from Rio Grande, the joint formation transited to the operational area at medium level taking on extra fuel from a C130 tanker. Descending to low level, the Etendard pilot detected a shipping target which he presumed to be HMS *Invincible* and launched the remaining Exocet before returning to base. The Skyhawk pilots pressed inbound following the track of the anti ship missile before detecting smoke on the horizon. Combat reports from each side differ with Argentinian sources claiming damage to Invincible whereas British reports suggest that ships were making smoke for decoy purposes. The Exocet missed its target after being decoyed or damaged by defensive gunnery fire. What is clear is that 2 Skyhawks were engaged by Sea Darts and destroyed before reaching the task force. The remaining Skyhawks found targets and dropped their weapons. During the debriefing, Argentinian pilots were convinced that they had attacked HMS *Invincible* whereas British reports suggested it was HMS *Avenger*. It was telling that the aircraft lost during that raid were lost to SAMs rather than to the Sea Harriers and underlines the complexities of holding alert from the deck even when under attack.

Debriefing air-to-air engagements, Royal Navy pilots admitted being surprised at the way the Argentinian pilots flew tactical formation at low level. It was reported that they flew a fairly tight finger or arrow formation, albeit at very low level and at 500kts and above. Such formations give little mutual support or cross cover within the formation and are only used by RAF and RN pilots to manoeuvre a formation in restricted airspace. It was generally the case that the British pilots flew 'battle formation' where aircraft operate in a combat spread, line abreast, at a range appropriate to the height and threat. It is universally accepted that the Argentinians would have posed a significantly greater threat to the Sea Harrier pilots if they had flown a more fluid card formation behind the attacking bombers. Four aircraft flying card formation sit in a square formation, literally at four corners of a card. Daggers armed with Shafrir or Mirages armed with Magic missiles sitting behind the bombers would have been well placed to take opportunity shots against Harriers pressing against the bombers. If an engagement between the fighters had occurred, the bombers may have escaped unmolested. As it was, the aircraft flying in the less tactical formations were easier to engage and suffered greater losses.

Like the Sea Harrier, the Mirage was equipped with a simple pulse radar, the Cyrano II, which had poor look down capability like other systems of its generation. Forced to transit at higher levels to save fuel, the Mirage and Dagger pilots sometimes found themselves above the Sea Harriers giving the radar advantage to the British pilots. From personal experience, detecting a target below your own aircraft using pulse mode makes radar manipulation and interpretation harder but it is by no means impossible. Despite this, it was often cited as a reason for the lack of success against the Sea Harriers. Returning to the issue of defensive aids, it was harder to determine whether they were fitted with, radar warning receivers. Although both the Mirage and Dagger had RWRs fitted when operated by their host countries, it was unclear whether they were delivered to Argentina under the export deal. Speculation by British analysts after the campaign was that the Argentinian aircraft did not have serviceable

RWRs which would have made life much easier for British crews had the fact been generally known. The tactical advantage of being able to lock up the threat with impunity is enormous. Lack of warning of an attack by incoming fighters, particularly outside friendly radar cover, gives the attacker a huge advantage allowing the ingressor little chance to fly a defensive manoeuvre until he gains visual contact. By then, an attacking Phantom or Tornado F3 would have launched a Sparrow or Skyflash missile. Even the Sea Harrier would have probably launched a visually laid AIM-9L Sidewinder.

Often ignored, the Argentinians continued to operate a handful of Canberra bombers until early 2000. Of the ten B62s and two T64 trainers delivered from the UK in the early 1970s, eight of them were deployed to Trelew, albeit nearly 700 miles from their potential targets. It acquitted itself well flying over fifty sorties against the task force, both day and night, for the loss of two aircraft. It had the dubious distinction of being the last aircraft to be lost to British action during the conflict. As it was not equipped with an air-to-air weapon, the Canberra was not a threat to the defending fighters. It did, however have a much longer range and could threaten the islands. At low level, the Canberra was easy to see and I trained against it many times. It presented a large radar signature so was easily detected on radar and was vulnerable despite a decent turn performance. It was however, in its element at high level where it had much better performance than the fighters ranged against it. With its large wing it could fly and, more importantly, turn better at higher levels than the Phantom or Tornado and could manoeuvre quite aggressively at those heights. This made it harder to engage successfully with a Sparrow or a Skyflash as defensive tactics could negate a shot quite easily leaving a fighter crew committed to a close in visual Sidewinder firing. With a tight radius of turn, even that could be problematic. Realistically, however, once detected, it was a case of survival for the Canberra crew rather than pressing home an attack. A wary fighter crew would disengage, reposition and wait for the Canberra to turn for home before pressing for a kill. Once it disengaged its slow speed was a huge disadvantage and it could be easily overhauled.

It is interesting to project a potential engagement between Phantoms and Tornados against Mirages or Skyhawks had a runway been built earlier. Unlike those between the Argentinian aircraft and the Sea Harriers which occurred over the islands at the limit of the Argentinians range, these engagements would have been further to the west. Combat air patrols would have been pushed offshore away from the western coastline to threaten the attackers before landfall meaning that the attacker's fuel reserves would have been higher. Despite that, the attacker faced a dilemma. Once engaged, the first decision was whether to jettison the weapons and abort the attack. By doing so, the weight of the weapons was removed and the aircraft could be flown closer to its limits. With a full weapon load, even an aircraft as agile as an F16 is more vulnerable. It is unlikely that an attacking pilot would retain the weapons but, if he did, the performance would be severely limited and a Phantom or Tornado would have been handed a significant advantage making a kill more likely. In forcing an attacker to dump the bomb load, a defending crew achieves a 'mission kill' namely, the aircraft might return safely to its base but at the cost of missing its target. Most Phantom or Tornado F3 crews might elect to disengage at that point leaving the fight for another day; guaranteed survival is a valid tactic. For an attacking bomber pilot, an air-to-air kill, whilst headline material, was not a mission goal. Unless presented with a simple shot, most pilots might seek to disengage and return another day hoping to avoid a confrontation rather than seek glory. In an air combat training engagement, the simulated opponents invariably operate from the same airfield or from separate airfields but similar distances away from the operating area. A Phantom or Tornado crew operating within 100 miles of base would have a huge advantage over a Mirage or Skyhawk pilot operating 300 miles from base. Pressing the engagement to absolute minimums was always easier when close to home as calculating the fuel requirement was more accurate. The greater the distance from home, the higher the fuel reserves which were needed plus the higher the weight of the aircraft, the lower the turn performance available. What is certain is that neither of the potential protagonists had diversion options *en route*. It was 300 miles across the sea to the western Argentinian bases and Stanley was further away than Mount Pleasant and still a significant transit. Fuel was life.

In a shock development in 1994, the USA made an offer to modernise thirty-six ex US Marine Corps A4M Skyhawks. As an air defence desk officer in the UK Ministry of Defence at the time this came as a big surprise as it significantly increased the threat to the Falkland Islands from the Argentinian Air Force. We watched this development closely and it caused much discussion between ourselves and the US Air Attaché in London given that the move was purely commercial. The only positive was that the Argentinians had not received long range fighters such as the F15 or later model F16s which would have seriously disrupted the balance. Perhaps with hindsight it was a blessing in disguise. Thirty-two A4Ms were selected from the 'boneyard' at Davis Monthan Air Force Base and a programme of work was contracted with Lockheed Martin to convert the first airframes in California and the remainder in Cordoba in Argentina. The contract also included spares and a mission simulator. The A4Ms were upgraded to A4AR Fightinghawk status which included a complete airframe overhaul and the fitment of modern avionics. The Westinghouse AN/APG66V2 radar was an updated version of the original F16 radar system and gave a limited track while scan capability and was integrated into a glass cockpit with hands on throttle and stick or, HOTAS, controls and a head up display. Modern digital avionics, including an inertial navigation system, were controlled via a Mil standard 1553 databus. Most significantly, the defensive aids system was upgraded to fit AN/ALQ 126B and AN/ALQ 162 jamming systems and AN/ALR47 chaff and flare dispensers. All these systems could be programmed to jam the Tornado's air-to-air radar and missiles. Intended primarily as a bomber carrying up to 9000 lbs of bombs on five hard points, the aircraft could also carry 2 AIM-9M Sidewinders and 2 x 20mm cannon with 100 rounds per gun giving it a useful air-to-air capability. In comparison with the old A4Bs and Cs which the force had previously operated this was a quantum leap forward and could have posed a significant challenge to the Tornado F3s which, by then, equipped 1435 Flight. Deliveries began in late 1997 and the first Argentinian built airframes were delivered in mid 1998. Fortuitously, a programme to upgrade the Tornado F3 to fit longer range and more capable AMRAAM and ASRAAM air-to-air missiles was already in train and, once delivered into service, the defensive balance was regained. The Argentinian protests of British escalation when Typhoon was eventually deployed rang hollow given this earlier improvement in Argentinian capability.

Despite concerns over the combat air capability, in the years after the conflict, the interaction was not between British and Argentinian fighters but between British fighters and Argentinian surveillance aircraft. Reacting to these intrusions fell to aircraft from the Quick Reaction Alert force as operations settled into those more reminiscent of The Cold War. All the combat aircraft which were forward deployed returned to their principal operating bases and, in order to threaten the islands again, they would have to be moved forward yet again. This would give advanced warning of military intent during times of increased tension. It would be likely to trigger a British response to reinforce the air defence assets in theatre should such provocation occur.

CHAPTER 4
RAF Stanley

Over the coming years there were a number of key events which shaped the nature of the military presence. It was decided that 23 (Fighter) Squadron would become the resident unit in the Falkland Islands so it disbanded on 31 March 1983 at RAF Wattisham in Suffolk and reformed at RAF Stanley in the Falkland Islands the next day. Over the coming years it maintained squadron strength with as many as eleven aircraft on the books during the 1980s and 'The Red Eagles' became a familiar name to the islanders.

My departure for Stanley on my first visit in the same year could hardly be described as trouble free. My wife was expecting our second child and kids are unpredictable even before arrival. My son had already given advanced warning that he was ready to join the family; early if need be! I was on notice to deploy 'Down South' and such plans are immovable so as the departure day came closer, there was more than a feeling of trepidation. Those who have served will know the 'faff' which accompanies an operational deployment. The Air Force system bursts into life, issues bags of equipment which may or may not be needed and fills each arm with every inoculation known to medical science. The paperwork which is essential before departure never seems to be needed in theatre. What becomes apparent is that the enemy is far less effective at generating combat stress. What I didn't know at the time was that my Squadron Commander had already been given notice that two Phantoms were planned to return to UK for servicing and that my pilot and I would almost certainly be the crew allocated to the task; but no cast iron guarantees. The Boss was doing his best to offer me an early return but as I climbed aboard the Tristar at RAF Brize Norton, I was not sure whether I would be home in a few short weeks or whether it would be four months later. Even if I stayed for the full detachment it meant I would be home in time for my son's birth but the timing was tight, even if he played ball. Such trials and tribulations are a regular feature of service life; I was no different and the same stresses are being experienced today as people are posted to overseas theatres of operations for their tours of duty. Ironically as soon as we arrived on 23 (F) Squadron, we were interviewed by the squadron Boss who made it perfectly clear that we had been posted in, specifically, to take a Phantom home to the UK. Life in the islands was hectic and stressful and he wanted fresh crews to undertake the long transit sorties. The crew who would be leading the return deployment had only been in theatre a few weeks longer than us and were already planning the details of the operation. The prospect of an early escape made the detachment a lot more pleasurable as well as providing a totally new challenge which none of us had ever faced.

Before I even set foot on the islands, I had to experience the process of getting there which was, in comparison with flying with a civilian airline, quite painful. All RAF air transport movements originate from one of the main transport bases and are controlled by the RAF Movements staff. For the C130 Hercules this was RAF Lyneham and for the VC10s and Tristars, RAF Brize Norton. After a road move to the departure airfield, everyone 'enjoyed' an overnight stop in the Transit Mess at Brize Norton. Colloquially known as 'The Half Star Hilton', it was a time warp; reminiscent of 'days gone by' fitted out with 1960s 'G Plan' furniture and a real 'blast from the past'. Once in the grip of the RAF Movements staff, life could be tedious and a serving Member of Parliament, coincidentally, a Territorial Army Officer made his views known quite forcibly in the press after a recent operational detachment. Despite being on base and a captive audience, a call at 'O Dark Early' to make a 9 a.m. take off was inevitable and predictable. Despite a typically enjoyable RAF 'Full Fry' breakfast, the short trip in a coach to the air terminal which followed the 3 a.m. morning call was a brief prelude to the hours of endless fun before we were finally called to board the Tristar. There was no deference to rank during the process and wing commanders would vie for space with senior aircraftmen in a budget airline style scramble for a seat. Onboard, in a move which was truly unfathomable, the entertainment system had been removed from the Tristar after the ex-airline jets were purchased from British Airways and Pan American leaving a good book or a 'walkman' as the only ways to while away the long flight southbound. The movie screens were retrofitted some years later after a pang of corporate conscience and a further lucrative contract. The interim stop was at Wideawake airfield on Ascension Island, known in true Air Force style by its acronym, ASI. The volcanic island sits just south of the Equator at about 8 degrees latitude. On my first deployment, the aircraft suffered a minor problem which required rectification before we could continue our journey to the Falklands. Normally planned for only a short stop, personnel were sometimes kept onboard during the refuelling. With a few extra hours to kill there was no choice but to allow us to disembark for a leg stretch even though the lack of facilities meant that we were confined to a tiny building

A 23 (F) Sqn Phantom escorts the Tristar.© Steve Smyth

with a small compound in the glaring equatorial sun. Despite the heat, the leg stretch was welcome yet it offered a tantalising glimpse of what we would be missing over the coming months given that the Falkland's climate was far from tropical. The mountains which flanked the runway towered above base and I took careful note as I knew the next time I would see them, or maybe not, would be in the pitch black of an equatorial night on my return trip in a Phantom. The slightly shorter second leg to the islands concluded with a pre-planned tradition as the Tristar was intercepted by resident 23 (F) Squadron Phantoms as it approached the coastline. Often this would be the first and last time that some of the new arrivals would see the Phantom 'up close and personal' so everyone flocked to the window seats to catch a glimpse of the armed aeroplanes on each wing. Even though I had thousands of hours on the aeroplane I still pressed my nose to the window and clicked away with a camera along with my fellow passengers. Invariably the intercept occurred well to the north and the Phantoms would remain in loose formation as the airliner made its initial descent. With typical cloud conditions, this normally meant a short period with each fighter tucked in close formation on the wingtip to descend under the cloud deck. Again, this was one of the few occasions when most personnel would experience the thrill of a fighter jet within inches of the wingtip as the Tristar positioned for finals. The Phantom launch was always timed to coincide with the arrival of the Tristar so after intercepting and escorting the huge transport aeroplane to within a few miles of the coast, the Phantoms would break away and continue their mission.

Until the opening of the runway at Mount Pleasant (MPA), the only air transport into the Falklands had been the venerable C130s as the runway at Stanley was too short to accommodate airliners. At 3,500 miles, the maximum unrefuelled range of the Hercules was short of the 4,000 miles between ASI and Stanley and well short of the combined return distance. The C130 was the first propeller driven aircraft to refuel from a Victor tanker so the test crews had many challenges to produce operating procedures which would work. Victor tankers would accompany the C130 down route passing sufficient fuel during interim refuelling brackets to allow it to complete its mission. Typically, these brackets would be about four hours into the flight and again at eight hours if necessary. As with all air-to-air refuelling operations (AAR) it was complex. A Victor would normally transfer fuel to fighters at a speed of 250 knots and, at a pinch, could slow to 230 knots. With every lever in the cockpit pushed forward to the firewall the C130 could maybe accelerate to that speed but not comfortably. To hook the two together in mid air needed a compromise and a manoeuvre known as 'tobogganing' was adopted. The Victor would approach alongside the receiver from behind and begin a descent allowing the C130 to push its speed up and stay in formation. Literally, as the name suggests, the pair of aircraft would descend as if riding a sledge down a hillside. Colleagues described refuelling brackets which finished as low as 5,000 feet above a very inhospitable South Atlantic before enough fuel had been transferred to the C130 to allow it to reach the islands. Even then, success was not guaranteed. With the unpredictability of the weather in the South Atlantic it was not unknown for a C130 to hold in the overhead at Stanley waiting for a gap in the weather which would allow it to land but, if unsuccessful, for it to divert to the South American mainland or return all the way back to Ascension. This obviously required the use of yet more precious tankers for the return trip and tested the mettle of

Looking across the RAF Fire Service vehicles, an airbridge C130 Hercules departs for UK from the main runway at RAF Stanley. © Steve Smyth

inherently nervous crews as they tried to rendezvous with their tankers in open ocean on the return leg. Some staggeringly long sortie times were recorded by C130 crews during this phase of operations.

The opening of RAF Mount Pleasant with its 8,500-foot runway meant that larger airliners could assume the trooping role. Before the Tristar was pressed into service, Boeing 747s of British Airways had been contracted for the run. Although manned by BA crews and initially flown from London Heathrow, eventually the flights began to be mounted from RAF Brize Norton to ensure the hapless travellers weren't swayed by the bright lights of London. Whilst there may have been a few complaints about the abnormal rigours of a military flight, most of us were just glad that the two trips had been in the comfort of an airline seat with food and drink rather than the austerity of the rear cabin of a C130 with a 'butty box' as our predecessors had experienced. Of course, a few personnel were still allocated a C130 flight as their mode of transport and, in this case, personnel who had previously flown in a C130 knew enough tricks to arrive at Lyneham prepared for the flight. The seats in a C130 were made of

A British Airways Boeing 747 gives passengers one last glimpse of RAF Stanley before departing.

thick webbing material and designed to take a paratrooper in full gear and were not particularly comfortable for a long-range flight. I had spent quite a lot of time as a junior navigator being shipped around Europe and the Mediterranean in the back of a 'Herc' and knew that a cheap hammock from the local camping store could be strung between the cargo load and the side of the airframe or above the tail ramp. With ear-plugs and a sleeping bag, relative luxury and a few hours sleep was assured. This secret was jealously guarded as there were a limited number of suitable 'camping pitches'. One thing was absolutely certain; when a Tristar arrived at MPA it was always a welcome sight. For those who were part way through their deployment it meant the arrival of their precious mail from home. For those at the end of their time it was their transport home. Not surprisingly, the complaints and criticisms of the trip out were never repeated for the return journey, although it was still a welcome relief to leave the gates of RAF Brize Norton, homeward bound. For new arrivals at the southerly end, the trip from the new airhead at Mount Pleasant to RAF Stanley was over rough, dusty, graded roads in an RAF coach and was designed to test not only your patience but the quality of your dental work. The short 30-mile trip took well over an hour and the pitfalls for unwary drivers were legendary and accidents frequent.

Imagery ©2012 Cnes/Spot Image, Digital Globe, Geo Eye, Map Data ©2012 Google

RAF Stanley was located on the peninsular east of Port Stanley.

Having driven the road many times in a Land Rover, the coach drivers did an amazing job to stay on the rough, elevated 'cart track'.

RAF Stanley had improved markedly by the time I first arrived a few years after the conflict, although it was still austere by normal standards. On the airfield, in addition to the runway extension, extensive areas had been graded to provide additional dispersals for the Phantoms. The main 23 (F) Squadron complex was relocated to the south-easterly corner of the airfield adjacent to the Runway 26 threshold. Entry and exit taxiways led from the apron to the main runway leaving a short backtrack to the 'piano keys' as the runway threshold was known. With the short runway and heavy Phantoms it was vital to use as much of the operating strip as was available. The dispersal, like the runway, was covered in AM2 matting to give a stable surface which would not be affected by the poor weather. Keeping the rubble and stones which were strewn across the airfield away from the delicate fan blades of the Rolls-Royce Spey engines of the Phantoms was the eternal challenge. Grouped around the manoeuvring area were the ramshackle buildings which formed the squadron complex. Comprising an eclectic mix of caravans, portakabins and tents, the buildings, nevertheless, gave the essential protection from the elements.

The main squadron building housed a crewroom which is also where the QRA crews lived for their twenty-four-hour shift. The main functions were the operations room where flight ops were controlled, the 'Line' where the aircraft were signed in and out by the crews and where the turnaround servicing was coordinated and engineering control where the rectification of snags was coordinated. They were situated close to each other and set up along the same lines as a UK based squadron. The operations desk was manned by the Duty Authoriser and an Ops Clerk and was the focal point for the aircrew. Flights were authorised here and the Duty Authoriser briefed the last minute updates prior to the mission such as aircraft, airfield and weather states immediately before the crews walked to the jets. In UK, these squadron areas would be quite large and personnel would cycle through as they went about their daily routine. Ops desk lurking was a well known tactic for picking up extra sorties which might appear on the programme but was frowned upon by 'The Auth'.

At Stanley, conditions were cramped and only essential personnel could be accommodated. Where possible, additional ramshackle cabins were provided to allow mission planning and briefings to take place but space was at a premium. Unless essential, everyone was persuaded to stay in the crewroom or to disperse to the operational sites. For most of us this was a novelty as there was always pressure in UK to show willing by engaging in secondary duties. To be encouraged to stay in the crewroom was a positive luxury.

Communications did not stretch to commercial telephones in the early days. A 'squawk box' linked the crewroom with Ops and a 'telebrief' terminal connected the QRA crews to the Sector Controller at 'Puffin' as the Sector Operations Centre at Mount Kent was known. The islanders communicated via the high frequency or HF radio network and a radio set had been installed alongside the telebrief. Using this, crews about to be released for their precious rest and recuperation breaks, or R&R, would contact local families who would take them in for an overnight stay providing a much appreciated feeling of 'home away from home' and a hugely welcome break from military routine. This was to be my first example of the islanders' hospitality. Links around the rest of the site were limited to field telephones installed by communications engineers. The noise of the small portable field set jangling away became a familiar sound. Running water was at a premium but a resourceful NCO had somehow acquired a water storage tank which was hoisted on a jury rigged support tower to rooftop height. A series of pipes led into a tap in the coffee bar area providing 'running water' for the QRA crews. The tank was occasionally topped off by a water bowser providing one of the early home comforts. The ramshackle heater which kept the chill off the room and provided some hot water was legendary and more than one of us was 'bitten' by the temperamental beast.

The 23 (F) Squadron Operations Building.

A 23 (F) Squadron Phantom launches on a training mission. © Steve Smyth

23 (F) Squadron Phantoms outside the 'rubs'. © Steve Smyth

The Squadron weapons instructor poses for the photographer aboard the C130. © Martin Stringer courtesy of Steve Smyth

Of course no QRA crewroom would be complete without the essential VHS video player and video tapes. The endless hours on alert were whiled away watching the latest – or not so latest – movies. Videos were sent from UK by the families and topped up by more films provided by SSAFA or NAAFI from the library which sprung up on base. The cult movie was undoubtedly Monty Python's *Life of Brian* which aired at least daily, if not more. In one of the more bizarre competitions, if the volume was turned down, squadron aircrew were challenged to recite whole passages from the film. Not only did new crews have to learn operational procedures but they had to learn the most significant passages from the film. To mark the epic achievement, a '1000 Hour Life of Brian,' patch similar to the flying suit badges commemorating milestones in their flying careers, was commissioned by the deployed aircrew.

The original runway surface was in reasonable condition but it had been damaged by the bombing raids. A rock quarry appeared in the north-western corner of the airfield and a massive rock crushing operation provided raw materials for the runway extension and subsequent repairs. The matting sections were laid over the graded foundation and rotary hydraulic arrestor gear systems (RHAGs) were installed along the runway. For normal operations, an approach-end RHAG, in other words the cable at the upwind end of the runway, was used. A mid-field RHAG at the halfway point and an overrun RHAG at the far end of the runway were also installed giving an element of redundancy. If the aircraft missed the first cable, it could engage the midfield RHAG quite safely. This minor emergency was more common than might be expected. The runway surface was quite rough and it was possible, despite hydraulic damping on the hook, for it to bounce and miss the cable. The actual cable was supported on large rubber grommets and sat about four inches off the ground. With just a small skip, the toe of the hook could ride over the top and miss the cable completely. In UK, crews would quite happily engage the overrun cable because a further arrestor system called a barrier was available to be used in extremis. This was a large net which would envelope the aircraft bringing it to a stop. In the Falklands, missing the cable was much more serious and crews were understandably nervous. The lack of a barrier and the fact that the conditions in the overshoot area were extremely hostile meant that a crew would 'bolt' if they missed the mid cable and, sometimes, even if they missed the approach end cable. In this situation, the pilot would raise the hook promptly to avoid a high-speed entry into the centre cable. Full afterburner would quickly re-establish flying speed and, after a minimal ground roll, the aircraft would fly a further circuit before a second attempt to land. It had been proven conclusively that a Phantom travelling at high speed could easily break the cable or even pull out the concrete structure which mounted the arrestor drums. On one occasion at RAF

Coningsby, a very experienced Phantom pilot mistakenly engaged the RHAG on take off and, as the Duty Officer Flying, I watched the whole incident from the air traffic control tower. He rolled as number two of a formation and, as the aircraft increased speed, for some reason, the hook lowered. The RHAGs at Coningsby were 1,300 feet down the runway and at that point in the take off roll, a Phantom would be travelling at almost 100 knots but, crucially, unlike on an arrested landing, would be in full reheat generating massive thrust. With the aircraft accelerating, the hook engaged the cable and pulled the jet, almost instantly, to a halt. Unfortunately, the stresses were just too great and the cable broke under the strain snapping upwards in a huge arc and slamming down back onto the concrete, narrowly missing a Hawk trainer jet parked on the parallel runway awaiting take off. The offending Phantom taxied back leaving a very embarrassed pilot and a slightly damaged RHAG installation.

At Stanley, the predominant winds were from the west so aircraft routinely took off in that direction which led to a natural shift of the metal matting runway sections towards the western end. The main offender was the Phantom. A Phantom landing was described as a 'controlled crash' given that the aircraft was fitted with a robust undercarriage designed to land on an aircraft carrier. Add to that the fact that that the pilot did not flare before landing so the momentum of the heavy airframe hitting the runway hard on each landing coupled with the stresses of an arrested landing caused the whole surface to creep. The sappers who were tasked with runway repair frequently had to unbolt sections from the western end and reposition them to the opposite threshold of the runway. Without this essential maintenance the runway was in danger of migrating into Port Stanley harbour. This was a long and back-breaking task so, in a unique piece of lateral thinking, C130s were tasked to either land in an easterly direction, if necessary downwind, or to conduct fast taxi runs down the strip followed by heavy braking. This persuaded the matting to shift back towards its original position delaying the inevitable surgery.

On the north eastern side of the runway a further pair of access taxiways led to the secondary squadron dispersal where further 'rubs' housed more of the squadron's aircraft. Similar to the main Phantom dispersal, it was covered in matting to provide a solid base on which to operate. The 'rubs' and a few small shacks allowed a brief respite for the troops from the cutting wind during servicing.

Back on the south side, the hub of activity was Air Traffic Control. The crews of the C130s of 1312 Flight operated close by with their aircraft positioned on the main parking ramp. They were joined regularly by other C130s operating the Airbridge. The main parking area had also been extended to take the extra traffic and, like the other dispersals was covered in the ubiquitous AM2 matting.

The civilian helicopters and the inter-settlement Islander passenger aircraft also joined the C130s making for a busy operating area. By now, the Harriers from 'Hardet' had returned to UK leaving a further dispersal midway down the runway on the north side from which the search and rescue and transport helicopters of 78 Squadron could operate. With such a high operational tempo space was always at a premium.

Given the austere conditions, supporting the Phantoms was a constant challenge and not just at first line on the squadron. The Engineering Officer from my old squadron in Germany was posted in as the Armament Support Officer for the air-to-air weapons and, crucially, the motor transport pool. He described the challenges. With the poor storage facilities and limited spares resupply, by early 1982 many of the air-to-air missiles were being returned unserviceable to Armament Support Flight from the Squadron. In the UK missiles were flown only occasionally on a QRA mission. The hammering which they were encountering by being flown daily was unlike anything which the Phantom force had experienced before. He set about building a more robust storage facility from any precious building materials his team could find. Typically, this was bits of AM2 matting, ISO containers and scrap metal and wood. Ingenuity was the watchword. The missiles and gun pods were slowly rotated back to UK for deeper servicing. Ruggedised, waterproof containers were imported to store the Sidewinders. From that point on serviceability improved and it began to be possible to carry out much of the work on the island rather than rely on UK based facilities. Within months availability was much better and by mid 1983, the missiles were passing their twenty-eight-day maintenance checks and most problems could easily be fixed in theatre. A 'Rub' hanger was allocated to the team and role equipment from each aircraft type serving on the islands was slowly added to the programme. This gave respite to the heavily over tasked Airbridge. Without this type of resourcefulness and lateral thinking the apparently efficient veneer would have hidden a raft of problems which would have threatened the effectiveness of the defensive force if it had been attacked again by the Argentinians.

Often forgotten but the detachment relied on the fleet of ubiquitous Land Rovers and a fleet of requisitioned Unimogs to move the daily mass of people and materiel around the site. Like the weapons, the vehicles took amazing punishment given the rudimentary state of the rapidly installed roads and keeping them going was vital but by no means guaranteed. Getting around the airfield was a test as the majority of the roads were not intended to take the sudden increase in traffic. Transport was at a premium. A graded perimeter road snaked around the airfield from the northside 23 (F) Squadron dispersal, past the Squadron and continued past the technical site and ATC before winding onwards towards Port Stanley. As it crossed the lagoon where the accommodation barges,

The Missile Servicing Flight at RAF Stanley. © MOD Crown Copyright (1982) courtesy Anthony Howell.]

The Suu23 Gun Bay at RAF Stanley. © MOD Crown Copyright (1982) courtesy Anthony Howell.

known as the 'coastels', were moored, temporary car parks sprang up alongside to take the vehicles of those lucky enough to be allocated transport. With so many deployed personnel, the roads were chaotic and tested the ruggedness of the military vehicles to the limit. I certainly learned to respect the Land Rover as a design as it took the ruts in its stride.

Although the Phantoms provided air defence by mounting combat air patrols some miles distant, the main task of local base defence, both in the form of infantry on the ground and by providing the base defence zone, fell to the RAF Rapier Squadron. When the British Commander accepted the Argentinian surrender, the Argentinian Government was slow to accept an end to hostilities formally so there was still a real threat of rogue air attack and RAF Stanley would have been a key target. No 63 Squadron, RAF Regiment, normally based at RAF Gutersloh in Germany set up 'Black Eagle Camp' on Sapper Hill and established a defensive ring around the airfield deploying Rapier fire units in tactical locations. The missiles, manned by the RAF gunners, provided the firepower for the base defence zone which protected the capital Stanley from hostile air attack. For peacetime operations, the missiles were located in small camps within close proximity of the airfield making transits to and from the sites easy. However, on base and in the open, the fire units would be visible and vulnerable to air attack. Deployed forward into the local area, they would be dug in and camouflaged making them almost impossible to see from the air should the airfield be attacked. Unlike the problems experienced by their predecessors during the conflict, these later sites were carefully surveyed and gave a good view of likely attack sectors. At the first hint of tensions, the individual fire units would be dismantled and moved rapidly to other pre surveyed sites around the local area outside the airfield boundary. Easily transportable on wheeled vehicles the Rapiers provided a formidable capability. A combination of Phantom CAPs and the forward located Rapier hides ensured that any attacking aircraft would be engaged before they could overfly their target and release weapons. Not since my RAF Germany days had I been able to see Rapiers operating in the field. Typical of the enthusiasm of all deployed units, when I dropped in to see a fire unit I was eagerly welcomed and the complexities of operating this modern anti air weapon were laid out, warts and all.

The Rapier was surprising simple in its basic operating mode. The gunner peered through an optical sight which was mounted on the missile launcher. The fire unit commander could aim a 'pointing stick', literally as its name suggested, at the incoming threat aircraft which provided the gunner with a bearing. By slewing the launcher to the bearing he would carry out an elevation search to detect the target visually and be able to cue the missile for launch. The IFF system (identification friend or foe) interrogated the target electronically looking for a friendly response. Without that, but backed up by a visual identification, the target could be engaged. Once the missile was committed, the gunner kept the crosshairs on the target using a small joystick and the missile would fly into the line-of-sight following guidance commands from the fire unit. The Rapier was designed as a 'hitile' in that the missile was intended to impact on the target negating the need for heavy proximity fuses and allowing the use of a very small warhead and a contact fuse. Later, the introduction of the Blindfire radar gave the Rapier a much needed all weather capability. Although the radar tracked the target, the operator could monitor the tracking using his optics and, if he detected electronic jamming, could override the system to ensure the missile was not seduced. If properly located, the Rapier was a very effective weapon. Like the fighter crews, the Rapier crews spent long and tedious shifts on alert in case of attack.

Operating the Phantom from RAF Stanley was a unique experience and I recounted the story of my night currency ride in *Phantom In Focus – A Navigator's Eye on Britain's Cold War Warrior* (Fonthill, 2012). Despite the fact that the Squadron was on a war footing with rules of engagement which allowed us to use the air-to-air missiles against a hostile aggressor, we still had to train. With a squadron-sized detachment, the flying effort was similar to that of any UK based squadron with one major exception. When aircraft broke which they inevitably did in the austere conditions, the logistics back up was at the other end of a very long resupply flight. For that reason, the flying programme was more cautious than back home. Keeping the jets serviceable was easy in some ways yet more challenging in others. With personnel away from home the lure of home life was less pressing and the ground crew would work cripplingly long hours to make sure the jets were up and serviceable for the next day's flying programme or to meet the Q commitment. Unfortunately, this was tempered by the spares situation. All squadrons detached away from base carried a 'Fly Away Pack' which contained all the essential spares that were likely to be needed on a routine basis. This would include the obvious items like line replicable units for the radar system and avionics, through spare wheels to something as large as a Rolls-Royce Spey engine. The components which broke on a more regular basis tended to be better stocked. The pack which was deployed to Stanley was even more comprehensive than the norm but, inevitably, it could not contain every single item that could break on a Phantom. Surprisingly, something as large as a spare engine would always be in theatre yet a smaller part, such as a duct for the boundary layer control system, might take weeks to deliver. When a snag was generated that required a spare part which was not available in stores, a 'D State' was generated which began a complex logistical resupply procedure. The request was flashed back to UK and the location of the spare part was identified.

It was then shipped from that base or stores depot to RAF Brize Norton to be put aboard the next Tristar or C130 bound for The Falklands. Amazingly, I have seen a demand placed in the morning arrive on a Tristar the following afternoon. Typically though, a 'D State' often meant an aircraft would remain on the ground for a few days, perhaps weeks, awaiting the vital spare part. *In extremis*, particularly if another jet was on a routine service, the engineers would 'rob' the part from one jet to fix another. Although this got one aircraft flying it doubled the engineering effort involved as the time to remove the spare was added to the task time. It also ran the risk that, as more parts were removed from the hapless victim, it became known as a 'Christmas Tree' and could take some time to reassemble even once all the parts could be provided. With ten aircraft available there was more likelihood of producing a 'Christmas Tree' than with only four available.

The daily flying programme followed along squadron lines. With typically eight aircraft available on 23 (F) Squadron, two aircraft were always sitting on alert on QRA so an ambitious programme would see three waves spread through the day. A four ship would be planned for the first wave turning into another four ship around lunchtime into a final four in the afternoon. As aircraft went unserviceable during the day, the later waves would be trimmed down to fit the remaining aircraft. If night flying was planned the whole programme would slip right as a single shift plus a 'swing' shift could only cover a twelve-to-sixteen-hour day. A four ship could carry out reasonably useful tactical scenarios, normally 2v2 where one pair was nominated as fighters and the other as targets. Drop that to a three ship and 2v1 or 1v2 was the order of the day. The basic fighting unit was a pair so, normally, this would mean the singleton would act as target. On the occasions when only one aircraft remained serviceable, and this was by no means rare with the temperamental Phantom, other flying units such as the C130 or the helicopters would be co-opted to act as targets. Whilst the other crews loved fighting against the Phantoms, or conducting 'affiliation exercises' as they were known, the sorties carried a huge penalty in terms of fatigue life on their airframes and the fun was invariably rationed.

A typical sortie was never boring. A pre flight briefing lasted about thirty minutes and included the sortie domestics, intercept profiles and details of which 'playmates' were allocated. One of the unique Falklands aspects was that the airborne aircraft, being armed, could be pulled off a training event and sent against a QRA target at any time. Only the QRA camera would be missing but navigators often carried their own 'Box Brownie' in the cockpit which could be deputised. During the pre flight briefing, the lead pilot would cover the mechanics of the sortie, called the domestics, whilst the lead navigator would brief the intercepts and techniques. For a sortie in an operational theatre, the assumption was that everyone was conversant with techniques so that part would be glossed over but any refinement of tactics which might be different to the norm would be covered. Bearing in mind, the crews were drawn from across the Phantom Force, different squadrons often used different tactics so it was often advisable to brief a baseline. In theory, as all crews belonged to No 11 Group, 11 Group standard operating procedures, or 'SOPs' should cover it; in theory! In practice there were huge variations. Crews would then 'out-brief' at the operations desk giving the Duty Authoriser the chance to update any changes in aircraft allocation, weather, timings or serviceability. At that point, crews would 'walk' to their aircraft. This was a generic term; the Americans would 'step' for their aircraft whereas Brits 'walked'. For some that meant, literally, a short walk across the metal matting if the jet was in one of the 'rubs' adjacent to the squadron. For others it was a ride in a Land Rover around the perimeter track to the remote dispersal on the north side of the runway.

Transport permitting, the ground crew would always be at the 'rub' in advance of the aircrew to fire up the external power set, open the canopies and prepare the aircraft. The navigator climbed into the cockpit first, checked a few switches in the rear cockpit before climbing into the front and doing the pre-power on checks. Somehow, with an aircraft with a full warload of live missiles, that process was so much more important. It was underlined how vital proper checks could be at RAF Leuchars in the late 1970s. As a Phantom was prepared for QRA the continuous wave radar was selected to 'standby'. This was the guidance radar for the Sparrow missile. As the system powered up, a Sidewinder missile left the aircraft striking the ground some distance ahead, cartwheeling along the ground, before coming to rest in a small river alongside the airfield. Luckily, all parking slots for armed aircraft are surveyed to ensure that the area ahead is aligned on a safe heading for this very reason. There was no damage or injury and, apart from a few red faces and a large and unnecessary bill to the taxpayer, no harm was done. The paradox was that the CW selector had absolutely no effect on the Sidewinder launch circuit. It was later found that a 'no volts' check on the weapons circuit had not detected a stray voltage. When the weapons system was powered up, the simple pulse which a Sidewinder needs to fire was present and the rest was history. On a more normal start up, once power was applied the navigator returned to his own cockpit to align the inertial navigation system while the pilot finished his walk around checks and physically checked the weapons.

Strapped in, the crew completed pre flight checks of the aircraft systems and avionics before checking in ready to taxy. By now, fifty minutes had elapsed from beginning the briefing; quite a contrast to a QRA scramble which required the crew to be off inside ten minutes. Invariably, take off was to the west at Stanley so the taxy to the runway was short needing snappy pre-take off checks before departure. Take off may be in close formation or as a stream. For a formation take off, the pair would remain together until reaching 350 knots at which stage the pilots would do a 'playtex'. In this manoeuvre, the aircraft would turn away from each other in a violent break out, hold diverging headings for about fifteen seconds before turning hard back onto the original heading. This would put the formation in tight defensive 'battle' formation at the earliest opportunity and immediately ready to engage any attacker. The reason for the name of the manoeuvre may not be immediately obvious but it had its heritage in a 1970s ladies' underwear advertisement. The strapline – excuse the pun - was 'Buy Playtex because it lifts and separates' which is exactly what the manoeuvre did to the formation!

The westerly departure at Stanley was directly down the harbour and normally the formation would remain at low level along the waterfront. Never once did I hear a complaint from a Stanley resident about jet noise, although it must have been a feature of life for some years after the conflict. Low-level transits to the operating area were the norm even if medium level intercepts were planned. As soon as the formation was airborne the crews 'chopped' to a tactical frequency for the transit which was monitored by all air traffic in the islands. If the formation had flown a stream departure, the trail navigator would find his leader on radar and either he or his pilot would call a turn and a reversal allowing the No2 to slot into battle formation as quickly as possible. This ensured a modicum of deconfliction as each aircraft passed a position report as they reached significant landmarks around the islands giving a broad picture of who was flying and where. Once in the operating area, another frequency change would take the formation onto the tactical fighter frequency where the crews checked in with the fighter controller tasked to run the mission. The crews would then begin the tactical intercepts which had been planned at the briefing. Given that all the crews were operational and the airspace was virtually unrestricted, the target aircraft would have free range in height, speed and could evade without constraint. If the target crew could avoid being intercepted and reach their nominated target unmolested it was almost a badge of success, although for real it would have had dire consequences. Preventing that outcome was the order of the day and was hugely challenging.

Once the fuel dropped below a pre-briefed minimum the crews would recover to RAF Stanley. The preferred arrival was a 'visual run in and break'. The procedure had its roots in the Second World War when it was designed to put a formation of aircraft onto the ground as quickly as possible yet retain fighting speed for as long as possible. Some of the early wartime procedures were cumbersome and kept formations close together making them unwieldy and vulnerable. From an entry point known as 'initials' which was five miles from the airfield on the extended centreline, the formation would adopt 'battle formation', line abreast at about one mile spacing. Flown at fighting speed of about 400 knots, the break height varied depending on local conditions. In UK where local residents may be noise averse, it was a respectable 1,000 feet. At Stanley where the residents around the airfield were all military personnel it was a more tactical 500 feet or maybe lower if OC Ops Wing was not watching. At about the midpoint of the runway the pair would simultaneously execute a hard turn downwind pulling up to circuit height which washed off the speed bringing the Phantom back to circuit speed. Once below 250 knots the undercarriage was lowered, the flaps extended and the hook lowered to bring the speed back further to 'on speed' of about 150 knots. The finals turn was a constant arc aiming to touchdown just beyond the 'piano keys' leaving a short run to the approach end cable. For a normal arrested landing in UK, the navigator would watch over his shoulder to confirm that the hook had caught the wire. With the short cable run out at Stanley, the head was firmly locked to the shoulders and the go forward lever on the ejection seat was firmly locked. Anything less could result in the side of the navigator's head colliding with the radarscope as the force of retardation bent the navigator's back due to the suddenly much heavier flying helmet! This was a painful manoeuvre and best avoided. The pilot technique was also markedly different. Aerodynamically, the brake parachute could be popped at up to 200 knots but, for a normal landing, was deployed as the wheels touched the ground. With only 6,000 feet and few risk-free options, the chute was deployed before touch down while still airborne to slow the speed yet further. 'On speed' depended on how much fuel remained. An additional 5 knots was added for each 1000 lbs of fuel remaining so on a short runway, the ideal was to be as close to minimums as possible. For the Phantom the baseline speed was 140 knots. By flying an accurate 'on speed approach' and holding the aircraft on power, if the hook missed the cable it might theoretically be possible to stay down and stop in the available runway length, albeit with very hot brakes. To make the technique work, a decent headwind was needed but, with predominantly westerly winds at Stanley, that was normally not a problem. Even then, with cables at the midpoint and in the overrun, it might still be likely that one of the later cables would do the job. If all failed and the aircraft left the end of the runway on the ground, there was no option but to eject.

The unpredictability of a fast moving aircraft passing over an unprepared surface left too much to chance and the overrun at Stanley was like the lunar surface. A 'Martin Baker Letdown' was preferable to a collision with a large rock. Thankfully, during the time at Stanley no one was forced to make that decision. With a carrier strength undercarriage, the arrival was brutal and the

A Phantom on short finals with the hook down and the chute deployed. This photograph was taken by Jeff Bell, the navigator of XV484 lost in 1983. It is included as a tribute to my fellow navigator and a genuinely nice man.

Phantom smashed onto the runway killing yet more speed in the process. The hydraulic dampers on the hook hopefully kept it firmly in contact with the metal runway before it engaged the cable about 1,300 feet from the threshold. From 150 knots on short finals, it was a mere 14 seconds from touchdown to full stop. Holding the aircraft on power, the pilot would keep tension on the cable before chopping the throttles and allowing the tension in the cable to pull the aircraft backwards slowly. Retracting the hook at that point just as the tension eased allowed the aircraft to disengage from the cable without help from the arrestor party and it could then be taxied back to dispersal to allow the fire crews and arrestor party to re-rig the cable ready for the second Phantom in the formation. The short taxy back to the squadron dispersal was across the same AM2 matting which linked the runway with the dispersals. After checking in with Eagle Ops to pass the serviceability state the pilot would taxy back making a wide arc in front of the nominated 'rub' and lining up in front of the open hangar. Another of the spoils of war was pressed into service for this phase of the sortie as a number of captured Argentinian 'Unimog' vehicles were used for pushbacks. If the engines were closed down outside the 'rub', a short time had to be allowed for the gyros in the inertial navigation system to run down. If not, they would vibrate themselves to an early demise. For that reason, one engine remained running and once the tow bar was hooked to the nosewheel, the aircraft was pushed carefully into position inside the 'rub' before closing down.

QRA sorties were common but, to the best of my knowledge, we were never tested by fast jet intrusions. At Stanley, the Q aircraft were normally held on the ground and rarely flew other than for practice scrambles and currency. This of course reflected the wishes of the squadron commander at the time and a less risk-averse commander might press the limits by flying Q more often. In the UK where training sorties were flown without live weapons, preparing and accepting a QRA aircraft was more complex and time consuming. An aircraft nominated for Q had to be blown through, the weapon system tested and the missiles loaded. Sidewinders were easily loaded by hand but Sparrows and Skyflash missiles had to be loaded using a piece of special-to-type ground equipment. At Stanley all aircraft flew live armed so they could be put onto QRA extremely quickly. This made the operation 'down south' inherently more flexible.

As I arrived for my first detachment the Station hierarchy began to wrestle with the difficult problem of planning station exercises. The concept caused much debate. Operations in the islands presented some unique tactical challenges in the air as well as particular problems for station support personnel. It was hard to keep the finely tuned operation working even when everything was going well but, add the problems caused by combat operations and trying to maintain tempo with an 8,000 mile logistics tail, it became incredibly difficult. Taxying out to the main runway was straight forward but simulate a bomb crater and simple tasks took longer. In the air there was a strict delineation between live operations on QRA and training sorties, perhaps driven by the loss of a Jaguar to a Sidewinder at RAF Wildenrath in 1982. If an aircraft was armed it was for a purpose and there should be no confusion. For training, a 'switches safe' call was always made during a practice intercept at 10 miles from the target and armament circuit breakers in the rear cockpit were pulled as an additional safety measure. This was a final reminder to crews that they carried lethal weapons. Downloading the weapons for exercises at Stanley when the station was still on a war footing was not an option which could be considered as it would leave the airfield vulnerable. Switching between live armed and unarmed would cause yet more confusion. If exercises were to be conducted, that hitherto sacrosanct boundary would have to be crossed and live weapons would have to be carried in a training environment where real tactical problems would be set. Putting crews under that extra pressure might be the difference between safe and sorry. In the end, a station exercise was held and, as in UK, the various elements of the war machine were put through a carefully scripted scenario. In the air, however, things were a little more cautious. Although a Phantom was used to provide a pseudo 'pop up contact' simulating a Mirage intruder, things erred on the side of prudence and the Rapier squadron was warned in advance that it was a drill. The true 'pucker factor' is never present when the exercise is warned in advance so we were left with a distinct feeling of pointlessness. In the event, the Station executives were happy that we had been 'drilled' but most of us questioned why reactions would be any different as we were already on a war footing. Perhaps the benefit was felt more in the ground play?

There was one story which had its motives rooted in charity rather than ill discipline, although, whether the plan was thought through fully is debatable. Until the AN/ALE 40 chaff and flare dispenser system was fitted to the Phantom, a contingency plan had been tested by the RAF Central Tactics and Trials Organisation. This involved packing a standard service envelope with chaff and taping the bags inside the speedbrakes. This would allow the pilot to deploy a single one-off chaff shot as a defensive measure by simply popping the speedbrakes at an appropriate moment during a defensive manoeuvre. I remember seeing the archived trial report still marked 'Secret', during a later tour as a trails officer at the Air Warfare Centre. Even then it caused a chuckle but it could be a valid and cheap countermeasure providing it could be used at the right time. Idle aircrew minds are a dangerous thing and the old contingency plan was clearly in somebody's mind at one time.

The islanders often invited crews to stay overnight and the quid pro quo was that we would try to take a small 'goody bag' along with us. Speaking nicely to the Warrant Officer who ran the Officers' Mess kitchen usually produced a few items 'in lieu of rations' which we would have eaten had we stayed in the Mess. We could offer this as a thank you to our generous hosts for the hospitality we received. Fruit, which was impossible to buy in Stanley, was a prized gift. Unfortunately, the ships bringing fresh produce to the islands only docked occasionally so it was not always available. One crew were invited to visit a settlement but the fruit had run out. Having been hosted in the usually fine manner, the crew promised to 'deliver' some fruit the following week but left the precise details unsaid. On their return to Stanley, the boat from UK had docked and some highly prized lemons had arrived. The crew were on the flying programme scheduled for a low level interception mission so, before the sortie, they fired up the engines, popped the speedbrakes and loaded a couple of lemons into the speedbrake bay. The plan was to fly past the settlement at some stage and drop the gift for their hosts. As with all plans, it failed to survive first contact and they were pulled off from their planned mission and vectored at medium level towards an incoming contact by the sector controller.

No amount of hopeful protestations could prevent the task so the crew pressed on with the mission trying desperately not to use the speedbrakes. One of the indisputable facts is that the air temperature drops off with height at the rate of about 2 degrees per thousand feet so the outside air temperature at 15,000 feet is typically minus 20 degrees Celsius on a Spring day. At those temperatures, lemons in an unpressurised bay freeze hard! The crew now had a dilemma. They could jettison the precious cargo or attempt delivery and, being fighter aircrew, they chose the latter. Once the interception was complete they descended to low level and made a slow pass past the settlement popping the speedbrakes at the appropriate time. The crew fully expected the owner to have to 'dig for victory' to retrieve the lemons once they landed in the soft peat surrounding the house. Reportedly, the by now frozen, lemons struck something hard on landing, skipped across the settlement, through the wall of an outbuilding and were never seen again. I heard from a former colleague that a similar incident had occurred with a Mars Bar and, given that he had been shown the hole in the roof of an outbuilding, I have no reason to doubt that the tactic was tried more than once. Suffice to say that once the airborne delivery method was uncovered by the squadron supervisors the practice was not encouraged.

Reflecting on operations at Stanley, perhaps the most memorable contrast was air traffic control. Shortly after my arrival in 1985, I visited the control tower which had been toned down with drab green paint and an RAF Stanley sign fixed to the upper wall of the building. Cargo pallets and ground equipment cluttered the immediate vicinity and vehicles came and went every few minutes. As Duty Officer Flying I sat at the desk in local control and, around me, RAF air traffic assistants went about their duty dressed in camouflaged combat kit. Listening on my headset, the Local Controller passed constant instructions to the variety of aircraft ranging from fast jets in the circuit to C130s arriving from the north to helicopters which clattered in and out at regular intervals. In all, it was a bustling airfield with hundreds of movements on an average day. When I returned for a liaison visit as OC 1435 Flight some nine years later, the difference could not have been more evident. The tower had been returned to its pre war state and wore a new white paint scheme. A bright red Range Rover fire vehicle was parked on the deserted apron and the formerly bustling offices below the tower were marked 'Arrivals' but equally deserted. The heavy military equipment had been replaced by a simple baggage trolley. Climbing the stairs, which I had last done such a long time before, I poked my head into the local control room and startled the controller who had his headset around his neck and his feet on the control desk. We chatted for some time without him needing to don the headset. The planned arrival of an islander from a distant settlement was not until much later in the afternoon so we were undisturbed. Air traffic control had reverted to

Above: The 'Coastel' accommodation barges moored in Stanley Harbour to house military personnel. .© Steve Smyth

Left: A 4 man room in the 'Coastel'.

The control tower at Stanley after the conflict.

The control tower at Stanley returned to civilian use.

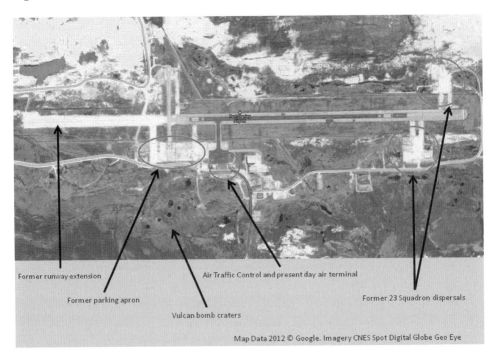

Former runway extension

Former parking apron

Air Traffic Control and present day air terminal

Vulcan bomb craters

Former 23 Squadron dispersals

Map Data 2012 © Google. Imagery CNES Spot Digital Globe Geo Eye

Stanley airfield returned to its original state.

a much simpler lifestyle serving an island community with a regional air shuttle. The bustle of military operations had moved thirty miles inland to RAF Mount Pleasant. Walking the former site of 23 (F) Squadron, at ground level it was hard to even visualise where the buildings had stood.

RAF Stanley served the Nation well and it provided a home for a variety of aircraft types for some years. The Phantoms of 23 (F) Squadron left RAF Stanley in May 1986 allowing the islanders to return to normality. The matting was torn up and removed leaving just the earthworks to mark the temporary role as one of the busiest military bases in the South Atlantic.

CHAPTER 5
Operations at RAF Mount Pleasant

Building a new airfield on the islands was inevitable and the location which was selected at Mount Pleasant was reasonably predictable. It had to be close enough to the capital, with access to a deep-water port, particularly during the construction phase to allow materials to be imported. Most importantly, it had to take the pressure away from the local inhabitants. The airport at Stanley was never big enough to cope with full-scale military operations nor was it sustainable to drop thousands of British servicemen into the local community and expect any sort of normal life for the islanders. Mount Pleasant, or MPA, opened in early 1986 having cost £276 million to build. The Phantoms of 23 (F) Sqn moved onto the base on 1 May of that year, which coincided with a roulement as some of the original aircraft were returned to UK for servicing. The squadron moved into the new dispersal on the eastern end of the airfield and ran as a squadron sized operation until 1 November 1987 when the numbers were reduced as a conciliatory gesture by the British Government. Downsizing to four aircraft meant that the unit was reduced to Flight status and it adopted the 1435 Flight numberplate. A realignment of command structure saw all the flying units come under the control of Wing Commander Operations with each flying unit being commanded by a Squadron Leader. Not wishing to repeat the mistakes of 1982, the Government continued to reinforce the base for short periods by redeploying additional Phantoms under the banner of Exercise Fire Focus usually timed to fit in with the regular servicing roulements. Such exercises ran in March 1988 and February 1990 but in July 1992, following the decision to retire the Phantom from operational service, 1435 Flight's last Phantoms were scrapped on the islands. It would not have been cost effective to fly the airframes back to UK for disposal so the airframes, XV472, 'Faith', XV442, 'Hope', XV461, 'Charity' and XV466 'Desperation' met an inglorious end when they were destroyed and dumped into a pit near the Air Terminal. The airworthy airframes were, literally, torn apart by heavy plant machinery and, from then on, only divers from the local sub aqua club were able to see the 'retired' airframes. One Phantom escaped that fate. XV409 was repainted as 'Hope' and placed as the Gate Guardian outside the Air Terminal where it was seen by hundreds of visitors as they disembarked from an airliner on arrival. Ironically, XV472 was the aircraft in which I flew my first ever Phantom flight at RAF Coningsby back in 1975. When I returned to the islands in 1994 I had no idea that it had met its fate only yards away from where I climbed off the Tristar. It is a small world. The base sub aqua club often made diving trips down into the pit and it was possible for divers to see the wrecks of the Phantoms. Had I known that XV472 was down there I would have speeded up my efforts to gain my diving qualification to allow me to make a dive. It would have been a strange way to be reacquainted with my first ever Phantom.

What I had also not realised at the time was that, due to radical downsizing of the Air Defence Force in UK, this was to be my final flying tour. With command slots disappearing fast, I would never realise my ambition of commanding a full squadron but my experiences in The Falkland Islands would be just as dramatic and just as challenging. As Deputy Commander of the Tornado F3 Operational Conversion Unit, I was responsible for the day to day running of the flying operations where all new crews who would fly the Tornado F3 were trained. The OCU was a huge outfit by UK standards being twice the size of a normal squadron. At peak strength, the OCU had twenty-six Tornados on charge with forty instructors and up to thirty student aircrew at any one time. The OCU was supported by over 150 ground crew, again much larger than a normal squadron. The pace of life was hectic and the pressure to graduate courses on schedule was relentless. In comparison, 1435 Flight with its four Tornados, ten aircrew and fifty-five ground crew was a tiny outfit. The difference was that, being 8,000 miles from home and three hours behind UK time, there was little, if any, daily hands-on control from HQ 11 Group who exercised operational control of the detachment. My task was stunningly simple. I had four aircraft to defend the islands from air attack and, in a worse case scenario, I had to be able to hold a rear-guard action for about twenty-four to forty-eight hours until reinforcement aircraft and crews could be flown in. To do so I had to guarantee to hold two aircraft on constant ten minute readiness, 365 days a year, to guard against potential air intruders. There were absolutely no excuses for a failure to do so. Within those broad guidelines and in keeping with the battle plans, I had almost total autonomy.

The Falklands Operations Wing was set up differently to other RAF units in the UK. Because the numbers were smaller, each aircraft type was technically a Flight. In the UK, a squadron was equipped with twelve aircraft and commanded by a Wing Commander who was responsible for just over 130 personnel. 'Down

South', each flying unit had, at most, four aircraft, and was commanded by a Squadron Leader and half the number of troops. 1435 Flight had four Tornado F3s, 1312 Flight had two Hercules and to make matters completely confusing, seventy-eight Squadron operated a Chinook and two Sea Kings. The Officer Commanding Operations Wing was in command of the flying effort and was also the Air Defence Commander reporting to an RAF Group Captain Station Commander. He in turn reported to The Commander British Forces Falkland Islands; a joint appointment. As my immediate supervisor, OC Ops also had to supervise the other flying units and the Rapier missiles so his time was shared thinly. That said, he was a Tornado F3 pilot so, I seemed to see him quite regularly as he flew his allocated hours, and a few more, with the Flight. Mine really was an expensive 'train set'; small but perfectly formed. Few stations around the Air Force had such a diversity of types and roles.

My arrival on a Tristar was only the second time I had set foot on the airfield at Mount Pleasant, although I had arrived at the Air Terminal on my first tour in 1985 and had made a single approach to the airfield in a Phantom. As we heard the call from the Tristar cockpit that we were shortly beginning our descent into Mount Pleasant, 2 Tornado F3s slipped into close formation on each wingtip of the passenger aircraft. Fully armed, it was yet again a reminder of the task in hand and the responsibility I faced over the coming months. The initial impression as I looked down again at the coastline that I had not seen for eight years was of a holiday island. From the air, the Falklands landscape looks pretty and I could have been lulled into a false sense of arriving on a holiday charter but for the rather more austere cabin of an RAF trooping flight. As the Tristar dropped onto final approach, the sandy beaches gave way to slightly less attractive scrubland before the jet settled easily onto the long main runway. The arrivals process was rather more relaxed than a civilian airport and in stark contrast to departure. I was met by the outgoing OC1435 Flight who was wearing the biggest smile I had ever seen. I was to learn myself in just a few short months that the arrival of your replacement was indeed, a red letter day and much anticipated.

The short journey from the Air Terminal to the accommodation block passed in a blur, albeit navigating across the bone shattering potholes which pockmarked the islands' roads brought back memories; instantly! I was shown to a room in the accommodation block, known affectionately as 'The Death Star' for reasons that will become apparent but I was advised not to unpack as I would inherit the Boss's room once my predecessor departed which was closer to the squadron 'lounge'. There was little time for pleasantries as we immediately returned to the Land Rover which would be my means of transport for the coming months and we made our way over to the Squadron. There would be time to settle in later. Away from the relative 'luxury' of the accommodation area, the roads took on the more familiar character which would mark my time on the islands. The paved surface around the accommodation ended quickly replaced by a rutted, graded rock surface which the Land Rover's suspension took in its stride, albeit with plenty of teeth jarring lurches. The roads were rudimentary but were well packed down and took some amazing punishment from both users and the climate. Occasionally, a large bulldozer type contraption would drag a blade across the surface and rearrange the displaced rocks back into the ruts reforming a useable road surface. Barely wide enough for two vehicles to pass, my first journey around the airfield perimeter felt as if it might be my last. The greeting I received at the operations building was to become another feature of the detachment:

'How long have you got to do? .... No one has that long to do!' delivered with a smirk to every newcomer.

At that precise point of my detachment I may have missed the humour, although I confess to using the line myself as my remaining time at Mount Pleasant began to shorten. Even so, my aircrew served only five week detachments, so it would be a while before I got my own back; on the aircrew at least.

The handover was extremely short and my predecessor announced that he was booked to return on the Tristar flight departing in two days' time. The thought of taking command within such a short timescale was daunting. I thought that, having been an instructor for so long, my operational colleagues would be way ahead of me in tactical thinking. What I'd forgotten was that the core business down South was QRA and I had sat on alert in the Q Shed for many more hours than most of my younger colleagues. My experience was just as relevant as the more complex operational profiles on a squadron. What was also soon evident was that many of my aircrew had passed through the OCU during my time as an instructor suggesting that the experience levels on the squadrons had become diluted. I knew most of the faces.

The operational procedures came back very quickly. During the early handover, the flying aspects such as operating from the airfield and the detail of the operational task were almost glossed over. That would come once I got airborne. More emphasis was placed on the supervisory aspects. The Squadron supervision operated almost identically to a UK squadron, albeit on a smaller scale and on a rotational basis. The most sobering thought at that early stage was that within four weeks, because of the rate of rotation of the crews, I would be the longest serving aircrew member on the Flight. Luckily, true 'newbies' who had never operated from the islands were increasingly rare but it was a sobering thought nonetheless. Much time was spent discussing the practicalities of supervising aircrew from other squadrons operating in the free environment of the islands and the challenges that brought. Fortuitously, I had spent much of my previous years on both the Phantom and Tornado as an instructor and latterly, a supervisor. Many of the deployed aircrew had passed through my temporary control at some time and I had served on squadrons with many of them. I was used to monitoring aircrew with random experience levels and that was huge advantage in retrospect. I also had a number of squadron leaders and experienced flight lieutenants planned to deploy during my time and knew that some wise heads that I could trust would be on the Flight. I already knew who I was to fly with. Each UK squadron allocated crews to meet its commitment to the Falklands roster. As I was to spend four months deployed, four pilots would rotate through the unit and had already been allocated by the Operational Conversion Unit planners. They were all instructor pilots and were extremely experienced on the Tornado F3.

Ironically, my first pilot had become famous as he was the pilot responsible for shooting down the RAF Jaguar with a Sidewinder missile in Germany in 1982. Rather than adding to the pressure, I felt completely relaxed in his abilities. He was a fine fighter pilot who I respected enormously and, just as important in the confines of the islands, a true gentleman and a nice bloke. His unfortunate incident never once crossed my mind as we went about our business armed with four Skyflash, four Sidewinder missiles and the gun. In another ironic twist, my second pilot was another good friend who had steered me through my conversion exercises on the Phantom as I joined 92 (East India) Squadron in Germany on my second tour. The irony was that in my early days in Germany he had trained me in the Central Region Air defence role. Despite his huge experience and skill I was now his Boss. I had already begun to mull over a spoof which would allow me to return the favour for some of his 'comprehensive' debriefs in the past.

My third pilot, although a relative youngster was extremely talented and went on to become the Tornado Display Pilot. My final pilot was one of the OCU's elder statesmen and was just as relaxed and capable. After three months away and just as island fever was setting in, I learned to listen to his sage advice. All in all I was well served by the pilots with whom I flew.

One of the first warnings I received was to set the tone. My predecessor explained that one of his crews had transgressed just a few weeks earlier during an air refuelling detail. Although he explained the broad facts, apparently it was a special request from OC Ops Wing that he hold off on the details until I had been offered 'guidance' by my new Boss! The 'bombshell' which was delivered almost as a parting shot was that two of the aircraft were planned to rotate towards the end of my tour of duty. That meant that we would have to prepare two aircraft to return to the UK and accept their replacements whilst keeping our aircraft on the required readiness states. During that week, the Flight would swell in size as the additional crews were absorbed on strength. Inevitably though, the flying rate would be limited during the rotation as caution would be the order of the day. I was to be refamiliarised with a 'Trail'.

That night I was acquainted with the delights of 'The Death Star'. Named after the fictional space station in the Star Wars movies, the building was a labyrinth of small accommodation blocks linked by a maze of corridors to protect the inhabitants from the climate. Looking more like an industrial facility than an accommodation block, in reality it provided a level of comfort which had, hitherto, been missing but its modern functional construction was a far cry from a typical RAF Mess back home. In the normal way, individual messes were provided within the complex for the officers, the non commissioned officers (NCOs) and the airmen and soldiers. Naval personnel tended to live aboard their ships and took rooms only temporarily. Huge kitchens turned out meals for the detached personnel and, given the undoubted problems of acquiring fresh produce so far from home, did the usual magnificent job. Some fresh produce arrived aboard the Tristar, some aboard the regular supply vessels and some was sourced around the island but, even so, there were few complaints. The usual public rooms such as the bar and the ante rooms were located close to the main entrance. The accommodation was much further afield and some blocks were a good ten-minute walk from the entrance. The main corridor linking the mess to the accommodation is reputedly the longest corridor in the world being 800m long. Although the Q1 and Q2 crews lived in the QRA Shed for their twenty-four-hour duty, a further crew was always on 60 minutes' readiness back at 'The Death Star'. A Land Rover parked close by an exit door provided a quick getaway when the hooter sounded closely followed by the alert bleeper as the crew would have to rush over to the squadron to prepare the Q3 aircraft in the event of unserviceabilities with the two primary jets. The authoriser in the crew would go to the Tower in case supervisory information was needed or operational decisions had to be taken. The other member of the Q3 crew would return to squadron operations. With the punishing schedule, for most crews, true relaxation without the risk of callout was limited to a few nights a week. Off duty crews often 'played hard' but there were no byes if alcohol intake was over indulgent. The rule was to be there, on time. The Engineering Officer and, of course myself, were on permanent call which somewhat dictated the nature of my social life. Individual rooms in the complex were austere but comfortable in comparison to those experienced by our predecessors at Stanley but the view from the window was consistent. The weather outside could change from summer to winter within minutes.

My arrival interview with OC Ops Wing was a very swift grounding. I had known him for some years, although we had never served on the same squadron, and I held him in high regard. The welcome was warm but he then briefed me on the recent incident in which a Tornado had been flown rather too aggressively when departing from the Hercules tanker causing a good deal of grief to all concerned. The Tornado pilot had dropped back before accelerating to high subsonic speed. As he passed the lumbering Hercules, he had pulled up from below the nose, by then, almost transonic. His idea had been to give the C130 crew a spectacle but the transonic airflow caused severe wake turbulence subjecting the Hercules to a 3G jolt which was beyond its normal operating limits. The offending Tornado crew were firmly dealt with but my predecessor had been left under no illusions that the remainder of the squadron should be reminded of the limits – and the penalties of transgression. I left knowing that I needed to keep a tight rein on flying discipline whilst still maintaining the combat edge; this was the eternal compromise. The flying was always aggressive in the Falklands and, rightly so. It was important that, should the Argentinians ever consider laying claim again that their first welcome would be a smoking Skyflash missile. Crews practiced hard, flew low and intended to win. The challenge as the Boss was to ensure that the divide between professional, aggressive capability and licensed hooliganism was clear. Despite best efforts I was to have to deal with my own, albeit less dramatic, example during my tour of duty.

The Tornado Dispersal sat at the north-eastern end of the airfield. The buildings were of modern construction and painted a tactical green. A small Operations and Engineering complex was the hub of the squadron and provided offices and working space for the squadron personnel. The aircraft operated from 'housies' which was a take on the term HASs, or hardened aircraft shelters. As the shelters were built of traditional steel and alloy rather than the concrete structures of the Cold War, they adopted the appropriate nickname which was a twist on their more muscular cousins. A quick look at Google Maps shows the split complex with sixteen shelters built around a loop taxiway. The short runway dissected the two complexes. Given that the Flight operated only four Tornado F3s, the normal operations were conducted from the most easterly section of the dispersal. Quick Reaction Alert was the whole focus of the flying activity and the QRA aircraft were operated from the first two 'housies' closest to the runway with the alert personnel living in the 'Q Shed' for the duration of their twenty-four-hour duty.

The shift pattern was brutal and was set within a ten-day cycle. The cycle began with a 24 hour QRA duty and ended on day 9 with a final QRA duty. In between, days on QRA were interspersed with days when the other crews flew the remaining two aircraft on training sorties. In addition to the two alert crews, a further crew was nominated as Q3 which meant that they were on the more relaxed sixty minute readiness. It did, however, mean that the bar was still off limits for that period of duty as they may be called upon to man an aircraft. The final stint on QRA finished at 7.30 a.m. on day 9 leading into two days' R&R. In practice however, the next stint of QRA began at 7.30 p.m. on day 10 so there was never actually a full day off duty. For that reason, aircrew rotated on a five weekly basis, the logic being that the airbridge flight was regular and a shorter rotation meant that routine peacetime requirements such as check rides and simulator sorties could be planned around the operational detachments. The downside of shorter detachments was that they came around with regular monotony and one or even two per year was not uncommon. Overall, most crews preferred the shorter yet more regular detachment as it disrupted normal life less than a long detachment. The Boss of the Flight, the Engineering Officer and the groundcrew spent a full four month detachment in the South Atlantic and some served for six months. Some of the Station executives such as OC Operations Wing and the Station Commander spent a full year on the islands but were able to take their family along living relatively comfortably in a small 'married patch' adjacent to the 'Death Star'.

I flew my first familiarisation sortie 'split crew' with a pilot who had already been on the islands for a few weeks while my own pilot flew with the navigator from the other crew. The familiarisation followed a typical sortie pattern starting with an Exercise 'Fiery Cross' into random practice intercepts against the other Tornado F3 and finishing with a practice diversion to Stanley airport to reacquaint us with its new configuration. By now, Stanley had reverted to a 4,000-foot concrete runway which was quite useable for a Tornado F3 with its thrust reverse system. Although we could land quite comfortably in that distance, getting airborne again in a fully armed aircraft would have been 'sporty'. Prudence said that if forced to use Stanley as a diversion, a lighter load for takeoff might have been advisable. Even so, having a bolthole in the unpredictable climate was a boon.

The following day I flew with my new Boss, OC Operations Wing who was a current Tornado F3 pilot and we completed a full practice QRA scramble to run through the procedures which by now, were lodged well in my mind. Surprisingly, as an OCU instructor, although I had not held QRA in the Tornado before — I had only operated in exercise conditions — the procedures were ingrained and came back very quickly.

My log book shows a variety of activity in that first month. As well as my own pilot, I flew again with OC Ops Wing and the Station Commander, another experienced Tornado F3 pilot and old colleague and Flight Commander. In addition to a familiarisation sortie with a newly arrived pilot from 111 (Fighter) Squadron, I flew plenty of the typical intercept sorties and took part in an exercise named 'Cape Petrel' in which my Tornados acted as 'Orange Air' to exercise the base defences. Affiliation exercises with the Hercules in which we trained the crews to react to fighter attack, affiliation exercise against the Lynx helicopter from HMS *Newcastle* and ship air defence exercises with HMS *Newcastle* and HMS *Scylla* which were visiting the islands completed the first month's activity. Of course no month was complete without welcoming the new arrivals by arriving alongside the Tristar.

My first task on the squadron was to look at how QRA was operating. Up to that time, QRA crews decamped from the Q Building to the Squadron Headquarters to brief their training missions. Although the crews carried radios, the aircraft were a healthy sprint away from the briefing rooms and covering the distance, perhaps carrying helmets and lifejackets, cost a valuable minute or more of the allotted ten minutes readiness time. It was a risk I didn't think was worth taking, although, I could not have anticipated the biggest friction that the decision would cause. There was a small room on QRA which was easily transformed into a briefing room but, at the time, it contained the exercise equipment which the groundcrew (but rarely the aircrew) used when cooped up in the Q Shed. As a stop gap, I decided to transfer the machines up to the squadron HQ but immediately the mutterings began. If the Q shift wanted to exercise, the line managers would need to spring them for a short time. It was unpopular with the troops but, there would have been little point having the aircrew in close proximity but having to wait for ground crew to arrive from the HQ. In the event of a scramble, efficient teamwork was vital and the risk of failing to meet the scramble time was just too great if any problems were encountered on start up. I was surprised how important such small essentials could be in the austere environment and learned from it. In parallel, I began lobbying the Station Support Wing to provide a new portakabin to be used as a QRA briefing room which would allow the exercise equipment to be returned to Q. There was a suitable hard standing just outside the Q Shed which looked big enough to take a small extension cabin. Electricity and communications could easily be piped in from the existing accommodation so there seemed to be few problems other than the inevitable lead time to identify a suitable building and have it erected on site. It was during the 'siting board' for the new QRA briefing room that my fist 'leadership challenge' occurred.

I had invited members of the Station administrative staff over to the dispersal to look at the planned location. Bright and early, the appropriate experts assembled and we were joined by my immediate Boss, OC Ops Wing. As we began the discussions, the first pair of the day taxied out from the dispersal and made for the threshold of the easterly runway. As the mundane discussions of footings and services for the building droned on, I heard the sound of the pair roll down the runway and lift off for their sortie. The norm on any sortie was to begin by running an exercise known as 'Fiery Cross' which had the Tornados simulating Argentinian fast jets attacking the base allowing the Rapier crews to practice their engagement procedures. The pair would leave the base defence zone and return a few minutes later at high speed at low level from any direction and complete a simulated air attack on the airfield. Inevitably, the QRA Shed was a popular target. During this run, Rapier crews would track the incoming 'hostiles' and take simulated missile shots against the aggressors. It was always good to know that these drills were simulated as we had no desire to provide a real target for the Rapier missiles which sat armed and ready on the rails every day. As I waved my hands in an appealing fashion pointing out where I felt the footings should be placed I heard the brief noise of an approaching Tornado. Little is heard in advance of an overflight but the suppressed sound of an approaching F3 was enough for me to glance upwards to catch the sight of one of my jets flashing over the top of QRA cranking into a tight turn at a height which looked suspiciously lower than the briefed minima. Luckily, unlike the scene from *Top Gun*, I wasn't holding a cup of coffee but I could not suppress the natural reaction to flinch at the sound of the jet noise. Luckily my Boss, OC Ops Wing who had been in deep discussion about an esoteric aspect of the cabin site had missed the low pass so I was able to make a disarming comment about noisy jets and the incident passed without further ado. One of the pilots had been a brand new first tourist on his first detachment to the Falklands whereas the other was a seasoned weapons' instructor with many hours on both Phantoms and Tornados. I felt sure I knew who had 'misjudged' the pass and began to rehearse the inevitable 'bollocking' I would have to deliver to maintain flying discipline. As I was part of the Q1 crew, the duty authoriser was 'invited' to send the crews to the Q Briefing room as soon as they had signed in. As the crews assembled, I opened with the inevitable, 'What were you thinking?' explaining that the 'siting board' with most of the Station hierarchy had been on the dispersal during the pass. I began to home in on the junior pilot who I was sure was the guilty party when the experienced pilot coughed and admitted that it was him. After dismissing the remainder of the crews, a quick one-on-one determined that he had misjudged the height producing the sporty results I had witnessed. No harm was done and transgressions on heights were inevitable as crews strove to maintain an edge and adjusted to the rigours of flying 'Down South'. The important thing was to maintain a balance between combat effectiveness and discipline. I can safely say, however, that I learned yet again not to judge too quickly. The matter was solved on this occasion in a gentlemanly fashion by a large donation of beer to the squadron bar; with dire warnings to set an example as a further transgression would have been more serious.

As Boss of the Tornado Flight I held one of the most important 'cards' on Station as I was the sole arbiter of who received back seat rides in the Tornado

F3. I could be extremely popular at times but, equally, unpopular if the decision went the wrong way for the prospective 'aviator'. Flying passengers was extremely important in order to get the message across to those who supported the flying effort about what we did and why we did it. It was not, however, easy to set up given the permanent QRA commitment and limited aircraft numbers. Aircraft had to be disarmed and careful briefings delivered on what to touch and, most importantly, what not to touch in the back cockpit. The, apparently, petulant demands from 1435 Flight air and ground crews for certain things to be delivered at absolutely no notice was often put in perspective when the new 'back-seaters' were trussed up in flying kit and strapped into the cockpit. We often received quite a lot of sympathy when the passenger was poured back out of the cockpit after the trip, frequently looking a little green around the gills or clutching a 'sick bag'! Whichever way the sortie went I never heard anyone say they didn't enjoy the experience, although many admitted that it might have been somewhat more pleasurable if it had been shorter and they hadn't felt airsick during the flight.

I often heard crews at home in the UK say that flying in the Falklands was boring but I could never understand that school of thought. Granted, the numbers of available Tornados were small and it was a challenge to launch more than a pair of fighters at the same time so training against multiple fast jets had to be done during sorties back home in UK. That said, the diversity was still exciting. On most days you could chose to go against a C130 or a helicopter target which were demanding profiles in their own right. I'm not sure I ever tired of pulling alongside the 'Timmy' as it made its descent into the airfield seeing the faces pressed to the windows of the airliner as they caught their first glimpse of a Tornado in the air.

Flying infractions allowed me to set up a spoof on my 3rd pilot who was an old friend and mentor, an experienced weapons instructor and hugely respected by the young crews. In any event, I owed him one after a particularly lengthy debrief during my staff work up as I returned to the Tornado F3 after a ground tour. After the *Top Gun* moment during the 'siting board', I had made it clear that I could not tolerate being cavalier with the rules on my watch. I was on notice, so were my crews. I wanted aggressive flying to the limits but not beyond. Shortly afterwards, my pilot pushed a little too hard on one sortie and we went below the minimum height with a young pilot as wingman in battle formation. All was perfectly safe but later in the bar, I took him aside and explained how, if I was to retain credibility, I could not be seen to be saying 'do as I do, not as I say'. To his credit, as a true professional, he flew strictly to the rules for the rest of his detachment, although I sensed the occasional frustration. The incident set me scheming as I had a few old 'debts' to settle with my old mentor. As the day of his departure neared, I began crafting a carefully prepared end of detachment debrief report. I found all the appropriate extracts from previous appraisals such as 'this officer has struck rock bottom and continued to dig' and 'I would follow this officer but only out of curiosity'. Armed with the spoof report I had my PA call my pilot across to the office but left him to stew outside for 10 minutes or so. This was completely out of character as my door was always open and we were big mates. He waited patiently as my PA, in an unusually reflective mood, shook her head explaining that I was a bit grumpy today and I'd been locked away for hours. When I finally called him in, I read out the spoof report verbatim starting with minor criticisms which might have been plausible but leading towards the more jocular. I watched as his face dropped and he became increasingly quizzical. My line was totally out of character. A giant of a man, I could see him moving from confusion to distress to anger and, luckily, my poker face broke before he had the opportunity to grab me warmly by the throat. He had realised by then and immediately saw the funny side as I gave him his real report which obviously extolled his skills and virtues and reiterated how much he had helped me with maintaining the professional edge of the Flight during his short time on the islands. Thanks goodness we parted still friends! We've since shared many beers so I must have got away with it.

The weather was without doubt the biggest challenge and it was not uncommon to see all four seasons reflected in a single day. With nothing to stop the predominantly westerly winds from the point where they blew off the Argentinian mainland to the point at which they struck West Falkland, gales were a fact of life. With the majority of sorties flown at 250 feet, low-level turbulence was always present and it was unusual to experience a truly calm day. Equally, most of our air-to-air refuelling was flown at much lower altitude than in UK and heights of 5,000 feet and below were common. At these low altitudes, the refuelling basket was invariably lively and taking on fuel became a joust. There were some very interesting airflow patterns over the ridgeline to the north of Mount Pleasant airfield. If the wind came around to the north it would set up an eddy pattern over Pleasant Peak which would swirl over the airfield making for some difficult conditions on final approach to the main east/west runway. Pilots became adept at handling the various conditions but supervisors became paranoid about potential changes in the weather and tried hard to predict the unpredictable. The Duty Officer Flying, normally the QRA commander, was always conscious of the state of readiness of the C130 tanker to ensure that it could always be available to provide fuel for the Tornados if they were forced to hold off for adverse weather. At least the ability to transfer a full load of aviation fuel to a pair of thirsty Tornados allowed a modicum of thinking time waiting for the weather to clear.

The whole of the airspace around the islands was a large low flying area and far from receiving noise complaints, it was more common to receive complaints from the islanders if they didn't receive a visit from a Tornado every week or so. Unlike the UK where the intercept areas were well delineated to deconflict from airways and controlled airspace, no such problems existed down south. There were no civilian airways. Practice intercepts could be flown in any area, oversea or overland and at all heights from surface level to the stratosphere. If we planned overland intercepts, the area to the south west of Mount Pleasant over Lafonia was flat and free of inhabited areas. On West Falkland, A4 Alley and the plain to the west was always a favourite and the ground was reasonably flat and good for manoeuvring at the merge. Some of the coastal islands provided outstanding terrain masking and a Tornado could drop in between the rocky outcrops and disappear from radar for some time during the run in. If we operated with the Control and Reporting Centres at Mount Alice or Byron Heights they preferred us to operate over the sea and to the west of the islands where their radar picture was good. As you can imagine, being able to see low level fast jets in that area was important to them so they were keen to practice. The SOC at Mount Kent, however, often pushed us out north or south, again because even though they could see the picture from the CRCs, their own radar head had better coverage in those sectors. In reality, the airspace was extremely flexible and was always available, as were the controllers with whom we operated. The controllers certainly enjoyed more chances to exercise close control of their fighters than they did back home in the UK.

Working with the Navy was one of the more interesting aspects of life in the South Atlantic. With the slow decline in numbers of ships, it had become difficult to arrange training events in the UK. The ships the Navy retained were invariably operating in distant waters or on refit in home port. The only regular maritime exercise was known as a JMC or the Joint Maritime Course. Unfortunately, these were normally run in the Iceland-Faroes Gap working with a combined NATO task force which meant that sorties were extremely long, supported by AAR, lacked targets and could be extremely boring. Given that the fleet could be hundreds of miles off the coast, it was difficult to ensure that bombers and fighters were in the operating area at the same time so it was quite common to spend two or three hours on combat air patrol and not see another aircraft. Targets to intercept were often at a premium and avoiding the small airliners which plied the regional airports could be a challenge. Many an Islander aircraft dropping into a regional airport or a beach strip has been unaware of a Phantom shadowing a short distance behind. No such limitations existed down south despite the smaller numbers of assets. Training could be focussed where it was needed and everyone was keen to provide training opportunities for each other.

Luckily, during my time at MPA, our deployed ship was HMS *Newcastle* which was a Type 42 destroyer whose primary role was air defence for the fleet and complementary to our own mission. That meant that it carried a full complement of fighter controllers who were always keen to work with our Tornados. Unlike JMCs, the ship could operate within sight of the Falklands coastline and often come back into port in the evening. Not only could we work with the controllers but we could also share stories and experiences over beer in the evening. Equally, the ship's crew had to remain current on defensive techniques and we were able to use our aircraft to simulate key threats, in particular, the Exocet sea-skimming missile.

Just as with the Navy, it could be difficult to liaise with our parent operations centres. For RAF Coningsby, the parent sector operations centre was RAF Boulmer in Northumberland. The drive was well over three hours and invariably entailed an overnight stay taking crews off the flying programme for two days. Inevitably, this meant that visits could only be scheduled to meet the annual 'stat'. In the Falklands no such limitations were evident and crews could hop aboard one of the helicopters which visited the sites daily and, an overnight stay during the break from QRA was a positive bonus.

One of the features of life in The Falklands was the variety of squadron bars which sprang up around the 'Death Star' and across the dispersals. Each unit had its own little drinking hole; The Queen Vic for the Hercules crews, Lot 22 for the helicopter crews, Steamers Bridge, The Cat's Cradle, Sharkey's and Shady's to name but a few. For 1435 Flight aircrew, the hub of social activity was its own bar called 'The Goose' named after the Upland Goose which was the main resident of Mount Pleasant before the arrival of the airfield. Two rooms had been allocated as a communal lounge where aircrew on stand down could listen to music and catch a few beers still dressed in flying suits, away from the more formal surroundings of the Officers' Mess. To appease the leadership, it was technically not a bar as beer wasn't sold. A fridge in the lounge was stocked by Flight members and guests were invited on a personal basis. TV was an impossible luxury as even The British Forces Broadcast Service was in its infancy on the islands. Only video films were available to while away the time. Given that films were a staple for QRA, it was rare to see a movie in The Goose other than during the day for off duty crews which smacked of 'Coals to Newcastle'. Dinner times were fairly traditional from between 6.30 p.m. to about 8 p.m. after which most officers would gravitate towards the Officers' Mess Bar. Between cease work on the Squadron and dinner time would see a constant stream of the crews not involved with QRA catching an early pint in the Goose.

The main feature was obvious as you walked along the corridor. Artwork representing the squadron badges of every squadron which had provided crews for 1435 Flight decorated each wall. The insignia ranged from fine renditions of squadron patches to some particularly uncomplimentary cartoons. As Squadron Boss, it was quite enlightening to see how some squadron crews viewed the Operational Conversion Unit which had been my most recent posting. The cartoon for 65 Squadron, latterly 56 Squadron was of a pair of aged aircrew one of whom was being pulled along in a wheel chair. I suspect that it was not an OCU artist who came up with the design but even so, the OCU instructors who manned the Flight along with their squadron counterparts were happy enough to sign the cartoon. A pub sign which showed a male Upland Goose held pride of place at the entrance to the bar .... sorry, Lounge. On the opposite wall were fixed the flying patches of every aircrew member who had ever served on 1435 Flight. Pinned to the wall in crews of pilot and navigator, the badges were a permanent reminder of time spent at the outer reaches of the former Empire. Particularly poignant were the badges of those who had lost their lives in the service of their Country. These badges were reaffixed upside down to mark the loss. On entering the bar, the history of The Goose was immediately apparent. A large frieze showing a Phantom intercepting the Argentinian Boeing 707 Intelligence gatherer adorned the wall. Each of the Phantom squadrons was represented by a cartoon badge with each squadron representative clearly enjoying a rendition of a squadron song. Close by was another poignant piece of artwork and I defy anyone who ever entered The Goose to deny a small lump in the throat which it evoked. In an earlier accident, a Phantom crew were lost when conducting a practice intercept mission against another Phantom. In the days before the crash, the crew had been preparing a new piece of artwork for The Goose. The Phantom spook which was the informal logo of the Phantom Force had been painted in outline. The caption below was to have read 'Death before Dishonour'. The crew died before the painting was completed leaving only the outline of the word 'Death'. As a tribute to their memory, the artwork was covered in Perspex and left in the state in which it was on the day of the accident. I hope it will be preserved as a lasting memory to the crew for as long as the RAF occupies The Goose. Other slightly less emotional but equally morbid trophies littered the lounge. An ejection seat recovered from one of the Phantoms which had been scrapped on the Islands was mounted on a stand and occupied pride of place in the corner. Its donor aircraft now lies at the bottom of a water filled pit at MPA. Wreckage of Argentinian aircraft lost during the conflict had also been recovered during 'rest and rehabilitation', or R&R trips and joined the RAF memorabilia. The windscreen of an A4 Skyhawk sat next to the gun port of a Mirage III. The inscription on the windscreen said simply: 'Windscreen of A4 C215 brought down by 40mm gunfire from HMS *Fearless* on 27 5 82. Crashed 10nm NW of Port Howard. Mariano Velasco ejected.'

The remainder of the detail had worn with age but recorded the parameters of the A4 at impact. Still visible were 480 knots and 45 degrees nose down. Researching the crash in Jeffrey Ethell and Alfred Price's excellent book *Air War South Atlantic* revealed that the aircraft from Grupo 5 based at Rio Gallegos had been tasked to attack an equipment dump at the old refrigeration plant in Ajax Bay. The attack had been driven home and two bombs had killed five task force personnel and injured twenty-six others leaving four more unexploded bombs in and around the plant buildings. Unfortunately for Velasco, as the A4s returned over Falkland Sound, they were hit by fire from both HMS *Intrepid* and HMS *Fearless*. The aircraft was struck on the wing damaging the hydraulics and causing a fire in the rear fuselage. The crippled aircraft flew on for only a few more miles before it proved uncontrollable and Velasco ejected suffering only a sprained ankle. The legacy of the attack proved more complex. The plant had been used as a makeshift hospital to treat the wounded. Two of the bombs landed close to the operating theatre. The bomb disposal officer had to make a life and death decision to decide whether the bombs were armed with delayed fuses. To evacuate the hospital would have cost more lives in the freezing conditions but to stay ran the risk of further explosions. In the end the decision proved to be the right one and the medical staff worked on almost certainly saving the lives of the injured. The experience must have been harrowing at the time. Seeing the stark mementos of the doomed aircraft tells little of the human stories which surrounded their losses.

Artwork in the 1435 Accommodation.

Right: The 56 (Reserve) Squadron
artwork.

Below: My own flying badge.

Beer on tap was a luxury too far and the impromptu events held in The Goose relied on the ubiquitous 'tinnies' stored behind a makeshift bar. There were however, many stories of wild parties which emerged over the years and occasionally made press headlines. The *Sun* newspaper published a lurid account of misbehaviour which was picked up by *The Merco Press* published on 4 December 2012 in Montevideo. It led with the sensational headline: 'Sex, Drink, Scandal? and Duty' and made interesting reading:

> Allegations of promiscuous sex and excessive drinking by servicemen and women in the Falklands Garrison has met with mixed reaction in the United Kingdom with a reminder that whatever happens in off-duty hours, the tri-service force remains at a high state of readiness to deter any military threat, which is its reason for being based there. The Ministry of Defence says allegations of misconduct are being investigated and, where proved, disciplinary action will be taken. Military chiefs here challenge and deny what they reject as an unrepresentative, jaundiced and potentially damaging picture of rowdy behaviour, published in the large circulation Sun Newspaper, based on a dossier it says was sent by an RAF officer who had recently served there. The Ministry of Defence stresses the professional and strict training of the armed forces, and their readiness for combat if required.

The article added balance by underlining the good reputation the forces enjoyed amongst the islanders:

> The Falklands Government has frequently praised the garrison for its generally good behaviour and its help to the civilian community. It has a long record of coping with emergencies and saving Islanders' lives by medical evacuation to hospital in Uruguay and the United Kingdom. The Falklands Government Representative in London, Sukey Cameron, emphasised the strong rapport and co-operation that exists between the local population and the military and mutual support for each other's welfare and charities. Servicemen have built up a record of good behaviour in their contacts with Islanders, who have welcomed many of them to stay in their homes. The timing of the article comes just before a 20th Anniversary mass visit by veterans of the South Atlantic Medal Association (SAMA) who evicted the Argentinian invaders in 1982.
> (© The Merco Press)

Personnel on detachment work hard and play hard. At the first sign of tensions, the posture would change and social activity would take a back seat. Personnel would work extended hours to get the job done so apocryphal tales spread by misguided insiders paint a false story. That is not to say that incidents do not occur. The Commander of British Forces, at the time an Army General, was invited to The Goose for a beer by the Tornado Flight Commander. Two young ladies were twirling around something which looked remarkably like a pole from a nightclub. The Commander was heard to ask 'Good God, where did you get these two trollops from?' In a response which may have lacked a certain amount of diplomacy, the reply was, 'Sandhurst, Sir'. It would appear that the ladies were from the Army College on a short visit and enjoying life with the fighter crews.

I was by now two-thirds of the way through my tour and already flying with my old friend from RAF Germany days. A keen walker he persuaded me to take a trip across to West Falkland on one of our free days. We already knew that the R&R Centre at Shag Cove was closing for a few days as the resident personnel were returning to savour the delights of Stanley for their own R&R. We would be alone at Shag Cove but had only planned to stay for the day. We finished QRA in the morning and decided to spend the following day walking before returning to Q that evening. The morning of the trip dawned fair so clutching a bag of essentials, lunch and a camera we headed off to the air terminal to catch a flight with Bristow Helicopters who were responsible for moving personnel around the island. The service was set up to move essential duty personnel between the various units on the island so a regular shuttle ran between Mt Kent, Mount Alice in the South and Byron in the north. If there were seats available, they could be booked on a 'first come, first served' basis for off duty personnel and we had some seats earmarked. The islanders were always happy to see squadron personnel and would offer a bed for the night so the helicopter would drop in at the settlements *en route* dropping others off as it made its way around the route. We booked a return flight from Shag Cove for the same afternoon. We climbed aboard the S61 at the Air Terminal but by the time it set off from Mount Pleasant a shower had hit the airfield and we began to question the wisdom knowing we were due on Q that night. Typical of the Falklands weather, the shower passed quickly and within minutes we had popped out into bright blue skies and unlimited visibility. The flight was at low level and it made a nice change to see the islands from a different perspective. Flying around in a Tornado F3 we thought we flew low to the ground. Hedge hopping in the S61 proved just how hilly some of the 'flat' ground in East Falkland really was. After a short stop at Goose Green settlement and an interesting approach into Mount Alice where the GCI site sits atop a large isolated pimple of a mountain, we eventually made the approach into the helicopter landing site at Shag Cove. As we climbed off, the senior NCO who ran the R&R centre gave us a hurried briefing; it was clear his mind was on his own upcoming time off. The centre had been left open but he asked us to 'drop the latch' before we returned to Mount Pleasant airfield that night. The R&R staff had a full four days off so it would be unoccupied for a few days after our departure.

The day could not have been more relaxing. We took a short walk across the countryside which was covered in yellow gorse and bathed in sunlight. Late in the morning a Tornado F3 from 1435 Flight flew past and dropped the wing in greeting as it made its way down the coast. It was a stark contrast watching the aircraft from the tranquillity of the Falklands countryside knowing what was going on inside the cockpit. The walk took us across A4 Alley which was the shallow valley which the Argentinian pilots had used to such effect during the conflict. Running parallel to the Eastern coastline, a ridgeline shields the valley from the view of any ships operating in Falkland Sound. The Argentinian pilots dropped into the valley at the south-western end before routing north eastwards towards the Task Force anchored in the waters around San Carlos. A late pop over the ridgeline allowed them just enough time to set up their initial point for their run on their selected target. Critically, it gave the defenders the least time to take a sighting solution on their attackers and to prevent the attack. It was a tactic that was to prove lethal and a number of ships were lost in those days immediately following the landings when the Task Force was at its most vulnerable. Standing in the base of the valley it was clear why the tactic had worked as the ridgeline provided perfect cover. It could not have proved totally effective, however, as we came across the remains of a wrecked Puma helicopter which had come to grief on 23 May 1982. It was one of a section of four helicopters attacked by a flight of Sea Harriers from one of the carriers. The Sea Harrier pilots had found the formation and, after being threatened during an initial pass, one of the Pumas flew into the ground destroying the aircraft. An Augusta 109 was destroyed by cannon fire, at which stage the remaining helicopters had landed to seek refuge from their attackers. By then, out of ammunition, the Sea Harrier pilots had reported the intruders to another formation who destroyed the remainder of the helicopters on the ground again using guns. Which of the unfortunate formation we had fallen across was not clear but it was a sobering reminder of the intensity of the conflict which had raged just a few years before.

As the appointed time for the pickup drew near, we made our way back across the stunning countryside to the landing zone. It had been a fantastic day and we had both enjoyed the break but the next QRA stint beckoned. With perfect timing the helicopter appeared, popping up over the ridge which separated A4 Alley from Falkland Sound. Immediately alarm bells rang as, unfortunately, its heading was well to the north and it passed serenely by, climbing slowly. All was not well as we watched the helicopter disappear into the distance, its engine noise slowly fading. To say panic set in would be an over exaggeration but let's call it mild concern. We were on the wrong island, night was beginning to draw in and we had no mobile 'phones as they were by no means standard issue in 1994. Luckily, we had not yet dropped the latch as that was to have been our final task before boarding so we made our way back over to the R&R Centre.

An overnight stop was unappealing as there was no food, no heating and no means to summon a pick up. At that point, the bad situation became worse as the 'phones were dead. Try as we might, there seemed no way to reactivate them. Fortunately, part of the arrival briefing had been a mention that the radio had been turned off so after a short search we located the HF radio set that the staff used for routine communications. It was also stone dead! We scored our first success after a further search found a master switch which reactivated the 'phone which would have been a positive boon if we could have located a 'phone book. Back at MPA, speed dialling and on base extensions were the norm and it was rare to have to ring around the islands. The vagaries of inter settlement dialling was lost on us. Undeterred we began a series of test calls using vague dialling codes from memory until eventually we managed to contact the Duty Corporal for the Royal Marines Detachment at Moody Barracks on the outskirts of Stanley. He was immediately ordered, under pain of ritual execution, to hold onto the 'phone and to stay put until we had made contact with the QRA Ops Room at MPA! In true Army fashion he rose to the challenge and proved to be our saviour. Keeping the line open, he managed to make contact with the duty QRA crew who then contacted the RAF helicopter squadron. Naturally, OC 78 Squadron was delighted to launch the search and rescue Sea King for the short transit to Shag Cove to return OC 1435 Flight to QRA in time for the handover. Within thirty minutes the dark grey fuselage of the SAR helicopter hove into view and I don't think I'd ever seen a more welcome sight. The R&R Centre had turned from an idyllic setting to a place of potential incarceration and, certainly, embarrassment. As the helicopter touched down I could see OC78's grinning face knowing that my secret was safe with him . . . not! At the inevitable 'debrief' we tried to find out what had gone wrong. The S61 crew had known that the R&R Centre was closed for a few days so assumed that we would make our way to Shag Cove 2 which was an alternative landing site some two miles away. They had landed, looked for the F3 crew but finding nothing, pressed on around the route. Why they made that assumption when they had dropped two exercise-averse aircrew at the primary landing site will remain forever a mystery.

One of the 1435 Flight traditions was a weekly review known as 'The Claw'. Run by the ground crew, it was a look at life on the Flight and followed a strange format possibly more akin to freemasonry than the Air Force. It was held in yet another unofficial 'lounge' located on the 1435 Flight dispersal known as The 'Eyrie Bar' which was yet another reference to the Flight's heritage as the original mascot for 23 (F) Squadron was an Eagle. The name stuck despite the transition to Flight status in the 1980s and the adoption of the Maltese Cross. For most of the week the 'editorial team' collected snippets of information, preferably unflattering, to compile into a weekly review. The proceedings were opened by the Engineering Officer or ENGO, sitting on an old ejection seat from one of the scrapped Phantoms and wearing a strange helmet. One of the ground crew was selected to read out the weekly tale which was accompanied by catcalling and banter. Various awards were handed out including 'Donkey of the Week' for the biggest mistake and 'The Jack B'stard' Award for the foulest crime of disloyalty. To an outsider, particularly a sober outsider, the proceedings must have seemed macabre. To a crowd of Alpha Males and Alpha Females, it was an easy and, normally, harmless way to let off steam.

As Boss, I took plenty of banter but the hardest ribbings were saved for the ENGO who was the first officer in the chain of command for the troops. Mostly light hearted, I had to make sure it stayed on the right side of propriety as it was easy for banter to become personal. In the close community of detached operations, letting off steam was healthy. Ultimately, the ENGO may have needed to enforce discipline and knowing when to draw the line was surprisingly, one of the most difficult challenges I faced. It was on more than one occasion that I had to threaten to shut down 'The Claw' if it strayed too far which would have been amazingly unpopular. Successive Station Commanders had expressed disquiet at policing the unofficial crew room bars and any sign of impropriety or poor behaviour would have brought immediate action. Sadly, the bar met its demise when the exploits were published in the infamous article in the *Sun* newspaper in 2002. I wonder if the journalist and the disgruntled RAF officer realised the impact of their revelations on the captive audience on detachment? I can imagine the discussions which ensued and I suppose it came as no surprise that the leadership were forced to close the unofficial drinking clubs shortly afterwards. I can only imagine the mood at the time but no doubt other outlets were found to let off steam.

Following my helicopter exploits, naturally my pilot and I took quite a lot of banter from the troops. The review took a few swipes at us for alleged 'cock ups', the Bristow's crews for stranding OC1435 Flight on West Falklands and any other culprit where banter seemed appropriate. Afterwards, one of the squadron artists produced a cartoon which I still treasure after so many years have passed. I would happily post credit for the sketch but sadly the artist is by now anonymous. My pilot was awarded the 'Jack B'stard' Award for the week for failing to look after his Boss properly. The facts couldn't have been further from the truth but when did proceedings at 'The Claw' ever allow facts to interfere with a good story?

When I received my posting to MPA, the fact that I would have to spend Christmas away from my young family had been the greatest strain and was heart wrenching. In the event, it was just as bad as expected and nothing can ever replace the lost memories, although Christmas that year proved to be

A cartoon produced by the 1435 Flight Artist.

memorable for other reasons. In the run up to Christmas, Andy Green, who was to become famous as the pilot of Thrust 2, the car which broke the World Land Speed Record, had decided that the Operations Room on QRA needed some festive spirit. Anyone who has been anywhere near the Falkland Islands will know that trees are at a premium. Certainly, anything resembling a fir tree is in the flying pig category! With typical aircrew ingenuity, a collection of wire appeared which when threaded through a green pole, produced a structure which vaguely resembled a tree. Covered with green and silver tinsel, the 'twigs' were mounted in a pot and adorned with a single strand of fairy lights which also mysteriously appeared, presumably the result of a raid on the General Store in Stanley. Christmas ornaments were at a premium so the tree seemed a little sad for quite a few days. The arrival of the 'Timmy' brought a package from my family containing Christmas gifts. Whether luck or premonition, two small Christmas ornaments, which were presents from my children were included. Miraculously they survived the journey across the world and within minutes, the tree sported two new occupants in pride of place. One was a small bear in an upturned pot and the other, a white bear in a red bed both surrounded by miniature Christmas gifts. No one could accuse the Flight Christmas Tree of being the most cosmopolitan tree that year but it was certainly put together with ingenuity and a good deal of pride. Andy may have gone on to break world records at death defying speeds but the Flight Christmas Tree was undoubtedly his ultimate achievement.

Christmas Day deserved something special and we struggled to think of an appropriate gesture to mark the occasion. I was determined that we should fly on Christmas Day to ensure that the fact that we operated for 365 days of the year was not lost on the rest of the Station. The QRA team were a captive audience and the spare jets were prepared and serviceable so no one would be put to any extra work. A live QRA scramble seemed unlikely as we knew our neighbours in Argentina would also be celebrating the occasion. An intercept mission seemed somehow rather provocative on the day of peace so an alternative solution was needed. The local residents knew we were there defending their airspace but we decided to visit every major settlement on the islands, so I set about drawing a map which connected the dots. Taking in every major settlement, the resulting map with the short tracks connecting the dots, looked like a bloodshot eyeball. After takeoff, the first destination was, obviously, the airfield and a minor deviation from runway heading took in the 78 Squadron dispersal. Every sortie included a flyover of the airfield to exercise the Rapier crews providing a target for them to engage. I'm not sure how interested they were to take part on that particular Christmas morning but we duly obliged. After a right hand turn-out from the main runway we kept it tight along the foothills of the ridge which skirts the airfield to the north. Another turn down the line of the secondary runway with the RB199s humming a Christmas Carol lined us up with the accommodation block, or the 'Death Star'. Passing overhead the block was normally forbidden but OC Operations Wing was equally keen to ensure that it was not forgotten that operations would continue despite the celebrations. We had to practice approaches to the secondary runway which was much shorter than the main strip and the overshoot along the line of the runway passed sufficiently close to the accommodation to welcome-in Christmas morning, particularly at 420 knots.

As we pressed south, we passed over Mare Harbour saying Merry Christmas to the Navy who had sensibly returned to port for the day. We expected a good turnout at the radar sites and, true to form, the area surrounding the radar heads was packed and a few party hats and balloons were evident as we flashed past. Even our controllers went off frequency as we went by to make sure they saw the Christmas salute. What was truly rewarding was that, as we passed many of the larger settlements, we could see the islanders flocking onto the open spaces and waving wildly. Although, we were tight on fuel to take in all our planned sites, a few of the larger settlements warranted a second pass. On reflection, had this gesture been repeated around the local area in Lincolnshire, I'm sure there would have been a raft of noise complaints about the noisy Tornado which had interrupted Christmas Lunch. As it was, the only complaints were from isolated communities who heard about the flight and were miffed that we hadn't over-flown their own settlement. Our return to MPA was a little less dramatic and as we taxied back into the dispersal we had a final plan. With the ejection seats and weapons made safe, bone domes were exchanged for more suitable headwear for the festive season and we captured a unique Christmas pose, (plate 18).

After the morning's events, Christmas Lunch on QRA was slightly more austere than the feast which had been prepared in the Officers' Mess. Meals on QRA were normally eaten casually with a plate of food balancing on the knee of an immersion suit. For Christmas Lunch a table was laid and both crews dined on traditional turkey with all the trimmings. The fifteen-minute journey across the airfield in a hotlock insulated container didn't spoil the taste but, sadly, the celebrations could not include a glass of wine and the Loyal Toast was drunk with a soft drink. We all know that one of the Christmas traditions is a visit from Santa Claus and courtesy of 78 Squadron we were not disappointed. As lunch was settling, the sound of approaching rotor blades suggested that 78 Squadron were also flying on Christmas Day. As we assembled outside, the winch man was already hanging from the end of a strop dressed in a full Santa suit. He returned our earlier noisy greeting by tapping out a tune with his boots on the roof of the QRA shed.

Reminders of the conflict were never far away. As the time neared for the rotation of two of the Flight's aircraft I began to question my Engineering Officer on his plans for housing the additional aircraft on the complex. Only four Housies were in regular use as we needed to focus our efforts in the section of the dispersal closest to QRA. The more remote Housies had not been used since the last reinforcement exercise. One remote housey had been brought into action when an aircraft needed deeper servicing but one particular housey seemed neglected. Closer questioning elicited the fact that it housed a Pucara so ENGO was immediately despatched to collect the keys. As the access door was pulled open, a slightly dismantled but still camouflaged Pucara sat in all its glory. I had not seen a Pucara since my first visit to the islands many years before and, at that time, the hulks littered the airfield. This airframe had obviously been protected and was in remarkably good condition. I never found out how the aircraft found its way onto the Flight's dispersal nor did I find out how it arrived at MPA. I assumed it was one of the airframes airlifted into MPA by Chinook after RAF Stanley closed and its fate had originally been to act as target on one of the ranges. It survived for many years but like its predecessors, reportedly, it was scrapped in situ. It was one of the more unusual incidents of my tour.

The islanders celebrated their heritage on regular occasions during the year but links with the homeland were a common theme. 'Battle Day' is commemorated by a monument on Ross Road in Stanley and the islanders take an annual holiday on 8 December. During the First World War the German Fleet was sighted by a member of the Falkland Islands Defence Force and the British naval forces stationed in the local waters were alerted. The British victory which followed, laid the foundations for ultimate victory in the South Atlantic. On 8 December 1993 I was asked to provide two Tornado F3s to join a Hercules tanker as part of the Battle Day flypast and I was happy to help. After flying a training sortie we made sure to leave plenty of fuel for the flypast. Sitting on the wing of the Hercules, the task of navigating to the event and, more importantly, for ensuring that the timing over the top was correct fell to the C130 navigator. The parade had formed up along the sea front in Port Stanley and the flypast heading was selected to pass due west along the harbour. We were preceded by RAF and Navy helicopters. Somewhat slower than our own formation, they were less flexible and were less able to adjust their timing. The plan was that the helicopters would fly the same track as our own formation to arrive a minute ahead of us but then peel off leaving us an unobstructed flight path along the harbour. At the initial point, the Hercules navigator was on time and we eased into close formation on each wingtip of the tanker as the C130 navigator extended the refuelling hose. Once in close formation we switched off our powerful air-to-air radars to avoid irradiating the Hercules crew. It was never a good plan to upset the crews who provided your fuel! The calls from the helicopters made it clear that they were also hitting their timing so, with little to contribute, I was able to look out of the window and leave the hard work of maintaining formation to 'Biggles' in the front cockpit. I could see the landmarks passing by which had been so familiar during my earlier tour of duty operating from RAF Stanley. The run in heading took us south of Cape Pembroke and Port Stanley Airport, past the FIPASS mooring and along the harbour. The crowds along the sea front were easily visible from our vantage point and, as we passed the dais at the appointed hour, it was nice to reflect on the victories of our predecessors and the islanders continued freedom.

As I neared the end of my tour I had one of the more bizarre experiences, albeit one of the easiest problems to resolve. It was 5.30 a.m. and my pilot and I were still fast asleep in the QRA bedroom when the 'phone rang. Expecting the call to be a warning from the Duty Controller of QRA activity, we were both immediately alert and ready to react. The voice on the other end was in fact my Station Commander from RAF Coningsby in UK. I gestured to my pilot to stand easy and go back to his bed and began to exchange pleasantries. By now I had received my posting to the Ministry of Defence for a second tour of duty in London and I was wary that perhaps something had changed or that there was a problem. Nothing could have been farther from the truth. Knowing I was returning soon, he was placing his order for some perfume for his wife and asked if I could bring it home with me when I returned. He had found a brand which was now proving to be a favourite and needed the 'brownie points'. How could I refuse and I went back to sleep happy in the knowledge that the radar screens were clear.

Departure from MPA was bittersweet. Commanding a fast jet unit so many miles distant from the command element was a unique challenge. Decisions were never simple and consequences of errors could be enormous. When the time came to hand over to my own successor, I knew that I had to welcome him in a suitable fashion so a plan began to hatch in my mind. Flying all 4 Tornado F3s simultaneously had only rarely been done due to the need to maintain the QRA readiness states. It was a plan fraught with risk as I would be the first Commander of the Flight to fall down on the QRA commitment if it failed. Even so it was a valid challenge as I might have been called upon to launch all four aircraft at any time. We could legitimately hold the QRA commitment while airborne but what we could not do was have all four aircraft landing at the same time as they would all then be undergoing post flight servicing simultaneously and, by definition, off state. Equally important would be to maintain a running plot of serviceability states throughout the sortie. If a jet had a problem which would result in it being declared unserviceable during turnaround, I needed to know the minute that fault occurred in the air. In the event of a broken jet I would need a contingency to maintain the vital Q1 and Q2 aircraft on state. With that in mind I began to formulate a plan to put all four Tornados in close formation alongside the Tristar to say hello to the new OC 1435 Flight. The first, and not simple, task was to fire up all four aircraft and launch as a four ship. The F3 could be temperamental and the old joke among crews was brief as a 'six', walk as a 'four' and launch as a pair. To make the plan work, the first event would be to intercept the Tristar as soon as it came within range of the islands and deliver the greeting. The chance to run a couple of 2v2 intercepts was not to be missed as this would be a special event for the Flight. It would also be a good morale booster for the ground crew to see all their aircraft launch together. Of course, the occasion to run a four ship overhead the field could not be missed and, although we couldn't take in the CRCs on West Falklands, the SOC at Mount Kent would be easily reached. By now I was flying with the fourth pilot of my detachment, a wise and experienced OCU instructor whom I'd known for years. Little did I know that I was planning my final sortie in the Tornado F3 in his company but, in hindsight, I could not have asked for a more fitting end to my flying career. In broad terms the plan was to intercept the Tristar and escort it towards the islands. That meant maintaining formation until it began its approach into Mount Pleasant. At that point we would break off and reposition to the south of the islands for a single 2v2 air combat split, knocking off the engagement at a pre determined fuel state. The formation would then form up in a 'box 4' formation and fly past Mount Kent before overflying Mount Pleasant airfield and Mare harbour in close formation. At that point, I would nominate 2 aircraft to land and turn around after which they would assume the Q1 and Q2 commitment and call back on state. In the meantime, my remaining 2 aircraft would endure, eking out the remaining fuel. At this stage, my last jets would need enough fuel to be able to conduct a supersonic intercept against a target if a QRA commitment was called. The C130 tanker would be on alert throughout this phase ready to 'scramble' to provide fuel.

With my plan in hand I first briefed OC Ops Wing and was amazed when he smiled and enthused at the idea. After that, given that he was The Air Defence Commander, I was able to brief the Master Controller at Mount Kent who, with his own Boss's endorsement, also thought it was a great idea. As I briefed the aircrew and ENGO on the plan, not once did I get the usual aircrew cynicism. Motivation was high and RAF personnel always rise to a challenge.

As the engines spooled down after a faultless sortie, I climbed from my Tornado in the housey on 1435 Flight's dispersal where the duty authoriser had positioned the Land Rover. I bounced across the airfield around the rutted, graded road that ringed the runway that had become so familiar. The Air Terminal was on the other side of the runway at the western end adjacent to the Tristar hangar. The sight of the old Phantom, XV409, which stood as the gate guardian brought on a feeling of sadness at handing over the Flight. All that said, I wore the same wide smile that I remembered from my own predecessor as I waited at the arrivals hall for the disembarking passengers to be cleared through. I recognised the tired look and the slightly apprehensive air on the face of my successor. As I had done only four short months before, we dropped in briefly to the accommodation and settled him into his new room close to 'The Goose' before moving on to the Squadron to meet the current residents and show him around. Unlike me, he had flown on 1435 Flight from Mount Pleasant before and it was obvious that he would settle in quickly. My own ticket home on the 'Timmy' was booked for two days hence and, over the next twenty-four hours, I rattled through the checklist of things I needed to get over to him. Once I felt he had taken his fill of the information I had one final significant act of my own. I was returning to the UK to take up an appointment as the desk officer responsible for the Tornado F3 in the Ministry of Defence. I was unlikely to have a requirement for flying kit in that role so, to ease the stress on my baggage allowance, my last task was to return my flying kit to squadron stores so that it could be returned through the logistics chain. A sad, sad day indeed as, little did I know, it would be the

The 1435 Flight photograph, January 1994. © UK Crown Copyright (1994).

last time I would fly operationally in a fast jet. Command appointments were becoming increasingly rare due to downsizing of the RAF and I would spend the rest of my career in ground appointments.

Of course, any handover of command has to be captured in pictures and one of the Flight's Tornados was pulled from Housey 4 to act as a backdrop for the official photograph. As the shutter clicked I was captured at the head of my groundcrew who adopted a suitably serious pose, ranged in a neat semi circle. As I stepped away from the lens, the shot which followed was somewhat less respectable.

The last night in the Officers' Mess, fortuitously or not, was Burns Night. It was a good way to relax on the final night knowing that I had handed over and that any further decisions on operational matters were for my successor to make.

As I downed my second glass of malt I heard that the 1435 Flight aircrew had been called for a briefing from their new Boss. It was business as usual despite the festivities. For the first time in a few months I could actually relax. The scotch helped considerably!

As I checked in at the Air Terminal I was immune to anything the RAF Movements staff could subject me to, although a dull headache, the contribution of a certain Rabbie Burns, had something to do with my acquiescence. I had been presented with a memento which had been retrieved from one of the Phantoms which had been scrapped. There was a visible expression of glee on the face of the 'duty mover' as the item set off the metal detector in the check-in hall. It tuned to abject disappointment when I presented the appropriate export paperwork duly signed by the relevant authority on the island which authorised me to take it home. Climbing aboard the Tristar, despite having just completed one of the most memorable tours of my service career, I could not contain a huge smile. My lasting memory as the 'Timmy' headed north eastwards was glancing out of the window of the airliner to see a Tornado F3 pull alongside accompanied by a message from the Tristar Captain wishing me 'bon voyage' from my successor! I had been on the other end of the greeting many times. There ended my association with the Falkland Islands which had begun on a bleak and windswept dispersal as I stepped from a Tristar at MPA in 1985.

CHAPTER 6
Working with the Other Services

Living and working in the Falklands offered a rare opportunity. In the modern era of expeditionary warfare joint operations are the norm but the islands were one of the few theatres, particularly in the years after the conflict, which saw the Royal Navy, the Army and the Royal Air Force working in close harmony. It was a truly joint effort.

For most of my brief time, the Army presence, although co-located at RAF Mount Pleasant, had been scaled back to a Resident Infantry Company, or RIC. They shared the accommodation in the 'Death Star' with the RAF personnel but would regularly 'up sticks' and disappear into the wilds of the Falklands countryside to practice their field craft. I made one of the rashest decisions of my time in command in an effort to help the deployed Company. Normally tucked up snugly in bad, I agreed to provide a flight of Tornados to simulate a formation of Argentinian fast jets to be overhead the dug-in troops as dawn broke. As an air defence aircraft, the Tornado F3 was not equipped to drop bombs, although the aircraft had a secondary strafe capability using the 27mm Mauser cannon. Despite that, to improve realism, the infantry needed to experience the sights and sounds of an air attack to recognise the stresses of real combat so we adopted an unfamiliar role to assist their training programme. To avoid an early start for the regular flying team I decided to use the QRA aircraft for the task as the Q crews were already a captive audience. If we experienced any unserviceabilities during the sortie, we'd simply pull one of the other jets into the shed during the turn round and regroup when everyone was awake.

We had pre-planned the mission the night before and knew exactly where the infantry were located. The Army exercise planner wanted the air attack warning to ring out at first light so we needed to pre-position in Falkland Sound in the darkness. There were bleary eyes amongst the see-off crews as we fired up the engines in the dimly lit housies and it was an unfamiliar sight as we pulled away from the lights of the dispersal towards the runway threshold. After take off, we routed well south of the exercise area to avoid giving any advanced warning of our approach. The troops were dug in on the lower ground in the bowl formed by Rodeo mountain, Rabbit Mount and Big Mount about 10 miles inland from San Carlos settlement. Although we had a time on target I had warned the planner that we may have to delay to ensure there was enough light to fly safely at low level. At that time, we did not routinely fly with night vision goggles so the attack would have to be in 'day' visual conditions. As we let down over Falkland Sound, we could see the surface of the water clearly. We were quite legal to fly at 1,500 feet at night but the dawn light of a South Atlantic Summer was highlighting our entry point quite well and it was obvious that we could drop lower to our normal daytime heights as the early morning light lit up the coastline. The plan was to run down the inlet at Port San Carlos and hit the site at low level at high speed from the northwest. The mountains to the south rose to about 500 feet so depending on light conditions we would either remain at low level and follow the central valley or pull up and over the mountain ridge and egress at high level. We hit the target on time and overflew the point we had been given by the exercise planner. We saw little on the ground in the early dawn but could only imagine the pandemonium below as tired troops were roused, unceremoniously, from their sleep probably pulling on their kit and gas masks to start another tough day in the field. Sure enough, the flying conditions were fine and we followed the valley around the rocky outcrops returning in a westerly direction from Teal Inlet to hit the site again but this time from the north east. On a bomber squadron, the unofficial rule is 'never re-attack' but, in doing so, it gave the embedded air defence platoon the opportunity to break out their Javelin MANPADS and engage us on the second pass. During the second run, we could see vehicles careering through the countryside as the RIC reacted to the rude awakening. Had this been a real attack, hopefully, the CRC would have provided advanced warning and the MANPADS would have exacted some retribution before an aggressor even arrived over the target.

One of the more poignant duties was to recognise those who gave their lives during the conflict and I recall a particularly touching moment. On 2 December 1993 I was asked to provide a flypast for a memorial ceremony at the Blue Beach Military Cemetery at San Carlos close to the site of the original landings. The cemetery is the last resting place of sixteen of the casualties, including that of Lieutenant Colonel 'H' Jones of the Parachute regiment killed at Goose Green. Originally larger, sisty-four of the dead were repatriated to UK in 1982 leaving just sixteen at rest. Although not an anniversary, families of those lost were visiting the islands and it was appropriate to mark the ceremony of remembrance. At the end of a training sortie we set up a timing pattern to the north of Fanning Head with a pair of F3s. I had a time on target which would coincide with the last post and it was a matter of pride to meet the time exactly. I had only a short run in to the cemetery so I had to ensure that I met timing checks at each end of my holding racetrack. Each orbit took precisely four minutes so I could adjust the final orbit to ensure I set off from the initial point at exactly the right time to make my overhead time. In the event, the timing was perfect and we passed overhead to the second much to my relief. It was impossible to see the mourners below but I said my own words in respect of those who had given their lives and it was quiet in the aircraft as we flew back to Mount Pleasant.

The naval presence varied and was often reinforced by visiting ships. The deep-water port at Mare Harbour with its more snappy title of FIPASS acted as a depot for all the supplies which sustained the base at Mount Pleasant. The shore complex looked like any naval dock facility anywhere in the world. Considering its importance, the jetty which snaked away from the shore, seemed insignificant yet the long pontoon could accommodate a container vessel, the deployed warships and the tugs which supported them. A standing presence was provided by a deployed combat vessel which reinforced the resident patrol vessel, HMS *Dumbarton Castle* whose role was to patrol the local waters. Those were the days before oil was even mooted as a potential industry so her main task was to check on the hundreds of fishing vessels which plied the Falkland Island Protection Zone every day. During my second deployment she enjoyed a rather sedentary lifestyle. Midway through a patrol she developed problems with one of the main drive shafts from the engine and the ship limped home to begin a longer than expected layup in Mare Harbour while the engineers assessed the problem. It proved more complex to fix than originally expected and spare parts were ordered from UK. Unlike routine spares for our Tornados which could be shipped overnight on the Tristar, drive shafts for major warships are complex and specially manufactured.

The crew settled down to a life alongside as the logistics chain sprang into action. During their enforced vacation, the crew settled into a pleasant daily routine, although the Captain who was also a naval helicopter pilot, naturally took quite a ribbing over his inability to put to sea. Our offers of sending him home to carry out the Tornado conversion course while he waited for his ship to be repaired were taken, generally, with good grace. He did, however, win the prize for the most outstanding hospitality during my deployment. Trafalgar Night is a huge celebration for Royal Navy personnel and, with the enforced lay up, the hosting for that celebration aboard HMS *Dumbarton Castle* was exceptional. Being able to escape the routine of The 'Death Star' if only for a few hours was a prize to be celebrated. To enjoy the traditions of Trafalgar Night during the respite was simply marvellous. Sadly, I forgot about the naval tradition of relieving 'Crabs' of their hats and stupidly left mine hanging on the peg outside the wardroom. Finding a replacement forage cap in the confines of the Falkland Islands proved impossible and I was forced to have a replacement flown in on the Tristar from UK. It was a schoolboy error which I did not repeat and, for the rest of my stay, my hat stayed safely in my flying suit pocket when not in use. Towards the end of my detachment, the eagerly anticipated day arrived and the new shaft was fitted. HMS *Dumbarton Castle* left Mare Harbour under her own power and sailed into the local waters to test her newly repaired propulsion system. Naturally, we fired off a pair of Tornados to celebrate the occasion and they flew past the ship just south of the islands. The ship seemed to be making good headway. That evening in the Officers' Mess Bar we impatiently awaited the news from the test. Eventually, a very glum looking Captain arrived with a less than positive report as heavy vibration still plagued his ship and it was back to the drawing board on the repairs. When I finally left at the end of my four month detachment, the ship was still tied up alongside and, apparently, was only repaired some months later, albeit to a great fanfare. She was replaced in the Falkland Islands by HMS *Clyde* in 2008 and was finally sold to the Bangladesh Navy in 2010.

During my fist tour of duty at RAF Stanley I saw little of the deployed Royal Navy ship but my logbook records an air defence exercise with HMS *Danae*, an Exocet-armed Leander class frigate, on 18 June 1985. The ship had first deployed to the South Atlantic in the immediate aftermath of the Falklands War to escort the carrier HMS *Illustrious* returning again later the same year for a Falkland Islands patrol. In 1985, she made her third deployment and I had the opportunity to see her at very close quarters. *En route* back to RAF Stanley from Goose Green in a Bristow's S61 helicopter, we dropped a spare part for the engineers aboard the Royal Fleet Auxiliary vessel Diligence. As we put down on the raised helicopter deck, we sat within feet of the superstructure of HMS *Danae* which was moored alongside. Had we been as close in a Phantom I suspect words would have been exchanged!

During my second tour, I was even more fortunate. The capital ship was a Type 42 destroyer in the shape of HMS *Newcastle* which was an air defence ship. The Captain, who later became the Second Sea Lord, was a weapons controller by trade. We had a perfect ally as his early loyalties lay with the fighter community so it led to a wonderful professional relationship between the two units. The ship spent much of its time at sea but during its brief visits to port we were able to form a close working bond, particularly between the warfare officers and my aircrew. Although a warship protects its position carefully, it became a challenge to try to locate her on a regular basis. Our practice intercepts were positioned around the islands and our radars were constantly scanning the waters for the elusive contact. Our fighter controllers knew roughly which area the ship was operating and could vector us into the general area. If it was working close they would have a precise position. The radar contact from a Type 42 is surprisingly hard to locate in thousands of miles of open water despite its huge size. It certainly honed the Navy crews and made them conscious of their electronic emission control procedures. One stray transmission or erroneous lock-on from the Sea Dart system would bring a Tornado to investigate.

One of the training profiles which was regularly exercised, given the hard won experience during the conflict, was the anti-Exocet drill. The French made Exocet missile had exacted a heavy toll during the conflict and efforts had been made to resupply the stocks they had used. The ships needed to practice tactics and drills to ensure that they could counter a potential attack. When launched from an Argentinian Super Etendard, the missile would fly a pre-planned profile. Prior to launch, the missile carrier would pop up to medium altitude and attempt to locate the target with its onboard radar. Assuming the target was detected, those coordinates were updated in the missiles inertial guidance system before missile release. This allowed the weapons team onboard the ship its first opportunity to counter the threat. If the Super Etendard was detected by the ships air defence radar, a long range missile, Sea Dart in the case of HMS *Newcastle*, could be fired to intercept the firing aircraft. In any event, the emissions from the Agave radar would be detected by the electronic surveillance measures and would alert the Principal Warfare Officer to the threat. This vulnerable period for the firing aircraft was brief as, once the missile was launched, the Etendard pilot would turn hard away from its target and descend to low level to make his escape.

The Exocet is a sea skimmer so it immediately descended to within a few metres of the waves and followed a pre-programmed route to the target guided by its inertial navigation system. Being so low and having an extremely small radar cross section, the missile was invisible to the ship during this phase. Some ships were equipped with short-range combat missile systems such as Sea Wolf which could operate in automatic modes allowing rapid reaction. Every missile suffers from a minimum range limitation as the onboard safety interlocks need time to arm. For that reason the window was short and reaction had to be swift. At about the same time, the radar in the Exocet would fire up to provide terminal active guidance. If the threat had not been detected before that moment, the raucous alert of a terminal guidance threat would evoke rapid reaction from the ship's crew. The risk of late detection led to the deployment of CIWS or close-in weapons systems aboard RN combat vessels. The US built Phalanx and the Dutch Goalkeeper systems were fitted to most warships deployed in the South Atlantic. This allowed a final layer of defence at extremely short range. These CIWS are truly fearsome weapons based on the six-barrelled Gatling guns similar to that fitted to the British Phantoms during the Cold War. Fully automatic and radar laid, they dispense a high rate of fire towards an incoming threat and have proved to be extremely effective. In fact, the CIWS was not the final layer of defence which was left to the trusty 'Matelo' armed with a general purpose machine gun strapped to the ship's rail.

In order to replicate this threat, the C130 tanker was pressed into action as a 'missile carrier' with a pair of Tornado F3 'missiles' tucked under each wing. It would be apparent to anyone that this combination was not an ideal replication, given the size of the Tornado F3 although it could easily match the height and speed profiles giving a realistic flight simulation. The formation would select a run in heading and an initial point. At the appropriate range, with the Tornado F3s tucked in tight formation, the C130 would pull up to its nominated height and emit a few bursts from its mapping radar. At that point a simulated launch saw the F3s accelerate away from the carrier and descend rapidly to wave top height. Again, peacetime limits restricted the minimum height at which the Tornado crews were allowed to fly. The normal height was 250 feet above sea level although exceptionally, a 100-foot clearance could be given. Even at the lower height, the large Tornado was much more detectable than a sea skimming Exocet. Throughout the run in, the Foxhunter radar was left in standby mode so there were no radar emissions to confuse the tactical picture. At the range at which the experts assessed the Exocet would begin transmitting its terminal guidance, the Tornado navigator would fire up the Foxhunter in its short pulse mode simulating the missile. Although, the characteristics were quite different, training modes could be used in the ships radar warning system to make it appear like a real Exocet attack. To provide an even greater problem, the Tornados would widen and separate at close range to attack on different vectors. This gave the weapons officers a challenge in identifying and engaging targets on a multiple axis. Most of the profiles concluded with a short session of manoeuvring. The huge vessel was propelled by Rolls-Royce Tyne engines for routine patrolling but Rolls-Royce Olympus gas turbines could be engaged to provide increased performance. By placing the ship head or stern on to an incoming missile, a much smaller aspect could be offered against the threat. In simple terms, by pointing at the threat the ship appeared smaller and was harder to hit. Equally, if the briefed exercise was for the Tornado crews to act as an Argentinian bomber carrying dumb bombs, a wildly manoeuvring ship provided a much harder target to track. In any event, the sight of such a huge warship 'turning on a sixpence' was truly impressive.

Although not perfect, the profile provided invaluable training for the Navy weapons personnel. It was of little value to the Tornado crews, albeit good fun. There was no attack role for the aircraft which was armed only with air-to-air weapons so flying anti-ship missions was out of the question. Ironically, some

HMS *Newcastle* seen from the cockpit of a Tornado F3 during a mutual training exercise.

years later in its EF3 form, the Tornado was adapted to act as a SEAD platform to suppress enemy air defences. It took some effort and a good deal of patience to explain that, although we might have been engaged and 'killed' at ten miles during the run in, we were merely providing a target facilities service. It seemed that some of our naval colleagues thought that it was a battle between the F3 and the ship despite our lack of capability in the role. In reality, the greater concern was that, in the fog of war, identification systems might break down and a Tornado F3 could be engaged by a Sea Dart or Sea Wolf in automatic mode whilst on Combat Air Patrol or in hot pursuit of an airborne target. Close cooperation made this event less likely.

Being in such close proximity allowed regular liaison which was invaluable on both sides. RAF personnel were invited aboard HMS *Newcastle* for a familiarisation day. Luckily that day the weather played along which was by no means guaranteed in the Southern Atlantic Ocean. That meant that there were no limitations in demonstrating the full capabilities of the Type 42 destroyer. I was able to witness an Exocet drill both from the weapons control room and then from topsides. The Type 42 was well equipped with both surveillance and tracking radars. A Type 1022 D-band long-range radar and a Type 965 long range air surveillance radar gave the crew an extended air picture. Shorter range Type 996 E/F-band 3D target indication radar and Type 909 I/J-band fire control radars controlled the weapons. As the simulated Etendard pulled up into the radar coverage, the first paint of the 'hostile' radar was immediately detected by the onboard sensors alerting the weapons officer. Identification followed which set in train the engagement sequence and, a few barked commands later, a Sea Dart was allocated and fired. At this time the Principal Warfare Officer or PWO had to determine whether he had engaged the launch aircraft or the missile which would then determine his subsequent actions. Invariably, the launch aircraft would turn away immediately giving a surface-to-air missile fired from the ship little chance of success. It was a tactic we used ourselves in air-to-air engagements and was extremely effective. The sea skimming missiles would then descend and hug the waves which, because of their small radar return, meant that they may not be reacquired until much later in the attack. Whether that came before the minimum range of the Sea Dart or after determined how the ship would respond. Although a very effective weapon, being designed to intercept attacking aircraft, limitations in the Sea Dart's performance had meant it was replaced by the much more capable Sea Wolf system on later vessels. This later system was much better able to cope with the smaller Exocet type threat. If the sea skimmer penetrated the 'inner ring' it would be down to the close in systems to respond. This chess match was the daily life of the principal warfare officer or PWO.

Despite its role as an air defence piquet, one of the other major tasks of any combat ship is to provide naval gunfire support and a demonstration of the 4.5' gun was given. As the crew worked through the drill, various commands could be heard across the ship's tannoy. Eventually, the huge turret which held the massive gun rotated on its mount onto the nominated vector before the barrel elevated to its final firing position. It was to be an open ocean firing under clear range procedures. There was a surprising air of anticipation as we waited for the shot. The ear splitting sound as the gun fired was accompanied by a massive plume of smoke as the shell was hurled into the far distance. What was not evident from the demonstration is that the shell would land over twelve miles away and, at full stretch, the crew was, theoretically, able to send twenty-five shells per minute to a nominated target; an awesome capability. During the tour of the ship we had seen the huge magazines below decks which housed the Sea Dart missiles and the complex loading mechanism. From the vantage point on the bridge we were now able to watch the full firing sequence, albeit using a red drill missile rather than a war round. Like the Tornado, real missiles cost many thousands of pounds and were only fired on rare occasions in training. I had already seen the way in which the weapons officer had locked up the incoming 'Exocet' and launched the Sea Dart in the clinical environment of the darkened control room. What that exercise failed to provide was the actual noise which

1. A 29 (F) Squadron Phantom on alert at Wideawake airfield, Ascension Island. © *Peter McCambridge*

2. A 23 (F) Squadron Phantom gets airborne from the main runway at RAF Stanley. © *David Lewis*

3. Sunset Patrol. Dedicated to 'Banners', RIP Old Friend.

4. A 1435 Flight Phantom deploys infra-red decoy flares from its AN/ALE40 countermeasures dispenser. © *Paul Jackson*

5. XV426 engages the RHAG at RAF Stanley. © *Peter McCambridge*

6. RAF Stanley Air Traffic Control in 1985.

7. The 23 (F) Squadron dispersal taken from the cockpit of a Phantom.

8. A 1435 Flight Phantom, XV466 in loose formation over the islands. © Paul Jackson.

9. A 23 (F) squadron Phantom rolling at RAF Stanley. © David Lewis

10. A 23 (F) Squadron Phantom refuels from a C130 tanker. © *Edward Threapleton*

11. 23 (F) Squadron Phantoms holding QRA at RAF Stanley.

12. All quiet on the 23 (F) Squadron dispersal at RAF Stanley. © *David Lewis*

13. Threading through the outer islands at low level. The navigator's radar hand controller and radar control panel can be seen reflected in the canopy.

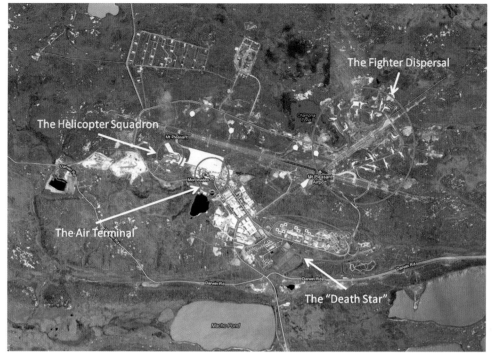

Map Data 2012 © Google. Imagery CNES Spot Digital Globe Geo Eye

14. RAF Mount Pleasant Airfield showing the main operational areas.

15. The 1435 Flight Fighter Dispersal.

16. 'Faith' and 'Hope' over Stanley Harbour. *UK MOD Crown Copyright*

17. A 'Measles' exercise seen from the cockpit of a Tornado F3.

18. Feeling festive after recovering to MPA after the Christmas morning flypast.

19. Christmas Lunch on QRA; soft drinks not champagne.

20. 78 Squadron Santa wishes 1435 Flight A Merry Christmas.

21. The 1435 Flight Christmas Tree.

22. A Tornado F3 conducts a 'Measles' exercise over Mount Alice GCI Site.

23. Wreckage of an Argentinian Chinook helicopter near Port Howard.

24. Wreckage of an Argentinian Puma helicopter near Port Howard.

25. Wreckage of a Dagger in 'A4 Alley'.

26. 1435 Flight
Operations.

27. Mount Pleasant
airfield from the
revetment alongside
Housey 1.

28. 1435 Flight
Quick Reaction
Alert with the
tunnel to Housey
1 visible in the
lower centre of the
picture.

29. ZE758, 'Charity' holding QRA. The Skyflash missiles are mounted beneath the fuselage.

30. Looking down on Housey 2 with a Tornado F3 preparing to taxy.

31. ZE758, 'Charity' holding QRA. The AIM 9L Sidewinder missiles are mounted on the wing pylon.

32. My cockpit prepared for a scramble. The shoulder straps are tucked into the ejection seat headbox for a rapid strap-in.

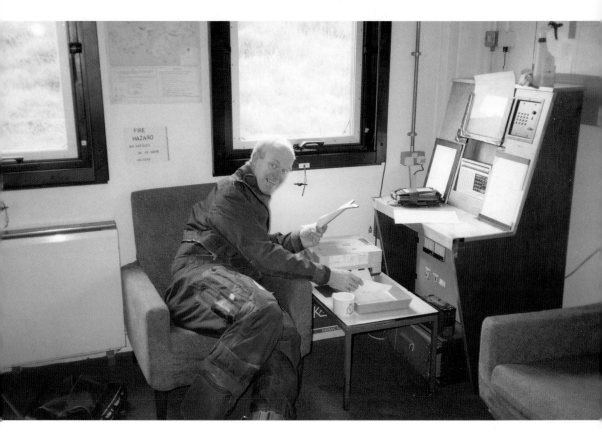

33. A relaxed 1435 Flight pilot holds Readiness 10.

34. In 'The Office' completing routine checks of the Q jet.

35. A 1435 Flight Tornado F3 in Housey 2.

36. Just airborne from the main runway at RAF Mount Pleasant.

37. ZE812, 'Faith' off the northern coast of East Falklands.

38. The Tristar descending through cloud before coasting in.

Above: **39.** HMS *Newcastle* leaves Mare Harbour with a drill Sea Dart on the rails.

Below left: **40.** A Tornado F3 pulls off after a simulated attack against HMS *Newcastle*.

Below right: **41.** A Tornado F3 on final approach to RAF Mount Pleasant.

42. A rare shot of all 4 1435 Flight Tornados airborne together. © David Middleton.

43. No. 1435 Flight Tornado F3s refuel from a C130 tanker. © *UK MOD Crown Copyright (1994).*

44. A Chinook helicopter lands at the Mount Alice Helipad.

45. Flying at low level over the Falklands coastline.

46. The 1435 Flight Corridor in 'The Death Star'.

47. The mural on the wall of 'The Goose', the 1435 Flight Lounge.

48. The 1435 Flight Aircrew Lounge, 'The Goose'.

49. A gun port from an Argentinian A4.

50. The windscreen from an Argentinian A4.

51. The air defence radar at Mount Alice protected from the elements by a radome.

52. The incomplete artwork begun by the crew of XV421 before they were tragically killed in a flying accident.

53. A Tornado F3 flies in close formation on a 1312 Flight C130 tanker during the Battle Day formation flypast.

54 to 56. The legacy of conflict. Minefields littered the islands for years after the conflict until finally cleared by bomb disposal experts. Stunning beaches were blighted by barbed wire preventing accidental detonation of the mines by walkers.

57. A Tornado F3 refuels from a 1312 Flight C130 tanker at low level over Falkland Sound.

58. A 1312 Flight Hercules flies low over the islands.

59. Some visits to the settlements could be 'spirited'. © *Ant & Biffo Tuson.*

A Typical Tanker Plan

60. A typical tanker plan.

61. A 23 (F) Squadron Phantom returning to UK refuels from a VC10 tanker over the South Atlantic Ocean.

62. No. 1435 Flight Tornados in formation with a 1312 Flight VC10. © *David Middleton*

63. No. 1435 Flight Tornados in formation during a rare 4 ship launch. © *David Middleton*

64. An albatross nesting on Saunders Island.

65. A Rockhopper penguin on Sea Lion Island.

66. Seals basking on the beach at Sea Lion Island.

67. King penguins at Volunteer Point.

68. 1435 Flight Tornados over the islands. © David Middleton.

69. Typhoon; the worthy successor now defending the islands.

70. The view through a Typhoon head up display.

71. The unrestricted view from the cockpit of a Typhoon which Phantom and Tornado crews never enjoyed.

72. Handing over command of 1435 Flight to my successor. © *UK MOD Crown Copyright (1994).*

would have reverberated throughout the ship during a live Sea Dart engagement coupled with the plumes of smoke from a launch. Having seen live footage from the conflict it took little imagination to visualise a real firing. The Sea Dart system sits under the foredeck of a Type 42 and the twin launcher boxes sit vertically when idle. Massive doors on the foredeck banged open with surprising force and the red drill missile was propelled upwards, mechanically, to be captured by the launcher rail. In a few seconds the launcher banged down onto an elevated trajectory and rotated rapidly onto the heading which marked the approaching threat. Denied the spectacle of a live shot, the drill seemed to fizzle out and it was some minutes before the Tornado, which had been the intended target, actually flew over the ship. The delay gave a good impression of the range at which the missile would have been launched to meet its target.

The final line of defence was provided by the Phalanx Close-In Weapons System. Based on the Vulcan six-barrelled Gatling gun which had armed the Phantom, this radar laid gun system provides a massive rate of fire which can be used with devastating effect against sea skimming missiles. Once detected by the integrated radar the gun slews onto the threat vector and sends 3,000 rounds per minute towards the target. As a terminal point defence system it is largely automated and relies on complex software algorithms to determine whether an incoming radar contact is a threat. It was easy to see why Phalanx was nicknamed 'R2D2' after the Star Wars character as it rotated wildly on its plinth firing at enormous speed against a simulated target. I had heard the noise before from the noisy confines of a Phantom cockpit but the whine of six barrels rotating at maximum rate of fire is simply unforgettable. Lastly, and easily forgotten, were the small arms weapons attached to the rails of the ship. The single barrel canons and light machine guns could be easily overlooked but some had been used to good effect during the conflict claiming a number of kills against Argentinian aircraft. A splash target was deployed and the small arms rattled away, directing fire at the bobbing target.

Once we entered the manoeuvring phase any semblance of normality ended. Used to crossing the Channel on a ferry, the sound of the Olympus engines at maximum power can only be described as fearsome. Anyone even vaguely prone to sea-sickness would have been well advised to pass on the experience as the ship heeled over in response to the Captain's commands to counter the incoming jets. I had no inkling that a major warship could manoeuvre in such an aggressive fashion and describe such a tight turning circle. As F3 crews, we could provide up to fifteen minutes close in manoeuvring against the ship but I could only imagine the rate of fuel flow with the massive turbines operating at 'max chat'. I suspect they would have given a Tornado RB199 engine in maximum afterburner a run for its money. Staying within visual range, and certainly inside five miles

Left: The Phalanx system (the white drum) on HMS *Newcastle*.

Below: A General Purpose Machine Gun provides a last ditch defence.

A Lynx capability demonstration.

we would attempt to set up a pass from either a beam aspect simulating a bomb pass or a head/tail aspect for a guns pass. The Argentinians had demonstrated the risks of such profiles during the conflict. Clearly, the ship could not outrun a fast jet and it was for the Captain to position his vessel to bring the maximum number of weapons to bear while leaving us the least favourable aspect to attack. At this stage, we were well inside the minimum range for Sea Dart so the gun systems were the key response from the ship. We were only too well aware of the devastating firepower of Phalanx and with a system on each side, our profiles, if flown for real, would have been naive and dangerous. Sadly, the CIWS was only fitted after the conflict or the attacks by Argentinian bombers might have had drastically different conclusions.

In response, a few Navy personnel, including of course The Captain, were offered back seat rides in our Tornado F3s. As I have already suggested, flying passengers was not as simple as it might seem. The aircraft had to be de-armed as I could not allow unqualified personnel to fly in the back seat of an armed aircraft. This put extra pressure on the groundcrew, particularly the armourers and the safety equipment personnel. I always took the opportunity to fly our own flight personnel if we went to the effort and, this compromise seemed to make the additional hassle worthwhile in their eyes. Inevitably, the competition for back seat rides was fierce and could cause friction amongst those who were unlucky. The more senior pilots on the flight were tasked for the familiarisation rides and the profiles could be adapted to fit the passenger. The bulky survival equipment and the hot and claustrophobic environment of a fighter cockpit limited the scope for many budding 'fightergators'. Sadly, it was too much for some and, often a very green face emerged from the cockpit after the flight clutching the mandatory 'sick bag'!

We obviously bonded with our fellow aviators who operated the Lynx helicopter which was the one and only aircraft which made up the ship's Helicopter Flight. Our first demonstration took place during the day at sea when the crew ran the agile little machine through its paces. Showing its role during anti Exocet drills the crew threw the small machine through a series of amazingly tight manoeuvres finishing with the obligatory bow to the visitors just off the port beam. As a thank you for the Captain's Tornado trip, or perhaps the hope of a future back seat ride, we received an invitation to join the Lynx on a training run around the island. At the appointed time, the small helicopter clattered across the airfield boundary and dropped onto the large aircraft servicing platform in front of the Tristar hangar. The rotors were shut down and the Navy pilot beckoned so my pilot and I made our way across the tarmac. There was little of the fanfare of flying from a civilian airport in UK. Dressed in flying suits we had open access to the movements area and we quickly strapped in with just a short safety brief. I was offered the left hand seat. The pilot cranked up the engines, engaged the rotor and we lifted off and headed west over the airfield boundary. Getting airborne in a Tornado we assumed that we held our height down in a punchy, tactical way.

From the front seat in a Lynx, the flat area just west of the airfield took on a whole new perspective. Deep ridges and gulleys suddenly appeared that even from 250 feet were all but invisible. The Lynx is an incredibly agile helicopter and we threaded our way around the lower slopes of Pleasant Peak and through a gulley into the broad valley to the north of the airfield. As with any helicopter flight around the islands the Lynx was delivering a load from MPA to a platoon from the infantry company deployed in the field. As we approached the designated point on the map we flashed over a group of soldiers who waved wildly. A short arc and we dropped into a field and heaved the package over the side. As we lifted, I could see the infantry retrieving the delivery as we dropped the nose and headed further into the hills. Our second drop demonstrated yet again the austerity under which some of the deployed troops lived. We made our approach to a hastily prepared matting helicopter pad marked with a large 'H'. A ramshackle collection of temporary cabins flanked the site with a few precarious looking walkways linking the buildings. The huts, miles from civilisation were the accommodation complex for the training firing range and Army personnel spent weeks at a time deployed away from the relative comfort of 'The Death Star'. The packages that were heaved out of the helicopter door were warmly welcomed and I suspect contained some precious mail from home. As we pulled away, the scars on the scrub suggested heavy tracked vehicles had passed by on frequent occasions. Looking around I suspect they might have been the only vehicles able to reach the site at times. The trip back through the gap was undoubtedly the highlight as we flew over a large lake on the northern side of Pleasant Peak at ultra low level, literally skimming the flat calm surface. The final task was to deliver a package to a remote antenna site on the peak surrounded by another 'portakabin city'. Deliveries complete, a final 'nap of the earth' run through the gulleys and we passed over the airfield boundary at MPA and dropped onto the huge dispersal outside the Tristar hangar.

The value of these exchange exercises is sometimes questioned. Accountants can place a price on such activity yet forget the value. Modern weapons systems are complex and expensive and the argument goes that they should only be used in their designated war role or training for it. I recall vividly my first Joint Maritime Course operating with a Navy ship off the northern coast of Scotland. After a dull three hours on CAP during which we saw very little 'trade', we returned to find that the ship had claimed us as a 'kill' during an attack by the opposing force. We had been providing the air defence for the ship so this revelation came as somewhat of a disappointment! By interacting, Tornado crews saw at first hand how the ship's weapons team worked suddenly appreciating their skills and their problems. We had the opportunity to present our own issues in how we operated and interacted with the ship. By flying the Navy personnel, they also realised the challenges of a fast jet cockpit when operating at low level. In my view, such interaction is simply invaluable.

One of the features of life on the islands was that each aircraft had a nickname. The Tornados were the 'Tonkas', the C130s the 'Alberts' which originated from the rather unflattering title of 'Fat Albert', the Bristow helicopters were the 'Erics' named after Eric Bristow the owner, the Chinooks were the 'Wokkas' and the Tristar was the 'Timmy' for no other reason than Timmy Tristar seemed apt.

1312 Flt operated two Hercules tankers which also had a maritime patrol role. When not allocated to QRA duties, the C130 would monitor vessels in the Falkland Island Protection Zone to ensure that they were who they said they were and that they were operating in accordance with the published procedures for the Zone. Most importantly, the C130s offered a long range search and rescue capability and carried multi crew life rafts which could be dropped to survivors in the water in the event of an emergency. I know of a number of vessels which declared an emergency close to the islands whose crews were happy to have an 'Albert' in close proximity as they battled with their problems. It was not unknown for 'Albert' to be sent to the South American mainland on a medical evacuation mission if personnel or islanders required medical treatment that could not be provided on the islands.

'The Erics' were the main workhorses and carried personnel and light loads between the operational sites and the settlements. The principal role was to move people from MPA to the radar sites at Mount Kent, Mount Alice and Byron Heights but, with typical flexibility, they would drop into the most remote village or settlement if it was even vaguely *en route*. Unlike a fixed wing aircraft, the ability to land in a field meant that the helicopter pilots could take a few more risks with the unpredictable weather. I remember vividly on my first detachment to the islands launching in marginal weather to visit a site on West Falkland. The first stop was to be Mount Kent to deliver stores and it provided an insight into how the helicopters operated but more of that later. We had been offered an overnight stay with a family on Saunders Island and, eventually, the Eric had dropped its planned loads and we were next. Saunders Island sits on the northern coast of West Falkland and the settlement is on the south-eastern side adjacent to a sheltered cove in the lee of Mount Egmont. There was little ceremony as our welcoming hosts met us at the helicopter and we moved away from the landing site carrying our overnight bags. With a quick wave, the pilot eased the Eric back into the air and immediately turned through 180 degrees away from the site. We assumed he was leaving but in true Falkland's spirit he returned for a very impressive pass over our heads before setting course back to Mount Pleasant. As fellow aircrew, the flypast was impressive but seeing the enthusiasm on the faces of the islanders who had greeted us was telling. Such visits made their day. We were delighted to break the routine of Mount Pleasant but they were genuinely pleased to see us. One of the unwritten rules was that for any visit to a settlement we would always speak nicely to the Mess staff and arrange to draw dry rations to offer as a gift to the hosts. When the regular boat arrived it would be laden with fruit which was always popular as it was otherwise almost impossible to acquire on the islands. In return we were treated to a dinner of roast beef or lamb cooked, invariably, in a peat fired Aga cooker, the likes of which I have never tasted before or since.

The airbridge was the essential lifeline back home. The main aircraft which provided the airbridge was the RAF's own Tristar known as the 'Timmy'. Purchased from commercial airlines, the British Airways aircraft were converted to air-to-air tankers. Following problems encountered when attempting to convert ex Pan American Airlines airframes, those aircraft were never adapted as refuellers and entered service as the C Mk2 carrying only passengers and freight. It was these aircraft which took the brunt of the South Atlantic airbridge

The 'Eric' lands at Saunders Island airstrip.

until Gulf operations added to the punishing workload. At various times, when the operational workload dictated, the Tristars were replaced on the run by commercial airliners. In the days immediately following the conflict and before the Tristars were procured, British Airways held the contract for the South Atlantic run. Long range Boeing 747 airliners were allocated and personnel used to enduring long hours in a C130 were, suddenly, enjoying the delights of airline meals served by BA flight attendants and a movie to while away the hours. This was positive luxury. Even so, an operational air pervaded and it was not unknown for departing BA crews to make a fast approach to the main runway followed by an overshoot to depart. Not only was it a nice way to get a last view of the airbase it did wonders for the morale of the people remaining behind knowing that it would be their turn soon.

No. 78 Sqn was an anomaly as it was the only unit which carried a squadron number plate for some years even though it had less aircraft than, for example, my own Flight. The only logic was that it operated a mixed fleet of a Chinook and two Sea Kings. The principal role of the latter was to provide search and rescue coverage over the islands and in the immediate coastal waters. With sea temperatures in single figures, it was only a matter of minutes before an ejectee would lose the effective use of his or her hands. Within ten minutes, if the survivor was unable to board the small dinghy which was carried in every ejection seat, even the best dressed aircrew would begin to lose consciousness and that would be fatal. The Sea King crews held readiness to be scrambled in the event of an ejection and provided that vital quick response.

The Chinook was another of the workhorses and transferred heavy material around the islands between the airhead, the port at Mare Harbour and the deployed sites. Being twin-engine, it was the only helicopter with the lifting capacity to position some of the larger loads such as radar heads and heavy containers. On one occasion I made a liaison visit to the Control and Reporting Centre at Mount Alice and the trip coincided with a sortie by a Chinook from 78 Sqn which was scheduled to move a large load at the site. We arrived at the squadron at Mount Pleasant in plenty of time to get a briefing on safety procedures. The loadmaster who was programmed to fly the trip took me aside and asked me if I was up for a 'ramp ride'. What I didn't realise at that time was that it was a set-up. When the Chinook is dropping stores or landing troops, the rear door is lowered to give the loadmaster a view of the landing zone. Equally, when the Chinook was operating on a fighter affiliation exercise against the Tornado F3, the ramp would be lowered to give the crew a good view of the stern hemisphere allowing the loadmaster to call defensive counters or to time when he would pop defensive chaff or flares. To ensure the loadmaster stays inside the aircraft if it evades violently, he is attached by a strop which clips to his harness and attaches to the side of the aircraft cabin. The length of the strop is carefully measured to allow free movement to the extremities of the ramp but no further. Nowadays, light machine guns are mounted in the doors close to the ramp and the crew are well versed in targeting insurgents when approaching a landing zone. We boarded the massive helicopter and the pilot ran through his checks and fired up the two huge engines which on the Chinook are mounted above and at each side of the rear fuselage below the aft rotor blade. The noise as they wound up was simply incredible and we were glad it had been suggested we bring along our flying helmets for the ride. The helicopter lifted into the air and after an exaggerated dip forward set off across the western airfield boundary and headed for West Falkland. As soon as we were safely airborne, the 'loadie' offered a harness which I clipped around my torso and pulled the straps tight. He waved a huge shackle which I clipped onto the harness and, from then on, I was attached to the Chinook. He eased over to the controls on the side of the cabin and, as he lowered the rear ramp, the view across the Falklands countryside appeared. It was truly amazing as we threaded our way westwards at no more than 100 feet above the scrub. Obviously well versed with the procedure he beckoned me across to the centre of the ramp and pointed at the lip. I gingerly eased my legs over the edge, facing the rear, literally balanced on the edge, albeit moving at about 100 knots backwards. The ground was rushing past at speed. It was a truly exhilarating experience and I sat mesmerised for what seemed like hours but in reality could not have been more than 10 minutes. Although I was firmly attached by the strop, there was no pressure and it, literally, felt as if I was sitting unrestrained on the ramp. No roller coaster could ever match the ride as the aircraft banked through its navigation turns at ultra low level and the horizon followed the manoeuvre. The pilot had pre-warned us that they would pull up from low level as they approached Falklands Sound and cross the water at 1,000 feet so as the aircraft began to climb I was fully expecting it. What came next, however, was a total surprise. I still have no idea what he used to make the noise but as we levelled at 1,000 feet there was huge metallic crash and simultaneously, the ramp lurched downwards. I started to slide gently towards the edge of the ramp before the strop arrested the movement but it was enough to give the biggest adrenaline shot I have ever experienced as my senses were convinced I would exit the Chinook via the gaping rear door. The movement of the ramp was brief and I scrabbled unmajestically to my feet and aimed for the safety of the cabin to be greeted by the smiling faces of the rest of my flight companions who were in on the 'loadies' joke. I can safely say, my ramp ride was an experience I'll never forget.

Often forgotten were the Islander aircraft of FIGAS or The Falkland Islands Government Air Service. These bright red British built aircraft operated on a commercial basis providing inter settlement transport for the islanders and delivered light freight and mail. Before the war the Company had operated a number of Beaver light piston floatplanes and a single Britten Norman Islander but they were casualties of the conflict. Initially captured by the Argentinians, they were subsequently destroyed. After the conflict the Islander was replaced and a fleet of five aircraft now provide an airline service between twenty-nine prepared grass strips around the islands. It is probably unique in that the aircraft can be booked on demand demonstrating the flexibility of remote life in an extreme climate. Flying from Stanley airfield, an early morning schedule departs at fixed times but for the rest of the day, residents or tourists can liaise with the airline to arrange trips to the settlements and be collected later in the day. Flying around at low level we often heard the pilots checking in as they passed the various reporting points but it was unusual to see an Islander in the air. In any event, it was always courteous to give a civilian flight a comfortably wide berth even though we would be talking to the pilot on the same frequency. I have no doubt the 'airline' passengers and pilots had a close view of a Tornado escort over the years but it was not something I ever tried.

I described how the Rapier operated in an earlier chapter and one of our main tasks was to provide airborne 'targets' against which they could practise their routines. To maintain his operational effectiveness, the detachment commander for the Rapier Flight was allocated a number of life-expired Rapier missiles and arranged an impromptu missile practice camp for training purposes on Bertha's Beach to the south of Stanley. As with any set piece event, invitations were issued to other units to come along and watch the activity and it made a welcome diversion from the routine. A Rapier fire unit had been redeployed from its usual location flanking the airfield at Mount Pleasant and was set up looking out to sea on the beach. Small radio controlled aircraft were used as targets for the missile crews and by the time we arrived, the drone had been airborne for some time and was flying short orbits out to sea. A Rapier fire unit had been set up. The major components were the actual launcher which held four Rapier missiles on side mounted missile rails on top of which sat a surveillance radar dish and the identification friend or foe (IFF) system protected by a small radome. The computers, electronics and an antenna which sent guidance signals to the missiles in flight sat at the base of the unit. The whole fire unit was designed to be towed by two Land Rovers. In parallel, the Flight's general purpose machine guns had been set up on firing plinths and the Regiment gunners were taking target practice at parachute flares launched from the firing point. Although the missiles were the set piece for the day, the small arms skills of the gunners were

A Rapier crew track a target prior to a practice missile firing.

A Rapier missile motor smokes as it prepares to fire.

also vital in order to carry out their role to protect and defend the airfield. The crews put the system through its firing routine. As the small drone headed towards the beach sounding like an angry bee, the Blindfire radar would nod occasionally. The gunner was cued onto the drone and, as he commanded the missiles to acquire, the launcher unit rotated rapidly onto the bearing and the missiles elevated into the firing position. After an uncomfortably long wait there was a crack from the missile, a puff of smoke from the motor and it sped from the rails. The first missile firing passed without drama and it corkscrewed towards its target, the flash as the live warhead exploded clearly visible from our vantage point. The second shot was less impressive. After the noise of the launch, the missile arched over the apex diving immediately back towards the sea exploding harmlessly only a hundred yards from the shore. Uncharitably, the watching crowd of cynics burst into a spontaneous round of applause earning dark looks from the fire unit commander.

Unfortunately for the RAF Regiment, the practice was to end in more embarrassment. The fact that some missiles failed could be excused as the rounds had exceeded their life span and a degree of failure was to be expected. Sadly, the way the fire unit had been set up left a tad to be desired. On the penultimate shot, the drone made its way towards the Blindfire radar and the aiming and firing commands were barked out by the commander. The fire command was given and, again, there was a short pause before the missile motor fired and the Rapier left the rails in a massive cloud of exhaust smoke and flames from the efflux. So far so good but as the smoke of the firing cleared there was a trail of flames snaking across the scrub which raised an immediate flurry of activity from the fire team. Two cans of fuel had been left immediately behind the launcher after tanks in a generator had been topped off and the blast from the rocket motor had knocked one of them over allowing the fuel to spill from the can. The flames rapidly grew in intensity fanned by the strong Falklands winds and a dark black smoke billowed from the base of the launcher. Fire extinguishers were rapidly deployed, the offending cans removed and the cables which connected the fire unit to the control station were pulled clear of the intense flames avoiding further damage. The fire was extinguished quickly and the drills resumed but the Flight Commander's embarrassment lasted somewhat longer than the short-lived flames. It was a rare mistake from a hugely professional team.

CHAPTER 7
Quick Reaction Alert

There should have been no doubt in the minds of the RAF personnel based in the Falkland Islands that the whole reason for the RAF presence was to support Quick Reaction Alert, or QRA. Immediately following the arrival of the Phantoms at RAF Stanley just after the war, a whole squadron supported the effort. It is well publicised that the UK now holds just 4 fighter aircraft on permanent readiness on the islands, a situation which has not changed since the decision was taken to reduce the presence as a goodwill gesture in 1988. For many years the alert aircraft flew fully armed, although occasionally, concessions allowed aircraft to fly with a partial load or even unarmed when there were overriding operational or training reasons. Air-to-air missiles have a 'carriage life' so the clock begins ticking as soon as that missile leaves the ground strapped underneath a fighter aircraft. After a certain time, the missiles have to be returned to the manufacturer for refurbishment to ensure that the stresses and strains of the flight regime do not detract from their serviceability. A peacetime limitation, a time-expired missile would be used if it was needed in anger as engineering calculations were generally pessimistic, although the risk of technical failure would be higher. During my tenure, the standard load was reduced to two Skyflash to reduce the toll on the missiles, although four Sidewinders were still carried. The loads could be varied easily during turn round so there was no real effect on the readiness posture. Typically, squadrons in UK operated with only half their declared numbers of aircraft available to fly on a daily basis. In the Falkland Islands no such luxury applied. There was, and is, one paramount rule that, whatever the conditions, two aircraft will always be ready to scramble within ten minutes to meet an incoming threat and those aircraft sat permanently on alert and were known as Q1 and Q2. To allow the other flying crews to stay current and, assuming spare parts were on hand, the engineering staff worked tirelessly on the third and fourth aircraft, throughout the night if necessary, to ensure all four were available in the morning. Protecting QRA was the primary role for 1435 Flight personnel and 23 (F) Squadron before it.

QRA at Stanley was a rudimentary affair lacking any of the permanent facilities typical of the main bases in the UK or Germany. Conditions on the airfield for the first few years were austere and cramped. The tiny municipal airport suddenly found itself home to thousands of extra personnel from all 3 of the armed services. Portakabin cities sprung up overnight to house all the vital functions which keep the defensive machine ticking over. For the newly named 23 (F) Squadron, the small collection of cabins provided just enough space for the crews who manned the Phantoms. Many of the trades which, traditionally, had their own workspace were squeezed into cramped rooms alongside each other. In the UK, it was normal for QRA to be located away from the squadron to ensure that there were no distractions from the task; namely the ability to be airborne within the declared readiness time. At RAF Stanley, there was no possibility of providing dedicated accommodation so the squadron crewroom housed the alert crews alongside the flying crews allowing no escape from the daily squadron routine. It took discipline to ensure that QRA crews were protected when the humdrum tasks were being allocated. That said, with an operational focus, even for the crews not sitting Q, the usual SLJs (or silly little jobs) typical of the squadron at home were minimised.

During the years immediately following the war, the alert Phantoms sat close by the crewroom on a makeshift apron constructed from the AM2 metal planking which covered most of the operating areas around RAF Stanley. Initially, there were no hangars or shelters to protect the aircraft from the harsh climate on the squadron dispersal. The best which could be provided was a set of waterproof canvas covers which shrouded the canopy and radome keeping out most of the water which would otherwise have found its way onto the floor of the cockpits. Although it was an analogue aeroplane, the Phantom electrics were temperamental and, if subjected to a soaking, the aircraft would show its displeasure on start up. Sodden radios or damp inertial navigation systems were the last thing the crews needed during the controlled panic which followed a scramble message. Crews made extra visits to the jet to inspect their cockpits and the inertial navigation systems were run up far more often than would have been the norm in the UK. For the groundcrew, the routine servicing which occurred every four hours was much more of a chore with aircraft parked outside and exposed to the elements. Suddenly, the relative austerity of a UK QRA facility seemed luxurious in comparison.

Life in the crew room was as relaxed as possible. Crews wore the usual thick underwear and protective 'bunny suit' under the heavy immersion suit but, as a sop to comfort, the upper half was undone and tied loosely around the waist using the arms of the suit to hold it in place. Crews tried to relax as best as possible. Thermal stress was easily possible if the suit was zipped up inside the buildings as it was designed to protect the wearer from the cold temperatures in the icy local waters not from the comfort of crewroom temperatures. In UK, QRA crews were sometimes allowed to dispense with 'G' suits as Q missions were unlikely to involve any hard manoeuvring. With a potentially more agile opponent such as an Argentinian Mirage, the concession to fly without a 'G' suit was not an option in the South Atlantic. The 'G' suit gave an additional 1G to 2G tolerance so it was an important piece of flying equipment if air combat was possible. With the heavy nylon fabric and the lacing which pulled the suit tight, the 'G' suit was uncomfortable when worn for twenty-four hours. It was designed to squeeze the legs when pulling 'G' and it did so even in the crewroom. For many years the 'G' suit was worn under the immersion suit so could not be easily discarded during the day. As the risk of encountering a hard manoeuvring fighter ebbed at night, the 'G' suit was sometimes removed. The bulky equipment would never be comfortable but crews found innovative ways to minimise the pain. On one exercise, a navigator who adopted a 'relaxed posture' was caught out. The hose which connected the G suit to the aircraft anti-G system protruded from a rubber seal in the lower section of the immersion suit. As he entered the crewroom he trapped the hose in the door and it popped out from the seal revealing a length of hose which had been liberated from an old 'G' suit. Sadly no longer attached to a working G suit he was forced to admit that comfort had outweighed professionalism on that particular exercise.

Similar to QRA sheds the world-over, a telebrief set was located in the corner of the crewroom giving a constant and direct link to the Sector Operations Centre at Mount Kent. A feature of life on QRA was the presence of the metronome, or confidence tone, which meant that the crews could be sure that the link was active. Taking the form of a regular ticking or an occasional bleep, the sound became embedded in the psyche after twenty four hours on 'Q' and would sound, subconsciously in the mind, for hours after handing over. It is a noise which is imprinted forever in my memory; a legacy even after so many years. The scramble message, when it came, was concise and slightly chilling, heralding the unknown. The short instruction gave a vector, a height and a control agency:

'*Eagle Ops alert 2 Phantoms..... Vector 270, climb angels 25, contact Puffin on pre-brief, scramble, scramble, scramble, acknowledge......*'

Mayhem!

Don the immersion suit. The free arm was pushed through the wrist seal and the tight rubber neck seal was pulled over the head forcing it down onto the neck. Heavy rubberised zips were pulled fast across the chest and the lower back. All this was achieved while running towards the crewroom door grabbing lifesaving jackets on the run. The Q2 navigator would acknowledge the scramble message and immediately follow the remaining three aircrew out of the door pulling on his own immersion suit as he ran. He was under most pressure as the ninety seconds it took to align the inertial navigation system would be the limiting factor in launching both jets on time. The short run to the jet was covered at breakneck speed despite the need to don the bulky lifejackets on the hoof. Climb up the metal ladders clipped to the side of the engine intake and jump into the cockpit feet first onto the ejection seat pan and drop into the seat. It was at this stage that you hoped you had left your flying helmet in the cockpit and not in the crew room. Pull it onto your head and clip in the microphone lead and plug in the personal equipment connector. As the ground crew fired up the external power set, check in with Wing Ops once the external power was online. The pilot in the front cockpit fired up the right engine before both crew were assisted to strap in by the flight line mechanics. The navigator began to align the inertial navigation system and checked in with the sector controller to get a final update if necessary. Once the groundcrew were clear the left engine wound up. Less than 2 minutes later, with a few rapid checks completed, both QRA jets would taxy off the slot to cover the short distance to the departure threshold completing pre take off checks on the roll. As the jet approached the runway, the local controller was expected to clear the take off but it was a formality. Nothing stopped a Q launch short of a major systems failure and the only way to prevent the jets from rolling was an authenticated cancellation message. Cold engines were persuaded into burner and the lumbering aircraft rapidly reached take off velocity and lurched into the air with gear and flaps travelling. Quite often, once the gear was up and the aircraft had settled onto its outbound heading, crews would carry out a little housekeeping to make sure nothing had been missed in the controlled panic. It was at this stage that I might finally get around to connecting the leg restraints for my ejection seat.

Although it took an act of God to stop a QRA scramble, occasionally, extreme weather or the risk of losing the aircraft could intervene. The risk of being unable to recover to RAF Stanley could mean that it was simply too great a risk to fly and a 'Mandatory' scramble state would be imposed to warn the QRA Controller. This highlighted the risk to the Air Defence Commander who had to balance the cost of potentially losing two aircraft and their crews against the value of the intercept. Perhaps, an inbound formation flying at high speed would mean that Q would launch despite the risk whereas a slower contact nibbling at the zone may not be of sufficient interest. The stakes could be high and the Commander's decision would attract scrutiny at the highest levels of command in the UK. I have no doubt that some of the intrusions into the Protection Zone by Argentinian surveillance aircraft when the weather at Stanley or MPA was marginal, were designed to gauge just what that tolerance was.

A 23 (F) Sqn Phantom taxies back after a QRA scramble is aborted due to extreme weather. ©
Edward Threapleton.

Crews return to Operations in appalling weather. © Edward Threapleton.

Falklands QRA was a sobering affair for both UK or Germany based crews in the early years after the conflict. Perhaps the most likely target in Europe would be a Soviet bomber *en route* to Cuba or a wayward light aircraft penetrating the Germany Air Defence Interception Zone. Neither was likely to need armed intervention, more the need to show a presence or give assistance. A wayward light aircraft pilot might need to be 'shepherded' away from the Inner German Border. Invariably, the Phantom crew would have the advantage. For the first time, Phantom crews faced the real possibility of a hostile opponent and the rules of engagement were set to ensure that they would not be disadvantaged. Although the likelihood of another Argentinian invasion was minimal, attacks by rogue formations bent on revenge was not out of the question. Bombers might be escorted by missile-armed fighters so tactical awareness was paramount. For a small attacking force, air-to-air refuelling might be available so a fuel advantage against opponents on the limits of their endurance was by no means certain. Precise engagement rules are always a closely guarded secret and are rarely discussed but it will come as no surprise that an aircraft flying at high speed and low level approaching from the West would have received a very unfriendly reception and the assumption would have been that it carried blue and white roundels with less than friendly motives.

This caused problems on more than one occasion. To keep forces sharp, it was important to test reactions. QRA crews and those manning the Rapier short range air defence systems were trained to react in accordance with the rules of engagement. Targets would be nominated and aircraft at the end of a mission would act as simulated intruders. Normally, key players within the command chain would be briefed as 'trusted agents' to ensure that crews under test were given realistic and challenging targets. The biggest challenge was to prevent 'simulatoritis' or the blasé attitude which could accompany a known and anticipated exercise. The most testing aspect in this complex post-war game was to channel the inevitable adrenaline and act efficiently and effectively. The command chain and its decision making capability had to be tested and proved. Using live-armed aircraft and war-ready Rapier missiles, there was no margin for error. It was not lost on us that a 92 Squadron crew had demonstrated the lethality of the Sidewinder only a few short years earlier when a crew had inadvertently shot down an RAF Jaguar in Germany. On that occasion it was a procedural error rather than a misidentification.

In the Falklands the lead up to a missile firing would occur beyond visual range so target identification would be from the ground, was vital and was a priority. If normal tactics were used, the Phantom crew would never see its target; they would simply be cleared to engage. The Jaguar shoot-down focussed the mind and influenced procedures as it was still fresh in the memory of decision makers. To test the system, Phantoms, and later Tornado F3s would route well to the West and drop down to low level beyond the coverage of the radars in the Control and Reporting Centres on West Falkland Island. The interrogation system, or IFF, was switched off meaning that the friendly electronic signals which identified the aircraft as one of our own, were not being transmitted. At a pre-determined point, the simulated intruder would pop up into radar coverage beginning the helter-skelter series of events which would lead to a live engagement unless stopped. As the intruder pressed eastwards, normally towards a key military target, command and control systems would be exercised and procedures practised and validated to ensure that appropriate clearances were sought and granted. Somewhere within that chain, the trusted agent would intervene at an appropriate time and terminate the exercise once procedures were validated or lessons were learned. One of the strengths of British doctrine, although in this case a potential weakness, was that in the event of lost communication, engagement decisions could be delegated to quite low levels in the chain. Ensuring that there could be no error was a necessary skill to balance the need for realism against potential 'own goals.' A blue-on-blue engagement was not out of the question in the heightened tension of the South Atlantic and had to be balanced against the need to remain sharp. Ensuring a 'trusted agent' was present at each level of the decision making chain was vital. The reassuring fact was that, ultimately, in the absence of a clearance to engage from the controller, crews would have been forced to close in to a range where a visual identification was possible. At the 'gravy strokes' there should have been no risk of misidentifying a Mirage for a Phantom or Tornado; or would there?

The fact that no Argentinian fast jet intruded into the airspace with hostile intent is a matter of record and our nervousness was never tested. The majority of intercepts were of intelligence gatherers who would push into the airspace to test the reaction posture and to record our communications, seemingly plying international waters innocently. The flight paths and behaviour were easily identifiable on radar. In 1973, the Argentinians bought three Lockheed Electras for transport duties buying additional airframes in 1983 for maritime patrol duties, using them until they were replaced by P3 Orions in 1994. A further airframe, operated by the Argentinian Navy, was known as the L-188W Electrone fitted with an Israeli signals intelligence suite. It was this airframe which popped up regularly in the Protection Zone over the years. As the crew probed the zone they were gathering signals and recording the electronic environment for analysis back in Argentina.

In the months following cessation of hostilities, the Electra was a regular visitor and was photographed by 23 (F) Squadron QRA crews on more than one occasion.

I found an interesting insight from the Argentinian perspective.

The Argentinian Electra intercepted inside the Falkland Islands protection Zone on 5 Aug 83. © Edward Threapleton.

A close up of the cockpit with media photographers at the windows capturing the interception. © Edward Threapleton.

The Electra on the Highway by Carlos A. Abella
'Encounters with the Phantoms'

> The ceasing of hostilities on the South Atlantic meant a difficult situation for aerial or
> maritime transit on the zone. Thus, on 05 Aug 83 aircraft 0693/5-T-3 was intercepted
> by 2 McDonnell-Douglas Phantom at 13.10 hrs and outside of the exclusion zone.
> The encounter lasted 8 minutes, and according to the British pilots' statements, they
> attempted to make the aircraft to change its course. The first incident of this kind
> had taken place on 25 Jul 83, when an Electra had been intercepted by Royal Air
> Force aircraft based on the Malvinas. In this case, the Argentinian airplane was on a
> mission from Rio Grande, bound for Trelew. These were not the only incidents and the
> efficient action of the Electras first and later of the Electrones, has meant frequent aerial
> encounters with the British Phantoms based on the Islands.
> (*Reproduced by permission of the Latin American Aviation History Society*)

A friend was scrambled against the Electra on that day, 5 August 1983, and he
described the incident from his recollections offering an interesting yet contrasting
description. As the number two of the pair of Phantoms, he was vectored by
'Puffin' against an unknown contact approaching the Falkland Island Protection
Zone. The lead aircraft was flown by the 23 Squadron Commander and his
navigator. The QRA C130 tanker was already airborne and, recognising that it
was a relatively slow speed contact but not knowing the intent of the intruder,
the controller separated the pair to allow the number two to refuel while the
lead aircraft was vectored onto the contact. The leader made the intercept and
began to shadow the Electra. Refuelling complete, the number two was also
vectored towards the contact which, by then, had penetrated the Falkland
Islands Protection Zone. Joining his leader alongside, he captured pictures of the
Electra using the QRA camera which was carried in the rear cockpit on every
QRA sortie. By then, the Electra was 30 nm inside the FIPZ. The crews made
contact on the international distress frequency using air defence interception
procedures and instructed the Electra crew to turn back onto a westerly heading
and escorted the intruder from the FIPZ. After landing at RAF Stanley, the film
was developed and the crews were surprised to see faces at the windows which
proved to be members of the Argentinian Press who were onboard the Electra.

With details of the FIPZ published internationally, it was, arguably, a
provocative act to penetrate the Zone so soon after the conflict, without notice
and for no clear purpose other than for publicity. Presumably, by flying into the
Zone Argentina was making a statement about the right to fly in international
waters but the FIPZ had been established as a consequence of hostile action. An

Electra flying on a direct track from Rio Grande to Trelew would be allowed to pass unhindered as it would be heading away from the Falklands and well outside the Exclusion Zone. There would be no reason for a Phantom crew to divert an Electra on a track parallel to the Argentinian coast routing in a northerly direction towards Trelew as it would pose no threat. Only an aircraft which had strayed into the Zone and was heading towards the islands would be ordered to change its track so the suggestion that the aircraft was merely going about its regular transport task is improbable. Even a maritime patrol would probably be allowed to operate without interference providing it posed no threat to shipping going about their legal business. For the Electra to be intercepted, it would have been flying a track towards the islands or would have penetrated the zone. To make an interception outside the zone was unusual as controllers would normally haul the fighter off before passing the zone boundary but it was not unknown to press the intercept to identify the target if necessary. An aircraft which penetrated the zone but then turned and ran once fighters were vectored towards, might be outside the zone at the point of intercept but having violated the zone would still need to be identified. This would occur in international waters if need be. Thankfully, sane minds prevailed and there was no incident that day. Such games of 'cat and mouse' have occurred between opposing forces for many years in NATO airspace during the Cold War so to see it occur in the South Atlantic was not surprising.

From a defensive perspective, the 'Electrone' was a significant problem. Equipped with electronic gathering equipment, the crews could sit some distance from the islands yet monitor the communications channels used by our forces. Sensitive information can be extracted from such intercepts giving vital information about operating procedures, force levels and capabilities. High Frequency (HF) signals can be collected at long range but Very High Frequency (VHF) or Ultra High Frequency (UHF) signals which are more often used by military forces are 'line of sight' signals and relatively short range. To collect these signals the gatherer needs to be closer to the emitters forcing the eavesdropper to work closer to the islands. Enforcing the Maritime Protection Zone was a military task but preventing a potential enemy from collecting useful intelligence was a personal challenge.

The reality of QRA was of hours of tedium spent watching endless movies or reading books punctuated by the occasional pandemonium of a scramble. Compared to Stanley, QRA at RAF Mount Pleasant was an entirely more organised affair. The airfield was constructed to provide a permanent base for the military personnel deployed to the islands. Not only did it improve the quality of life for deployed personnel but it gave the islanders a modicum of normality. Never again could the islanders enjoy their pre-war lifestyle but at least they were spared the close attention of thousands of troops on their doorsteps. A dedicated QRA facility was built adjacent to the 'housies' closest to the runway threshold. A small brick-built annex housed domestic and operational accommodation for the four aircrew and their associated ground crew. For the aircrew, life revolved around a small combined crew room and ops room. A small ops desk housed communications, telephones and a fax machine which passed the meteorological reports. A cabinet containing the operational information sat in the other corner. A weather state tote showed base weather and the conditions at Stanley. The supervisor occasionally checked the weather states for air bases on the mainland to see if QRA activity was likely. The lack of local diversions meant that monitoring the changing weather was less onerous than in UK as there were few places to go, however, the trends in base weather were critical and the consequences of lack of attention were more significant. Flying in marginal weather had serious political risks both for readiness and the potential to divert yet the weather could change in minutes. In the UK, weather trends could be predicted using the conditions at adjacent airfields as a guide. With 400 miles of empty ocean to the west there were few clues or warnings before a sudden deterioration in conditions hit the airfield.

Away from the small ops desk, there was ample space for the obligatory, yet essential, couches, tables, TVs and video players; DVD had yet to be invented. Two bedrooms, one for each crew were located across the hallway where crews slept during their twenty-four-hour shift. A telebrief repeater in each of the bedrooms ensured that there was no escape from the dreaded confidence tone or the potential scramble message. Along the hall, the groundcrew lived in a separate lounge as their sleeping habits could vary significantly from the aircrew and their shift patterns were different. Meals could be prepared in a small kitchen and, if the shift included a 'gourmet chef', basic rations could be requested which could be cooked on site. The QRA curry was legendary. In the absence of a budding Jamie Oliver, pre-prepared meals were delivered in insulated containers from the main kitchens on base and were surprisingly good despite the fifteen-minute journey across the airfield. Meals were a highlight to break up the tedium. A small briefing room was used by QRA crews to prepare for training sorties if the Q aircraft were used and meant the aircrew would not have to leave the confines of QRA until they walked for their aircraft. Once the sortie had been briefed, or if the hooter sounded, crews would make their way to their aircraft. A short uphill ramp led to the Q2 'Housey' whereas the Q1 'Housey' was a short sprint through a tunnel. Without a doubt, the tunnel was one of the more memorable ways to reach your jet and quite unlike the access route at any other flying base. In the event of a scramble, the crew-in was less calm. The 'Housey' doors would open and crews would scramble across the short space between QRA and the jet as quickly as their legs would carry them. To a casual observer it was a logical ordered procedure run at break neck speed. To the participants, it was more akin to a swan swimming. There was a calm practiced exterior hiding two rapidly paddling feet.

The daily routine on Q was predictable. Crew handover was staged so that at least one crew was on full readiness throughout the process. The first crew changeover was conducted in the morning with the second handover staggered until the evening. Once relieved, off going crews at the end of a ten-day cycle were scheduled for a nominal two days' rest and recuperation period. In reality that was impossible with the limited manpower available in theatre. Finishing QRA early in the morning, the crew could look forward to being back in the QRA Shed the following evening for yet another stint as the cycle repeated relentlessly. The schedule was punishing but for most crews who spent only five weeks on the islands, mercifully short.

Oncoming crews would complete a 'ceremonial' handing over of the aircrew 'Noddy Guide' which contained the mission data and, at that point, they became the alert crew. There could be no confusion over who held the vital commitment. The new crew would walk out to the aircraft and complete cockpit checks and radio checks to ensure all was working. The navigator would realign the inertial navigation system and set up the quick align mode ready for a scramble. Once ready, harnesses and helmets were placed in strategic positions ready to be donned quickly in the event of a scramble order. Normally, this meant the helmet resting on the cockpit rails and the harness laid out at the base of the steps but individuals had different preferences. One pilot was persuaded by his Boss that hanging his lifejacket on the seeker head of a Sidewinder missile was, although convenient, perhaps not professional. Leaving the kit close to the aircraft avoided a 100-yard sprint wearing the heavy equipment. Once prepared for a rapid scramble, known as 'cocked' in the trade, the cockpit was the domain of its occupant and no-one was allowed to enter without approval from the sitting tenant!

With limited aircraft numbers in the South Atlantic, QRA aircraft could be programmed to fly, although that had to be balanced against the risk of the aircraft returning unserviceable after a mission. If four aircraft were available, the Q jets could remain on alert whilst the remaining aircraft flew, allowing non-QRA crews to build up flying hours and maintain currency. If only three aircraft were serviceable, the QRA aircraft could be launched to provide a fighting pair or as a target but making sure enough aircraft remained serviceable tested the Commander's nerves. With only two jets, sanity normally prevailed and the readiness state would not be compromised. Luckily I never experienced the ignominy of having only one serviceable aircraft. At the earliest sign of tensions, reinforcement would render such procedures irrelevant.

As tensions eased, live Q missions became increasingly rare. Argentinian combat forces never probed the airspace seriously and the regular visitors were the Argentinian intelligence gatherers. I was not launched from ground alert on a live scramble during my whole period in command of the Tornado F3 Flight but being brought to cockpit readiness was a regular feature. I was, however, airborne in the Q1 aircraft on one occasion when an Argentinian 707 signals intelligence aircraft pressed its luck. It had been operating well to the west of West Falkland but slowly eased in towards the western airspace boundary. Either by design or by luck the 707 crew timed its penetration to a tee. We had been conducting a mutual intercept sortie over West Falkland when the CRC at Mount Alice identified an incoming track and gave us a vector towards the target. With hindsight, the approach was probably timed to coincide with our call to our controller that we were approaching combat fuel minimums.

Remaining at low level, I shut down the radar to avoid alerting the sensors onboard the intruder and we set our initial vector picking up the speed as we tracked across West Falkland. The fighter controller was providing good information on our target which was at high level to the northwest but had turned back westerly towards the mainland and was approaching the Zone boundary. We took a closing heading, swept the wings to fully aft and accelerated to supersonic speed as we coasted out. The converted airliner was well ahead and had a good head start and we were running low on fuel as we had already been airborne for over an hour. There would be no time to tank from the QRA C130 tanker or we would give the 707 the chance to make its escape without issuing a reminder of our vigilance. We made some rapid calculations and worked out that we could probably just make the intercept before the target left the Falkland Islands Protection Zone but we could not maintain supersonic speed which would have assured an interception. As we climbed it was obvious that the Argentinian crew were well aware of our presence and had probably been monitoring our fighter frequency so at that stage I fired up the radar and locked up the receding target. There was no reaction and I could see the contrail continue its course back towards mainland Argentina.

It was obvious that we had insufficient fuel to use afterburner to close the range so, after a few more calculations, we held a speed that we could sustain in cold power and decided we could probably just make the intercept, although by then probably in international waters. The range closed slowly and we decided that we would burn down to absolute minimums in order to make the pass and take a picture for analysis and to record the intrusion for the record. We would return on fumes but with important photographic evidence. Sadly, our controller had less determination than we and, at a range of about four miles, gave the 'haul off' call. So near, yet so far. It was with reluctance that we

The Argentinian Boeing 707 leaving the FIPZ at high level leaving a contrail in its wake.

complied making our way gently back to base. In the event, my only 'trophy' was a picture of a dot on the end of a contrail. That said, the Argentinian crew would have been under no illusions that their intrusion into the zone had not only been detected but countered. Had relations been less friendly, the target was well within missile parameters and we had plenty of missiles onboard. On that occasion, their only retribution would have been a photograph opportunity. The irony was that we heard the following day that while we had been chasing the Boeing 707 intelligence gatherer from the zone, our colleagues at RAF Akrotiri in Cyprus had been providing turnround facilities for an Argentinian C130 transport aircraft engaged in UN support duties in the Middle East! The world can be strange at times.

CHAPTER 8
'Trails'

No exercise or operation can be planned without allocating a codeword and deployments of aircraft between theatres is no exception. An allocation of a codeword to an operation begins as a highly secretive process but emerges into open use within months of its inception. For the RAF, the codewords are chosen from a random list held by a staff officer in the Headquarters at Air Command. A potential sponsor is offered a few choices which generally have the most bizarre names. Operation Granby was the codeword for the First Gulf War and within days it was splashed across most of the newspaper front pages. Operation Lampuca was the unlikely name given to the deployments of Phantoms between the UK and the Falkland Islands. Not unique to that route, a trip between key operational bases which was supported by a tanker was nicknamed a 'trail' and prefixed to describe its participants. Phantom Trail and Tornado Trail are easily identified but the nickname 'Tiger Trail' was given to the delivery flights of the F4J Phantom across the Atlantic when they were first procured from the US. The nickname referred to the squadron badge which depicted a tiger's head.

Deploying combat aircraft to the opposite side of the world places enormous strains on Air Force planners and presents challenges. Before aircraft are selected, the engineers study the maintenance history and the scheduled servicing plan. Some modification programmes must be undertaken at the major servicing facilities and, increasingly nowadays, that is with the manufacturer. The level and complexity of the engineering programmes are designated by the terms 'first line' to 'fourth line'. In the days of the Phantom, minor servicing was done at the main operating base at second line so it could be completed at Mount Pleasant, albeit the aircraft was unavailable to the flying programme during that time. Major servicing was done at third and even fourth line and, invariably, that meant RAF St Athan in Wales. A major servicing was a complex task and the aircraft was stripped down almost to its constituent parts. At certain times, modifications to extend the fatigue life were incorporated and these involved major reengineering of the actual structure. Take a look at the wing fold mechanism of a Phantom in a museum and you will see huge metal plates riveted onto the underside of the outer wing panel to add structural strength. These were added after the wing fold failures of the mid 1970s but were complex, required input from the manufacturer and the airworthiness authority and could only be done at a deep servicing establishment. There was no way such major engineering programmes could be implemented in theatre so the only option at that time was to conduct 'Trails' to return the aircraft to UK.

Later, planners began to think laterally, and with the end of the Cold War, giant AN124 Condor transport aircraft were suddenly available for hire on the international market and were taken on for the task. The wings were folded and the sections of the Tornado F3s were loaded into the vast cargo bay and flown back to UK. Ironically, such a solution was more cost effective than deploying the enormous tanker fleets which were needed to fly the aircraft home. At times, with heavy tasking of the tankers during the Gulf War campaigns, the tanker airframes were just not available so air transport was the only available option.

As engineering plans crystallised and a slot was allocated within a modification programme for a Falklands based aircraft, an aircraft was selected from the UK fleet to replace it. The candidate would be assessed and the servicing which was anticipated for the duration of its planned stay 'Down South' would be completed. Not only did this include 'minors' and 'majors' but the engineers would assess individual components which had a servicing requirement such as the ejection seats. Often the complexity of the requirements dictated that a candidate airframe would have just emerged from a modification programme itself. To ensure that the airframe was as prepared as possible, assessment went down to an intricate level of detail. Once the aircraft set off on its long journey south, it would have received everything possible to keep it flying for some years without needing major engineering work.

Tanker trails are elaborate operations which take a great deal of planning and I saw at first hand, the challenges of deploying over the vast distances between the UK and the Falkland Islands when I returned a Phantom, XV464, to the UK in 1984. 'Trails' begin many months before the actual event in the Air-to-air Refuelling Planning Cell in the major headquarters. Operations staffs set the roulement dates and decide how many aircraft need to be moved. They assess the expected weather *en route*, the distances and heights over which the trail will be flown and come up with a broad plan. Different aircraft types are able to operate at diverse heights.

The Phantom was most comfortable tanking at about 15,000 feet but could tank up to 25,000 feet, although with two external wing tanks and a centreline tank plus weapons aboard, it required a touch of reheat to hold its height as the tanks became full. With its smaller engines, the Tornado F3 was less able to cope as its RB199 engines were designed to be frugal and efficient and were optimised for lower levels. With the large 2,250 litre wing tanks and, especially if additional 1,500 litre fuel tanks were fitted on the cheek pylons, it could travel a very long way but tanking at 25,000 feet to extend that range still further was not realistic. For that reason, fewer tanks would give better performance at higher level even if that meant that extra refuelling brackets would have to be planned to keep the tanks topped off. There is, however, a fundamental dilemma when planning a long distance deployment. It seems logical that, if a fast jet needs two tanks of fuel to cover a set distance, the tanker only needs to fill it to full at the halfway point and the job is done. In reality this is impossible. For deployments to the South Atlantic, vast stretches of the route are many hundreds of miles away from the nearest suitable diversion airfield; so called 'blue water operations'. Fuel tanks need to be kept topped up to ensure that crews can divert sometimes long distances in the event of an in flight emergency or if the weather deteriorates at the planned destination. Although weather forecasts are studied in advance, the weather in the Falklands is notoriously unpredictable and can deteriorate at no notice mid way through a tanker trail. For that reason, the planner will plot the preferred route which may be affected by diplomatic constraints including such as whether a formation of combat aircraft is allowed to pass through another nation's airspace.

A four ship of Phantoms which took a short cut through Swiss airspace in the 1970s was particularly unwelcome and caused a flurry of diplomatic exchanges. After a diversion to France on the way home from an armament practice camp, the lead navigator joined the dots from where he was to where he wanted to go. Forgetting about neutral status, his route passed across Switzerland which caused not inconsiderable diplomatic traffic between Bern and London. On a more traditional deployment, the planner will calculate how much fuel is required and come up with the optimum plan to maintain the required fuel states at key times during the sortie. As an example, at optimum endurance speed at 25,000 feet, the Phantom would burn about 90 lbs of fuel per minute, although this improved as fuel burned off. The planners would use these generic figures and calculate a fuel plan which was then published to the squadron in the form of a 'Transop'. These planning assumptions would use typical headwinds and the broad figures would be validated by squadron experts at a later stage. It would be much closer to the actual deployment date, if not on the day itself, when actual weather conditions could be used and the plan would be finalised. For the 3,750 miles between Ascension and the Falklands, planners would typically include four tanker brackets but this could increase to five in the event of adverse headwinds. A typical tanker plan is depicted in the colour photograph section.

Trails are normally flown 'accompanied'; in other words in formation with the tankers. Depending on departure airfields, an appropriate join up is selected. If the aircraft are operating from the same base the tankers launch first and carry out a large orbit around the airfield to be back overhead the field as the fighters roll down the runway. This brings the formation together in the most efficient way without involving long tailchases which waste fuel. If the tankers and 'chicks', as receivers are known, are operating from different bases, there are a number of options to complete an in flight rendezvous. An RV point and time is planned and the lead fighter crew can control a simple intercept profile aiming to join in formation with the tanker. A much more complex procedure, known as an 'RV Delta' can also be scheduled. This involves the two formations pointing towards each other up to 100 miles apart. At twelve miles, the lead fighter turns the tanker onto a reciprocal heading and rolls in behind with both formations now travelling in the same direction. It is particularly useful if the tankers are positioned down route at a mid point in the deployment.

Once visual, fighters join on the left hand side of the lead tanker, the logic being that the Captain, who would be sitting in the left seat, could see the joining fighters as soon as they arrived. That said, even such a fundamental has changed at times over the years on the last occasion to standardise procedures amongst NATO nations. Once the fighters have joined in formation, the tanker controller, normally the lead tanker pilot, takes the formation to a quiet chat frequency and only the lead tanker then speaks to Air Traffic Control making it much easier to control the formation. Once at the transit height, the 'chicks' drift into a comfortable loose formation and fly in close proximity to the tankers at the same height. Choreographing and controlling the correct formation positions is important to ensure that the right aircraft are in the right position at the right time, particularly if a complex refuelling plan is needed. As the nominated bracket approaches, fighters are cleared in behind the appropriate hose and take their allocated fuel before disconnecting. At that point, they move to the opposite side of the formation allowing the next fighters in behind the basket. The actual refuelling sequence is intense so pilots take the opportunity to relax outside those brief moments of concentrated activity. Crews had various ways to while away the long transit sorties. With the advent of walkmans and iPods, small plugs were crafted which allowed music to be played over the intercom which made the tedium a little more manageable. The Tornado F3 was fitted with a cassette deck which was used to load data into the main computer but could deputise as a music player. Games of 'battleships' over a quiet tactical frequency were also popular and may have confused any 'snoopers'.

It was vital to consider emergency contingencies in the event of an aircraft systems emergency or a refuelling equipment failure. With aircraft coupling in mid air while travelling at nearly 300 mph, it was extremely easy to damage a basket when refuelling. With excessive overtake, I have seen probes forced through the spokes destroying the structure of the basket and allowing pieces of debris to be ingested into the engine. For that reason, one of the key planning factors is the single engine range or, in other words, how far and at what height a Phantom could fly if an engine failed. For a Phantom on a long distance transit, the fuel load was maintained artificially high, so with 15,000 lbs of fuel onboard, the single engine optimum altitude was 5,500 feet. At that height with three external fuel tanks the optimum mach number was M0.46 and you would travel about five miles for every 100 lbs of fuel used. These figures improved as the aircraft became lighter or if you chose to jettison the external fuel tanks. In the event of an engine failure at a distance from a suitable diversion, careful calculation and critical decisions might be needed in order to land safely. Obviously, in such an event, the formation could not maintain height if formation integrity was to be maintained. The aircraft with the failure would descend and his formation would follow. Another of the key planning factors is the 'point of no return' which is the point along the track at which time there is insufficient fuel to return to the departure airfield. If a fighter is flying from one airfield to another using only its onboard fuel, this point is easily calculated. When, refuelling in the air, fuel loads change as the tanks are topped off and such a simple system would not work. To achieve a workable solution, a number of 'brackets' are planned at regular points along the track which give a refuelling start line and a refuelling stop line. The lines show when the fighter will be cleared astern to take its fuel. The planned length gives enough time to receive the expected fuel offload but includes some flexibility should the 'plug-in' be difficult for any reason. The tanker plan assumes that the receiver will have taken on its allocated fuel before reaching the stop line and, therefore, a 'mandatory diversion point' is nominated shortly beyond that position. If the fighter has not received its allocation by then it would have insufficient fuel to complete the leg and would be forced to divert to an *en route* diversion airfield. In European airspace this is relatively easy to plan as there are many suitable diversions close by along most routes. When deploying to the South Atlantic or across the Atlantic Ocean, diversions are much less frequent.

As the destination approached, the recovery was normally flown unaccompanied. At an appropriate range, the lead tanker captain would clear the fighters back onto the main air traffic control frequency to make contact with the controller. Fighters would then depart and with sufficient fuel would fly ahead at a more tactical speed and land first. Quite often this could be as late as fifty miles from the destination and was often a source of frustration as the range to the destination wound down. Having received their fuel fighter crews were normally keen to land as soon as possible.

In *Phantom In Focus* I described, in detail, the recovery of two F4 Phantoms from RAF Stanley via Ascension Island to RAF Coningsby in 1985. The aircraft had been in the Falklands since the first days of 'Phandet' and were planned to enter major servicing programmes. The original plan envisaged four refuelling brackets spread evenly along the 3,950-mile straight line track between RAF Stanley and Wideawake Airfield on Ascension Island. Five VC10s would launch from the newly opened RAF Mount Pleasant at the same time as our two Phantoms and, after a join up in the climb, the Phantoms would refuel from the first VC10 which would then recover to the islands. After a further mutual refuelling bracket, another VC10 would transfer its own fuel to a VC10 before returning to its departure airfield. This would leave three fully fuelled VC10s with plenty of spare capacity to fly onwards in company with the Phantoms. The first bracket was planned within easy sight of the departure airfield. This would allow us to prove the refuelling systems on the Phantoms and make sure that we could take on fuel into all the fuel tanks and that they were feeding correctly. The Phantom had a complex system where fuel was fed into the fuselage tanks from the external tanks and the wing tanks. Failures were rare but not unheard of so, in the event of a failure, all the aircraft would return to the islands and regroup at a later date. Another bracket was planned abeam Uruguay with an emergency diversion option into Montevideo. The next bracket was even further from the South American coastline but the consolation would have been a night in Rio de Janeiro. By the time we hit the final bracket, we would have received enough fuel to complete the first leg of the mission and press on to our interim destination, Wideawake Airfield on Ascension Island in the dark. In the event of an emergency, the plan was that the whole formation would remain together and divert as one.

Unfortunately, like any military plan it did not survive first contact with the enemy even if, in this case, the enemy was one of the VC10s. On the trip south one VC10 was declared unserviceable at Ascension. In the plan, the margins were tight but the remaining airframes could carry just enough fuel to satisfy the planned offload. Enter the weather. With adverse headwinds forecast for the whole of the first northerly leg, there were insufficient reserves to hold adequate diversion fuel on arrival at the remote airbase in The Ascensions which is 1,000 miles from the nearest land. A hastily recalculated tanker plan which used a Falklands based C130 tanker to cover the first bracket, provided just enough extra fuel to compensate for the delayed VC10. Unfortunately, the unpressurised C130 could not climb to the same height as the rest of the VC10 formation so we were forced to descend to a lower level, tank from the Hercules before climbing back to 25,000 feet to catch up the larger tankers. Against the odds the plan proved sound and we caught the VC10s just before the critical second tanking bracket. The final refuelling was completed as night fell and we stayed with the tankers until top of descent before being cleared off by the lead tanker captain. The Phantoms landed first with the VC10s having, theoretically, the bigger fuel reserves, landing afterwards. The main risk was of a Phantom 'blacking' the runway by taking the cable rendering the runway unusable. In that event, the VC10s would need to hold off or divert to the mainland many miles distant. Such complex operations are never over until the last wheel is on the runway. The arrival proved interesting and after being released late, we were still too high as we approached the final approach needing an orbit to lose height. Although, the island is tiny, Ascension boasts some quite daunting mountain peaks which flank the single runway. Although I had carefully calculated my safety height, or the lowest level to which we could descend to remain clear of the obstruction, the descent into the inky black equatorial night was still a nervous manoeuvre. I felt an unnecessary feeling of relief as we rolled out on long finals with the runway lights in view having turned quite close to those peaks. The evening meal in the small Officers' Mess on the island, accompanied by a beer or two with the VC10 crews, was a pleasant affair after the long and sweaty journey. It was a vast contrast to the Falkland Islands both climate and surroundings.

After a 48-hour layover on the tropical island, by no means a hardship after the austerity of RAF Stanley, the formation continued to UK. This gave the tankers which had returned to RAF Mount Pleasant after the first tanker brackets the time to catch up a day later. By then, Wideawake was a much quieter place than in its heyday in 1982. Back to its more normal traffic flow, there was plenty of space on the huge parking area to accommodate our VC10s and the two Phantoms. The pre flight briefing had been done before leaving Stanley so just a quick weather check was needed on the morning of departure. With the outside air temperature already approaching thirty degrees, we had carried our immersion suits to the jets leaving it until the last minute to climb into the heavy rubberised survival suits. Although superfluous for the first few minutes of the trip, as soon as we left the safety of the territorial waters around Ascension Island we would quickly become reliant on them for survival if we had to eject. Even in the relatively warm equatorial waters, an immersion suit was vital to give that time needed to climb into the tiny single man dinghy carried in the seat pack of the ejection seat.

It might be a long wait for a rescue. The dinghy was connected to the lifejacket by a lanyard. Once in the water, the immersion suit provided that first line of defence against the cold water before you were able to pull the dinghy within reach and inflate it by pulling a small ripcord-like handle. Once aboard, blowing air into the floor and into a canopy which pulled up around the shoulders, you were provided with the protection from the elements which may keep you alive until the Nimrod search and rescue aircraft could locate you. Such thoughts were far from my mind as I pulled the rubber neck seal over my head, zipped up the suit and donned the heavy lifejacket. Within seconds, the exertion of climbing into the Phantom cockpit had caused overheating and I was already sweating; this would not improve until top of climb as the pathetic Phantom air conditioning system kicked in and pushed out some cold air. What should have been a routine start up began to get worse. As the countdown to taxi time ticked down, my inertial navigation system stubbornly refused to align. The gyros in the INAS provided not only navigational information but also fed the attitude instruments in the front cockpit. It was vital to have attitude but, with five tankers and another Phantom alongside I could live with an inaccurate navigation system. It was simply not worth delaying the formation departure to give navigation information. The attitude is the aircraft's position in relation to the horizon.

The state of the alignment process was indicated by a red 'ALN' light which flashed rapidly at first, slowing down as the platform became aligned with True North. For some reason, on that day the system in XV464 stubbornly refused to align and the relentless flashing of the caption was almost a taunt. The fact that it was an unusual fault was no solace. Eventually, after a good deal of pressing from the front cockpit I gave in and we decided that attitude would have to suffice. We would divert as a formation *en route* so if we had to use an airfield other than Coningsby we would have to rely on our flight lead or, hopefully, a trusty TACAN radio beacon. We checked in and called ready to taxi for the final leg back to the UK. Unlike the first sortie a few short hours earlier, we now had a full complement of VC10s so fuel was not a problem despite the much longer second sector. The plan for this leg had also been calculated to allow all the VC10s to continue along the route back to RAF Brize Norton. Simple tanker-to-tanker transfers would leave enough fuel in the final two VC10s to get us safely back to Coningsby. As with the first sortie, a tanker bracket was planned early on the first northerly leg to prove the fuel systems on both aircraft.

With three point refuelling hoses the VC10s were well placed to cover in the event that we damaged the refuelling basket making contact. The route took us through the tropics, more specifically the Doldrums and, even up at 25,000 feet which was our planned tanking height, clear air turbulence was a problem. One over-enthusiastic lunge at the basket in the turbulence could easily cause damage to the spokes. Ingesting debris from a refuelling basket which might then cause damage to the sensitive engine turbine blades could not be factored into the plan so caution was the order of the day. Nevertheless, a number of fallback plans were employed to ensure that the remaining aircraft could get the precious fuel into the Phantom tanks where it was needed by shifting fuel between VC10s if necessary. The route kept us in international waters but within striking distance of the coast to allow for a diversion in the event of an emergency. Further successful refuelling brackets off the West African coast abeam Liberia, Sierra Leone and Senegal gave further confidence that we would land back in UK as planned. The diversions were equally exotic with Monrovia in Liberia and Dakar in Senegal. Despite the huge runways, I had no real desire to experience an unplanned arrival with a sick Phantom. The fact that Conakry in Guinea was a regular stopping off point for the Tupolev Tu20 Bear Deltas of the Soviet Long Range Air Force gave us little confidence that it would be a much better place to visit. Eventually, after passing to the east of the Cape Verde Islands, the diversions began to sound much more familiar with Tenerife replacing Dakar. Although our return proved uneventful, during an Operation LAMPUCA mission the following year, a Phantom diverted into the Canary Islands with a massive fuel leak having declared a 'MAYDAY'. Somehow I suspect the pleasures of a few days on a beach as the aircraft was fixed may have been small compensation for what must have been a massive adrenaline shot during the emergency and subsequent diversion. The final leg past Morocco, up the coast of Portugal and past the Bay of Biscay seemed positively local. As we finally approached the south-western coast of the UK I was able to pick up the coastline on the radar giving a welcome feeling of confidence. My inertial navigator had set off on a diverging course many hours before and by now was somewhere over central Europe. The fact that Brize Norton TACAN eventually locked on and began to give a reassuring range and bearing was certainly welcome. Eventually, Coningsby TACAN was within range and we had a needle to follow to take us straight to Runway 26 at base. As we taxied back into the HAS site, the beer which was offered by aircrew colleagues was, without doubt, welcome but it could never match seeing the smile on the face of my young daughter. My son happily had decided to wait it out and was yet to hit the runway of life.

These sorties were some of the longest I ever flew in a fast jet only surpassed some years later by a ten-hour overnight epic to Oman in a Tornado F3. A surprising fact is that RAF Stanley lies at the same latitude in the southern hemisphere as Grantham in Lincolnshire in the northern hemisphere. On the first leg on 24 June 1985, we launched from RAF Stanley in broad daylight landing in the dark at Ascension Island just south of the equator some 7 hours 20 minutes later. The second sortie, on 26 June 1985, lasted exactly 9 hours. The flight time of 16 hours 20 minutes proved just how far the Falkland Islands really are from the UK. The flight literally spanned the globe. The fact that the sorties were flown completely over water with only a pin-prick of an island as a transit stop is as humbling as it is impressive.

As my time as OC1435 Flight came to an end, I was to be reacquainted with the complexities of a 'trail' yet again when two of my aircraft were scheduled to return home for major servicing. I had been warned on arrival and it was 'the elephant in the room' throughout my time 'Down South'. Due to take place in the last three weeks of my detachment, there was just a little part of me that hoped it would delay long enough to leave the challenge to my successor. The disruption to the carefully crafted programme and the risk of failing to maintain the QRA commitment with four of the six aircraft involved in the rotation was always in the back of my mind. QRA had to continue and the problems of servicing six aircraft from a spares pool designed to support four was more than an issue. QRA was my priority but I was concerned that others may think otherwise.

The first thing was to prepare the Tornado F3s which were to return to UK for their long sortie home. Critical to check was how much oil the engines fitted to our specific Tornados were using. The Tornado F3 was known to use oil at a rate which made long sorties difficult. The typical usage rate according to the aircrew manual was somewhat more than the predicted burn rate which meant that, in theory, the engine would run dry somewhere short of Ascension Island. A myth which had perpetuated in the Tornado GR1 force suggested that four hours was a maximum, a fact which we had disproved comprehensively by flying non-stop to Oman in 1986. Unlike that trip, however, it would be inconvenient if the oil ran out causing an engine to fail when the only diversion was many hundreds, sometimes thousands of miles away. The South Atlantic had fewer diversions compared to the Mediterranean. Every member of the formation was equally keen to make use of the only available runway at Wideawake airfield so putting a Tornado F3 into the cable would be a bad tactic and would not be well received. Theory aside, there was only one way to check the actual oil consumption and that was to fit the large 2,250 litre external wing tanks which were needed for the transit and to fly for up to eight hours. Prior to the early Omani deployment, we had mounted proving sorties where we flew the whole of the perimeter of the UK behind a Tristar tanker staying airborne for over eight hours. It was tedious but we gained a good idea of individual airframes and their likely oil usage. The same procedure would be needed again and it was with some trepidation that we began to look at repeating the exercise, although on this occasion it would be around the Falkland Islands plugged into a C130 tanker. There were few alternatives as most of the countries to the west of the islands, and one in particular were unlikely to welcome a visit from a pair of Tornados into their airspace. To the east, there really was only one destination, and that was South Georgia, the group of islands which were the first to be occupied during the Falklands War twelve years earlier. The C130 tankers occasionally conducted reconnaissance sorties down to South Georgia to check on shipping in the southern oceans and to show a presence. I had seen videos of previous trips and

A Tornado F3 conducting an oil calibration flight prior to a long distance deployment.

the scenery was truly spectacular. A plan began to hatch which might satisfy the needs of the test but might also provide a welcome relief in the form of a 'sightseeing tour' to South Georgia.

There was a major downside to undertaking the trip, namely we would be operating some distance away from the safety of the normal search and rescue coverage over icy Antarctic waters. Normally, we relied on the Sea King helicopters of 78 Squadron but their range was little better than 100 miles from shore. Over greater distances, the C130 could carry multi crew survival equipment known as Lindholme Gear and the crews had dropped life rafts to ships in difficulties around the islands over the years. I began to consider whether a trip to South Georgia would be viable if appropriate safety procedures could be put in place. As we planned to accompany the C130 there was no reason why 'Lindholme Gear' could not be loaded for the trip. As luck would have it, the sorties had to be flown in the week immediately prior to the 'Trail' to ensure than any consumption figures were as current as possible. 'Trails' in those days were always accompanied by Nimrod aircraft which provided long range SAR cover for the formation. It just so happened that the Nimrod was planning to visit Mount Pleasant during the week prior for local training and familiarisation. It would be available if the need arose. The maps were pulled out from Station Flight Planning Section and a few rapid calculations gave a distance of just short of 1,000 miles each way. Although well short of the 4,000 miles the aircraft would fly to reach the Ascension Islands, it was near enough half distance so it would be possible to extrapolate the readings. By then we knew that the oil usage was linear so if we flew to South Georgia and returned we should use about 50% of the required oil leaving a safety margin for the test should the usage be higher than expected. We worked a quick tanker plan with the experts on 1312 Flight and decided that 'Albert' could easily accommodate a pair over the shortened distance and have sufficient reserves for a hold off in the event of bad weather on our return. It could also accompany us for the whole trip improving the safety margin and complete one of its routine patrols. As always, Port Stanley airfield could provide a haven if Mount Pleasant was out for weather on our return.

The plan was to carry out an accompanied departure with the C130 and fly in formation to a descent point some fifty miles from the island. At that point, the two F3s would descend to low level to carry out a 'presence run' around the islands, say hello to the British inhabitants of the scientific community before climbing out and returning to MPA at higher level. It was hardly the most demanding sortie I had ever planned and certainly nowhere near as complex as the earlier Phantom Trail. We checked and cross-checked the figures and there was sufficient flexibility to cover contingencies. In our absence, the remaining F3s would provide QRA coverage so having all four F3s serviceable on the day was essential. Given that the two nominated aircraft were flying with external fuel tanks, they were not ideal for QRA duties during those final days in any case. The carrot was the thought of seeing some scenery other than that of the Falkland Islands.

The morning dawned and all the arrangements were in place. The C130 was serviceable, the Nimrod on standby and the F3s were fuelled, oiled and ready. The weather on the Falkland Islands was relatively poor but departure weather is rarely a limiting factor. What was more relevant was that the base weather was forecast to improve later but, unfortunately, the weather around South Georgia was little better than the local conditions. Given the likelihood that the latter stages of the trip would have been flown in thick cloud and that a descent to low level near the destination would have been impossible, there was little value in the exercise. I was truly devastated when it became apparent that the plan was stillborn and I admit to a feeling of impatience given that I had been confined for nearly four months and the thrill of a short escape was tangible. 'Island Fever' had become rife. Luckily, my pilot who had only been deployed for a couple of weeks and was hugely experienced was more cautious and proved to be a reliable sounding board. In reality, I was easily persuaded that the value was outweighed by the weather forecast. Reluctantly, the exercise was shelved and given the poor conditions at MPA the aircraft stayed on the deck that day, although, eventually, the weather cleared, exactly as forecast. In the event, the test was delayed and someone else drew the short straw and eventually flogged around the Falklands for a number of hours to prove the systems.

As the day approached, contact with the UK increased markedly. For most of my detachment, daily life had continued with little day-to-day contact with our Headquarters in UK. As the final planning was underway, daily 'phone calls at obscure hours became the norm. Suddenly we were popular again. One of the most significant aspects of a 'Trail' was that for the period of the roulement the numbers under my command swelled. I went from four aircraft, five crews and fifty-five groundcrew to six aircraft seven crews and an extra ten troops. My 'train set' was approaching squadron strength. It certainly gave an added air of hustle around the dispersal as the additional, normally unused housies were opened up to receive the inbound aircraft. Unlike previous roulements, the incoming detachment was self-contained. The Detachment Commander of the Tornado element was making all the operational decisions in coordination with the refuelling controller for the movements between theatres and I was happy to let them do so. My role was to ensure that QRA remained the number one priority, which was occasionally forgotten once the 'Trail' was underway. Nevertheless, it was a strange feeling having gone through the rigours of flying a 'Trail' nearly ten years earlier to be relegated to a more passive role on that occasion. I was advised throughout the deployment on the progress of the incoming Tornados. As with all such moves, four Tornados had been prepared in UK and had launched for Ascension but only the primary pair had left Ascension southbound with the spares turning back once the primary jets were serviceable and *en route*. The turn round at Wideawake had gone smoothly and the Tornados had set off on 12 January 1994 with their accompanying tankers for the long leg south. Of course no self respecting Squadron Boss could allow a formation of Tornado F3s to arrive into his airspace without the obligatory interception and welcoming committee and I was no different. Apart from that, they were unarmed and needed protection.

I launched the QRA birds to meet the inbound flight and they were welcomed aboard in an appropriate manner. Although I would have used the outgoing jets for QRA if it had proved necessary, the engineers had spent many hours preparing them, fitting the external tanks and we had flown ZG758 for a shakedown sortie in 'lima fit' at the last minute to prove some rectification which had been carried out. I felt guilty at the thought of wasting all that effort yet flying had to continue even if it was at a lower rate for a few days. In the event, the Q birds were serviceable and my Engineering Officer relaxed again, albeit at the expense of the occasional mumbling into his beer and a few more grey hairs on his young head.

During the short turn around at MPA, the new aircraft were accepted but with only forty-eight hours before our old jets took off for the return flight, there would be just enough time to remove the external tanks from the new arrivals, load the weapons and fly acceptance sorties. Routine snags would have to be managed. Even major problems such as an engine change would need to be managed locally. The first priority had been to deliver the replacements to Mount Pleasant. Once that had been achieved, the size and complexity of the 'Trail' meant that, once in motion, it would run as planned leaving us to pick up the pieces. It certainly helped having the whole formation operating from the same base unlike my earlier experience on my own 'Trail'. In retrospect, I do not recall any major dramas so it must have gone smoothly but perhaps my Engineering Officer has an entirely different recollection of those few days.

My logbook recalls the airframes I had on charge during that time. Before the trail we operated ZE812 (Faith), ZG790 (Hope), ZE758 (Charity) and ZE209 (Desperation). The first two airframes had been the originals which deployed on 6 July 1992 as the F3 replaced the Phantom. Three of the Flight's aircraft were named Faith, Hope and Charity after the three gallant Gladiator aircraft which defended Malta during the Second World War. With four aircraft on charge, an additional name was needed. With characteristic wit, or perhaps sarcasm, the name Desperation was adopted for the fourth aircraft.

ZE758 returned to UK in company with ZE209. ZG772 (Desperation) was one of the new replacements and, although few others would care, it held the accolade of being the aircraft in which I flew my last sortie in the Tornado F3 on 21 January 1994. The fact that its nickname was 'Desperation' seemed somehow ironic.

CHAPTER 9
Low Flying in the Falklands

'Jet Noise The Sound of Freedom'

The caption first appeared on a window sticker which was produced by the RAF Germany Phantom squadrons and was used to try to persuade a sometimes reluctant public in the early 1980s that there was a purpose to low flying. For the islanders this was undoubtedly a mantra. During two tours on the islands, and having met many of the locals, I never once met anyone who was not an avid fan and enjoyed seeing the aircraft fly past their settlement. A low flying complaint was unheard of and the only NOTAM, or Notice to Airmen, was to warn crews of a chicken farm where the noise tended to scatter the residents of the coops.

The Falkland Islands was a haven for low flying but why fly at low level in the first place? The height of the Cold War saw a proliferation of complex and capable air defence systems fielded by The Soviet Union. To be successful, NATO combat aircrew had to be able to penetrate those defences to attack their targets and doing so at medium level left them vulnerable to attack. Earlier surface-to-air missiles, or SAMs, were replaced by new variants. The early Vietnam vintage systems such as SA-2, SA-3 and SA-6 were replaced by SA10, SA-12 and SA-15 and the formidable SA-19 or 2S6 anti aircraft artillery (AAA) combined gun and missile system replaced the ZSU-23-4 gun. In the Falklands, the Argentinians fielded the capable Roland SAM and the Oerliken radar laid gun system with its Skyguard radar. If a fighter was not equipped with an effective electronic countermeasures system and flew straight and level at medium altitude, these systems were lethal as one RAF Sea Harrier pilot found to his cost. Flying back to the Task Force at 10,000 feet overhead Port Stanley, he had indications of being locked by a Roland. Climbing a further few thousand feet, he assumed he had climbed above the lethal engagement zone but the missile struck the aircraft causing its unexpected demise. After eight hours in a dinghy, during which time he had time to reflect on the quality of the intelligence assessments, he was picked up by a SAR helicopter from the ships.

The Skyshadow self defence airborne jamming system was fitted to the Tornado bomber to counter the Cold War threats but had been woefully under developed; although in 1987 there were two update programmes initiated and staff requirements were raised to gradually update the pod to counter new threats. The Zeus electronic warfare suite for the Harrier GR5 was innovative technology and was designed at the outset to integrate the radar warning receiver and the active jammer. It was software-driven and the concept was that the software could be reissued and updated as new threats emerged. Sadly, an element of hardware upgrading was also needed as missile and radar technology which it was designed to counter evolved. A staff requirement for a mid life upgrade which I drafted in 1987 was stillborn and an innovative company proposal in 2002 which upgraded the techniques generator was not funded. For this reason, the capability of the electronic warfare system slowly degraded through lack of money leaving Harrier pilots vulnerable to the modern threats. In the air defence community, the Phantom had never been fitted with an active jammer relying totally on a basic chaff and flare dispenser. Various proposals for the Tornado F3 failed to be selected for development due to lack of funding and it was only an American directive during the Bosnia operation which realised a hastily implemented jamming pod to allow the Tornado F3 to continue to operate in theatre. Although innovative, the jamming system was procured under urgent operational requirement procedures and was less efficient than another design which was available.

Against a background of obsolescent jamming equipment, our combat aircraft still had to be able to operate in hostile airspace. With the lack of electronic warfare equipment, if operating at medium levels, aircrews were extremely vulnerable to engagement by SAMs. The radar or infra-red trackers have a clear view of their targets at the higher levels and only a combination of jamming, chaff and flares with highly dynamic manoeuvring can defeat the missiles once launched. To manoeuvre in this way often means that aircraft have to drop weapons and external fuel tanks to extract the best performance from the airframe. This invariably results in a 'mission kill' as the crew can no longer prosecute an attack. Without comprehensive electronic warfare support, formations at medium level are easily engaged. Even the mighty United States Air Force and US Navy which invested heavily in support aircraft such as the EF-111 electronic jammer and EA6B Prowler aircraft armed with anti radiation missiles could not guarantee impunity. Although these specialist aircraft could suppress enemy air defences and give formations a better chance to penetrate defended airspace, British aircraft operating on National operations could not call on this help. For its part the UK had some old technology, such as the ALARM anti-radiation missile which could lock onto the emissions from a SAM and guide towards the radar which was threatening a formation. ALARM could be carried by one of the Tornado squadrons which specialised in the suppression of enemy air defences, or SEAD, role. Unfortunately, the Tornado was in its infancy and not available during the Falklands conflict. The Harrier could not carry ALARM and, although spending for major equipment continued, dedicated support aircraft and weapons systems were unaffordable within a constrained budget. All these factors meant that it was impossible to guarantee adequate protection to an attacking force. Furthermore, in the era of the 'Cold War Windfall', investment in defence projects was waning even further. For that reason, the RAF retained low level tactics to improve survivability.

There is one undisputable fact and that is that if a pilot can place a hill between himself and his aircraft, no tracking system yet developed can continue to track, although some are smart enough to predict. This usually results in a 'break-lock' and, if a radar guided missile is in the air, it loses guidance and becomes ballistic and, more importantly, harmless. This also applies to a seeker which uses another source on which to guide. If an infra-red guided missile is tracking on the hot metal of the jet pipes which are then obscured by a hill, again it loses lock. In tactical aviation parlance this is known as terrain masking and is one of the early skills which crews learn to use. In order to use terrain masking an aircraft has to be at low level. Another factor is the opponent. In order to operate effectively at low level crews require constant practice. New aircrew carry out an operational work up, normally on the Operational Conversion Unit, and are taught the techniques at 1,000 feet before progressing to lower levels. Operational crews train at 250 feet above ground level and, exceptionally, are cleared to 100 feet for key exercises. The difference between flying at these three heights is enormous. Against an opponent not properly trained, dragging them to lower altitude places them at a huge disadvantage. It is unlikely that an untrained pilot could operate his or her aircraft to the limit without a risk of hitting the ground. Many pilots could fly low but operating the weapon system at low level at the same time is much more challenging. This gives a trained crew a massive advantage. That said, it is not 'something for nothing' and weapons and radar systems are adversely affected by operating at extreme low levels. This means that aircrew must understand those limitations and fly their aircraft to militate against them. One key consideration is that, in order to detonate close to their target, air-to-air weapons are fitted with fuses. These can be contact fuses where the missile must strike its target or proximity fuses where electronics sense when it passes close to its target. The fuse then detonates the warhead. Weapon fusing at extreme low level is problematic and at levels below 100 feet, a missile which manoeuvres close to the ground may strike the ground in certain engagement regimes. Its fuse may also be confused by signals reflected from the

Flying low over Lafonia.]

ground and may detonate prematurely. Although manufacturers spend much time trying to alleviate these issues, for this reason, a missile launched against a target flying at extremely low level has a much lower probability of kill than against one flying at height.

Low flying tactics were tested extensively on operational test ranges in the UK and the USA and were proven to work. Given the lack of investment in jammers, British fighter and bomber crews flying at low level and were among the best in the world at exercising those skills. Given also the prowess demonstrated by the Argentinian pilots during the conflict, it was clear that any future fight in the air over the islands would be conducted at low level and the training regime supported that premise.

There were distinct differences in the topography. The southern part of East Falkland, south of Choiseul Sound was known as Lafonia and extremely flat. There were few visual cues to help the pilot with his height keeping given the total lack of trees and, to make matters worse, the ground was covered in a low scrub which resembled small trees giving an unusual visual anomaly. You could easily be seduced into flying very low thinking you were above a normal forest, yet the trees were only a few feet tall rather than many hundreds of feet. Only the radio altimeter showed the true story. To the eastern end of East Falkland sat the capital Port Stanley and a little further west the airfield at Mount Pleasant. Come further west and the major settlements of Goose Green and Darwin were close to Falkland Sound. Only a small strip of land connected this major landmass with Lafonia to the south. A major mountainous ridgeline ran west to east along the centre of the island. Moving northeast from Goose Green, Mount Usborne rose to over 700 feet above sea level and formed the backbone of the island. The ridge slowly dropped in height as it ran back east towards Stanley with the peaks of Two Sisters and Mount Longdon, which became famous during the war, ringing the capital rising to about 300 feet. In low flying terms, this ridge was a divider. There were no really suitable gaps through the ridge so unless you wanted to route around it to the east or west, the only option to cross was to climb above it.

To an intruding bomber pilot, cresting a ridgeline was anathema. To a fighter crew it could be used to your advantage. It could add pressure to an intruding bomber pilot if you wanted your presence to be known. Patrolling above a ridgeline might make an attacking pilot, who had yet to drop his weapons, predictable by forcing him over the flat ground to the south where he was vulnerable to detection and attack. It also gave a better view for your own radar which was less affected by the terrain shielding. If your intention was to remain undetected, the natural barrier made you invisible to an attacker to the south, albeit negated your own radar detection capability. If ground sensors could cue your attack, an undetected approach was possible. If an attacker approached from the north and crested the ridge to attack Mount Pleasant, it made them extremely vulnerable to a look up missile shot from either a fighter or a Rapier missile. Either way, the natural barrier could be used tactically by a defender as easily as it could by an attacker.

The north of East Falkland was different again. Deep inlets carved many years ago by the ice, cut sharply into the beautiful coastline giving some dramatic scenery. High peaks of about 400 feet in the centre of the island dropping to 200 feet towards the coast were spread evenly across the landscape. It was easy to drop into the many valleys around these peaks and be completely invisible to the air defence radars or your playmate looking for you on radar. Dotted across this landscape were hundreds of small airstrips which served the settlements and provided operating areas for the FIGAS Islander aircraft and the helicopters. Between the two major islands was the wide stretch of water known as Falkland Sound. This fifteen-mile-wide channel separated the two islands. Wider and clear at the northern end around San Carlos Water, the Sound was peppered with smaller islands towards the southern end. The biggest of these, Swan Island, although still only four miles long, was easily visible as you flew across the Sound and was home to a small community and served by a small airstrip. Immediately to its west was the most famous low flying feature known colloquially as A4 Alley. The eastern coast of West Falkland is protected by a mountain range known as the Hornby Mountains which runs from Fox Bay in the south to Port Howard in the north. As these mountains drop towards the coastline a dry river valley separates them from another ridgeline which rises again to 200 feet between the mountains and the sea. Covered in yellow gorse and littered with stones, the valley provides a perfect channel down which to fly making the aircraft invisible to anyone who is not down in the valley. The only way to detect a target down in A4 Alley is to set up a combat air patrol searching directly down the valley. This natural protection was used to devastating effect when Argentinian Mirage and Skyhawk pilots attacked the Task Force. The attacking aircraft would enter the valley at the southern end near Fox Bay and remain at ultra low level as they routed north eastwards towards the beachhead in San Carlos. Using the coastal ridge as a shield the fast jets would remain in the valley until Pax Port Howard before turning east for the short run in to their targets in San Carlos Bay. Relying largely on radar information from air defence ships or visual detection, the Sea Harrier pilots often picked the attackers up late unless weather conditions were clear. Despite this, an aircraft flying up A4 Alley was predictable and a visual observer in the valley could easily alert defenders to an attacker's presence. Needless to say, a run up A4 Alley was a must for any new fighter crew during local familiarisation sorties and was better than any roller coaster.

The main landmass of West Falkland is ringed on its western peripheries by hundreds of islands ranging in size from Weddell Island in the west, which is fifteen miles across, to the tiny Gid's Island near Chartres which is less than a mile in diameter. The most famous island, Pebble Island, also came to prominence after the SAS raids against the Pucara airstrip during the war. West Falkland is only slightly smaller than its eastern cousin. The mountains to the west were home to the two radar sites atop the peaks at Mount Alice in the south and Byron Heights in the north. Their positions gave their radar dishes unrestricted views over the air and sea approaches to the islands. Both stunning locations they are, unfortunately, completely isolated by geography. Although they can be reached by tracked vehicles, the main links in and out are by helicopter.

The island was peppered with reporting points which were chosen from the well known landmarks such as Fanning Head, Fox Bay or Swan Island. Unless we were operating with one of the fighter control sites we monitored the shared frequency as we made our way at low level around the islands checking in as we went. A call of 'Eagle 1 and 2 overhead Goose Green,' would immediately elicit a reply from anyone in the vicinity making the risk of a mid air collision so much less. Only when we arrived in our nominated tactical area would we chop

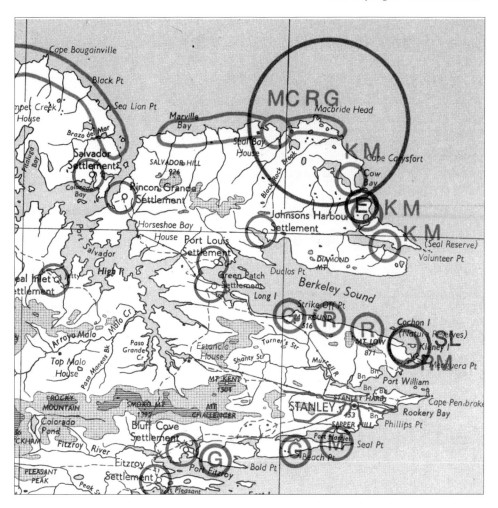

Wildlife colonies were marked on a Government map. © Crown Copyright (1985).

across to a quiet frequency for the intercepts. Once on that frequency, the fighter controller would monitor the shared frequency and give us updates as traffic moved around the airspace. Simple but effective.

The low flying rules were uncomplicated. You could fly at 250 feet above ground level anywhere around the islands. Exceptionally, we could be cleared to 100 feet for specific exercises such as Fiery Cross or ship attacks over the sea. Wildlife sanctuaries and breeding colonies were clearly marked on a map provided by Her Majesty's Government as were key settlements. It was vital to know where the areas of intense bird activity could be expected as a birdstrike with an Albatross was something to be carefully avoided. Equally, at key times of the season, jet noise and hatching were not happy soul mates so more care was taken to give the colonies a wide berth at these times. That said, my experience watching the wildlife on the ground was that they were largely indifferent to their human and mechanical neighbours.

The Tornado F3 had an excellent safety record at Mount Pleasant and despite the intensity of the low flying operations, aircraft losses were rare and only a few were lost over the years following the conflict. No Tornados were lost during its seventeen years providing air defence coverage and only two Phantoms crashed during the preceding ten years. Both Phantom losses were something of a mystery and I recounted the details of one accident in *Phantom In Focus* with the details published in an MOD Military Aircraft Accident Summary. I lost good friends in that mishap on 17 October 1983. A 23 (F) Squadron Phantom, XV484, was one of a three-ship formation which was scheduled for a practice interception sortie during operations from Stanley. The area across the centre of East Falkland between Stanley and Goose Green was ideal for this type of mission as it was relatively flat so the players could evade both during the intercept and, particularly, during the manoeuvring after the merge. In fact, with a combat air patrol at one end of the area and a start point at the other, the merge would occur quite close to where the airfield at Mount Pleasant now lies. On this occasion, the crew had been nominated to act as target for a pair of fighters manning a combat air patrol to the east. The weather was good with excellent visibility below a cloud layer which covered the planned exercise area. The fighters had already intercepted the crew of XV484 and the first engagement had been terminated. They turned back towards a start point near Goose Green and began another run at which time the navigators in the fighters on CAP briefly detected a target before it faded and never reappeared. In the minutes following, the crews in the remaining aircraft tried to make contact on the radio. Black smoke was seen above the cloud to the north-west but the crews thought that it was a peat fire which could often be seen around the countryside. When no radio contact could be established with the target Phantom, they assumed the worst and they alerted their controller who initiated a search and rescue operation. The wreckage of XV484 was found on the upper slopes of Mount Usborne 2 in the northern part of the exercise area. The aircraft had hit the cloud covered slope of the mountain about 500ft below the summit. The aircraft had been at tactical speed and had disintegrated on impact. The crew, neither of whom had initiated ejection, had been killed. I was simply stunned at the loss.

As with all military aircraft accidents a Board of Inquiry was convened but it was difficult to identify a cause. At that time, the Phantom did not carry an accident data recorder. They were able to determine that the aircraft had not suffered a technical failure and that it was in controlled flight when it struck the ground which meant that they had to look elsewhere for a cause. The Board members concluded that the crew might have been making a deliberate descent through cloud unaware of their actual position relative to the high ground. Some weight was lent to the conclusion as expert evidence showed that, at impact, the present position from the inertial navigation system, the INAS, showed them to be a number of miles south-west of the crash site which would have put the aircraft over the low ground in the area of Goose Green. They concluded that the crew should not have relied solely on the INAS to fix their position before descending through cloud. If the scenario was true it was a sound conclusion.

In the crewroom, the accident caused much debate and having flown with the pilot and worked with the navigator on many occasions, the conclusions did not ring true to me. There was no dispute about the facts and the Board was conducted in the usual thoroughly professional manner. The problem was why a skilled crew who operated at low level in poor weather in Germany every day of the week would let down through cloud on the strength of a potentially inaccurate navigation system position? The thought of doing so goes against all the airmanship lessons we were taught and, having flown with them, I feel sure the crew would not have considered such an action. In Germany, the pilot did much of the navigation as the navigator was fully occupied operating the radar, the defensive aids and carrying out visual searches in the aircraft's 6 o'clock. Navigating visually below cloud there could be no confusion over general position and the rising ground would have been evident from the cockpit. If they had popped up above cloud why try to descend again? Most of us would run the intercept above cloud to its conclusion. It is likely that the CAP position or a point close to it had been entered into the 'destination' which would provide a range and bearing towards which the crew would fly. In the Falklands when flying tactically in good weather, the INAS was little used. The navigation features were easy to see in that area and the target's start point was close to Falkland Sound and Goose Green which meant that the crew would have begun the run from a known location. Putting myself in the same position, once inbound, I would begin searching on radar for the incoming fighters and would react to signals on the radar warning receiver. A classic reaction to a fighter threat was to fly a 'notch' manoeuvre which was a turn through 90 degrees. This made it very difficult for the navigator in the fighter to see the target in pulse Doppler mode as it would be 'on the beam' with very little closing velocity. Holding the diverging heading for a short while would guarantee that the fighters lost contact which would not be regained until the target turned back towards them. Equally, if a fighter locked on, the manoeuvre would also break that lock so it was a very effective tactic. Over East Falkland a turn to the south would put the target over the flat plain. Unfortunately, a turn to the north would quickly put the target in the vicinity of the high ground. Tactically, being in the foothills would make the target harder to see, visually, so would be an attractive option. On the day of the accident, with a solid layer of cloud above, the crew would, more likely, have been held down below the cloud and would have had to manoeuvre underneath the overcast. With cloud on the slopes, a northerly heading could not be held for long and a turn back would be needed to avoid entering cloud. Timing that turn back would be critical. There was no logic for a Germany crew to climb above because that was not the way Germany crews operated. Indeed, if the decision had been made to go high, a rapid and significant change of altitude would have been more likely taking the aircraft to medium level. On 92 Squadron we flew at low level and stayed at low level. There appeared to be no reason to fly towards the high ground above cloud, and, particularly, not to descend back into that cloud.

Losing friends makes you reflect in more ways than the obvious one. I replayed a similar scenario in my own mind many times to try to decide what I would have seen in the cockpit and what I would have done. In a notch manoeuvre there would have been no reason to be looking at the radar. That would have come as we turned back towards the fighters. The view forward from the back of a Phantom was poor so I would have been seeing the hill shrouded in cloud and, as it grew closer, prompted a turn back east. At some time, the radius of turn would have been too great to complete the turn without going into cloud and, at that point, the only decision would be to 'abort' and climb up to medium level through the cloud. An abort manoeuvre was a rapid roll to wings level and a full afterburner climb above safety altitude. In that regime it would take seconds. Whichever way I looked at the problem I could not find a situation where I would have agreed to a letdown from above a cloud layer into cloud in an area of high ground while completing a 'notch' or even a simple radar turn. If I was above cloud and wanted to let down I would have headed south in the manoeuvre as Lafonia is completely flat. Assuming the 'notch' was flown below cloud, I could imagine my friend suffering sensory illusions which may have caused him to miss time his turn back eastwards. Only seconds of delay would have taken the aircraft too close to the cloud covered peak for it to complete the manoeuvre safely. I experienced such illusions many times and they could be totally disorientating.

The Board did their best with the facts available and in the absence of cockpit voice recordings or an accident data recorder, unlike we 'crewroom experts' after the event, could not speculate. No one will ever know what happened that day. Errors occur but I can, say without fear of contradiction that the crew were flying their aircraft to its operational limits and were professional to the last. Despite my own views, The President of a Service Board of Inquiry can only form a judgement based on hard evidence; an unenviable task at times.

Accidents often lead to speculation about flying discipline and low flying often produces situations where aircraft have a greater impact on people or property. Low flying is often conducted in remote areas to try to minimise that impact. The famous Red Flag exercise is conducted in the Nevada desert and low flying in UK is generally focussed in the less densely populated areas of the country. Being sparsely populated and with residents being so pro-military, the islands are perfect for this type of training. Unfortunately, ensuring crews stayed within the rules was a dilemma Commanders faced daily. Videos taken by navigators flying in theatre capture Phantoms and Tornados operating at extremely low levels, perhaps occasionally, below cleared heights as shadows on the ground may attest. It seems obvious that all a commander needs to do is rule with an iron fist but it is never that simple. To fly air combat at low level requires consummate pilot skills and supreme crew awareness. Pilots had to be used to operating the aircraft to its limits not only on bright blue days but often in marginal weather. Add then the pressure of having to meet a time on task to drop a weapon or the complexity of engaging a hostile aircraft at low level and the challenge mounts. Add the possibility of being engaged by a hostile surface-to-air missile during this phase and even the most capable crew is stretched to the limit. To achieve success meant total trust in the aircraft capabilities and an implicit knowledge of the aircraft's vices. Equally, navigators had to place total trust in their pilot not to fly into the ground as the options to eject became limited. Operating at low level in the back seat meant that much of the time was spent either staring at the radar or looking over your shoulder searching for threats. Engaging in either task meant that the proximity of the ground was hard to judge, although the sitting position was much better in the Tornado. To be comfortable in that regime, crews had to operate at, and inevitably sometimes below, 250 feet every day of the week. I have already alluded to the fact that there is a vast difference operating at 1,000 feet compared to 250 feet compared again to 100 feet. To be sure his crews would cope at the lowest levels the commander needed to exercise tolerance – but within constraints. Limits which have to be judged could be broken. Unfortunately the limits were sometimes stretched to breaking point – literally. One Phantom crew after finishing a training mission struck a mast at one of the remote settlements when returning to base at low level. After a particularly spirited pass it struck a transmitter mast at a point well below its apex destroying the mast and damaging the airframe. I can only imagine the discussions during the subsequent interview with the squadron Boss after landing. With such a serious incident, a Board of Inquiry was convened. In an extraordinary example of how protective the islanders were of the crews, the members of the Board arrived at the settlement to interview the owners but were politely asked to leave the farm without any discussion of the incident.

The other loss came as the Phantom was coming towards the end of its service life and the reason also remains something of a mystery but was probably a simple operational error or loss of situational awareness.

XV421 took to the air on 30 October 1991 as leader of a pair of Phantoms detailed to conduct practice interceptions. At the merge, as was usual, the crews began a series of manoeuvres with the nominated fighter attempting to engage the target to take a missile shot. The sea was covered in a solid cloud layer but the tops were relatively low at 1,500 feet and the weather conditions were clear above with good visibility. This set a false deck for the sortie. As the crew of XV421 manoeuvred, they were seen to enter the cloud at about 1,500 feet in a semi-inverted dive from which they never recovered. The aircraft crashed seconds later killing them both with neither of them having tried to eject. Another Board of Inquiry assessed the facts and looked closely at why the crew could have made the mistake which led to their loss. As always, the facts were hard to determine and, but for its imminent retirement, would have led to the fitment of accident data recorders in the Phantom. The leader had launched alone after his wingman had been delayed with an unserviceable aircraft. As they waited for the wingman to launch they made three practice interceptions against their Hercules tanker at medium level. When their playmate eventually arrived on frequency, they were vectored towards him by their controller for an intercept. Both aircraft were fully armed and the leader had refuelled from the tanker so both aircraft were still heavy. In this configuration, the Phantom could be a handful for any pilot and caution, until some of the fuel burned off, was always prudent. As the leader manoeuvred against his opponent, reportedly, it was obvious from the other aircraft that he had lost energy in doing so. The wingman called a warning to check height as he noticed his leader rolling almost inverted but the Phantom entered cloud shortly afterwards and contact was lost. Despite extensive search and rescue operations which must have been traumatic for those involved in such a tight knit community, very little wreckage was recovered and the cause could never be determined positively by the Board of Inquiry. The most likely cause was determined to be the infamous handling characteristics exhibited by the Phantom. Technical malfunction could not be ruled out and something as simple as a master caution alert which came on at an inopportune moment could be extremely distracting as I know from personal experience. Ironically, the aircraft's name was 'Faith'. By the time the facts were published the Phantom had retired from active service so little advice was relevant other than the obvious risk of dynamic low level operations. It did, however, prove a salutary lesson to crews of the Tornado F3 who by then had taken over the air defence role in the South Atlantic. Reassuringly, neither loss could be attributed to indiscipline.

CHAPTER 10
The Falkland Islands Air Defence Ground Environment

Every year in the UK we were scheduled to visit our local Sector Operations Centre as part of the annual training syllabus. This allowed us to discuss tactics and procedures face-to-face with the controllers who looked after us on a daily basis. At home that meant a four-hour car journey to RAF Boulmer on the Northumbrian Coast. In the Falklands it was almost easier; almost. The Mount Kent radar site sat atop the highest mountain in the Stanley area but it was certainly not easy to visit by any normal form of road transport. The other control and reporting centres at Mount Alice and Byron Heights were not even on the same island and there was the small matter of Falkland Sound in between. For that reason, a helicopter was the only viable transport option but it was a much quicker and far more enjoyable way to get there. The sites were both stunning in a strange yet bleak way.

My first visit to Kent, or 'Puffin' as we knew it, was during a short R&R break during my first detachment but I was only passing through and the brief stop proved a tad more interesting than I had expected. My pilot and I were *en route* to Goose Green for an overnight stay with a family but the helicopter had to stop at each site *en route* and spares were needed at 'Puffin'. As we lifted from RAF Stanley the weather closed in with a vengeance and it began to snow heavily. It would have been enough to stop our Phantoms in their tracks and I could imagine the QRA crews relaxing a little as a 'Mandatory' scramble state was declared. Such a state didn't reduce the readiness requirement but you knew that a launch in such conditions could only be for a real target and the body compensated with an adrenaline shot. The Bristow's helicopter pilot seemed unconcerned as we headed out across the airfield boundary in the murky conditions. I looked across at my pilot who was sharing the small cabin along with a few fellow passengers and, being a pilot, he was somewhat more nervous than me about being carried around in marginal weather. I was used to it! Ironically, he was also ex RAF Germany so had spent most of his previous tour operating at low level at 420 knots in some of the worst murk imaginable. Even so, the lack of a direct input into the controls seemed to unsettle him somewhat.

Tracking down Stanley Harbour the weather picked up a little as we cleared the snow shower and we assumed we had run out of the worst of it, although we had little view forward from the cabin. As we crossed the end of the natural inlet the ground began to rise and we could see the valley sides narrowing as we eased through the gap between Mount Longdon and Two Sisters. The valley floor steepened and the cloud base began to squeeze us from above. In flying parlance, a gap between the hills and the cloud is called a letterbox; literally a gap through the wall. We had been planned to land at the helipad on the summit but as the cloud already covered the peaks and the murk was closing in again, the pilot came up on the intercom and announced that there was a minor change of plan and that we would be landing on the remote pad. When the cloud made it impossible to land at the radar site, a pad some distance away on the lower slopes offered an alternative on which to set down. Not only was the cloudbase dropping but the visibility was getting worse and, inevitably, we slowly flew into it by now literally hugging the ground and crawling up the slope a few feet above the surface. I'd been close to the ground during my career but never that close with the aircraft still airborne! There was obviously a great deal of local knowledge involved and I have no idea where a helipad appeared from in the gloom before we gently dropped onto it.

With no sign of human habitation, we waited for a few minutes with the rotors still turning before a BV206 tracked personnel carrier emerged from the gloom and pulled up alongside. The pilot had obviously been chatting to the controllers in the radar site to coordinate the landing. The door was pushed open by the crewman, a huge box was unceremoniously dumped onto the pad along with the obligatory but vital mail sack full of letters from home. As the BV206 pulled away back into the murk, the engine note picked up and we lifted from the pad. Lifting might be over-describing the manoeuvre as I swear that the helicopter hover-taxied back down the hillside until we popped back out into the clear(ish) weather and set course for Goose Green along the northerly slope of the ridge. I suddenly became very aware of the skills involved when I considered the ability of a helicopter crew to navigate in some appalling conditions which would have forced an emergency pull up in a fast jet. I certainly gained huge respect for both the helicopter crews on the islands and the poor blokes who spent their lives in the murk on top of the mountain providing air defence radar coverage. I visited many times on later occasions but looked down from the rather warmer confines of a Phantom or Tornado cockpit whilst engaged in a 'Measles' tracking exercise.

The reason for locating the radar heads in such remote sites on the hilltops was to give the early warning radars which provided the air picture on the

A BV206 Tracked personnel carrier which provided access to the radar sites in the harsh conditions.

Falklands the best possible vantage point. From their lofty peaks, the radars on West Falklands looked out over the western approaches and gave uninterrupted coverage of the airspace down to extremely low level. At ground level the radar beams emanating from a radar dish send back clutter if they strike the ground close to the installation. This causes a blank area close to the actual head known as the 'dark area' in which it is impossible to see any targets. By positioning the radar dish at higher levels, this limitation can be lessened. At the end of the conflict, there were two long range radars operated by the Argentinians; an AN/TPS 43F radar operated by the Air Force and an AN/TPS 44 operated by the Army which had provided the air defence air picture for the occupiers. Both were captured and the TPS43 was taken into RAF service and returned to the UK in 1984. It served with various units, although at times it was difficult to procure spares as the Argentinians had not paid the bill and the US contractor spent some time trying to persuade the UK to stump up some cash! It was finally phased out in the late 1990s. The TPS44 had been damaged by naval gunfire and never saw service after the conflict. For reasons of supportability, the RAF deployed our own Type 94 radars built by Plessey in the UK and called the AR3D. These were delivered to the islands by sea and airlifted by Chinook helicopters out to the remote locations. During my few visits to the mountain sites, the wind always seemed to be blowing and it must have been a feat of airmanship and flying skills to locate these huge payloads with absolute precision into their operational locations at the limit of the Chinook's performance.

To the north, No. 7 Signals Unit at Byron Heights sat almost on the end of a finger shaped promontory on a dramatic ridgeline at the top of a large peak. The local spot height of 621 feet was almost the highest spot, certainly on that part of West Falkland and, approaching from the south west in a fast jet, it offered a dramatic sight. No. 751 Signals Unit on Mount Alice was ostensibly less remote as, looking at a map, it was surrounded by hills and mountains and deep glacially-carved inlets. Even so, the term is relative. On my visit to Alice, after a drop off at Fox Bay, the next stop was the southerly radar site. The powerful Chinook helicopter threaded its way around the coastal strip before pulling up towards the peak and dropping easily onto the helipad. As usual, there was little fanfare as the rotors stayed turning and we were beckoned across to an ISO container with the caption 'Mount Alice International Air Terminal' emblazoned across the side of the metal shack. Another sign asked you to declare your morale, sense of humour and spirits. The Battersea Park bus stop which was fixed to the side of the 'Air Terminal' was little used as the bus service was somewhat infrequent. However, this did not stop one comedian suggesting that the resident infantry company visitors should queue at the bus stop for the run into town. A few squaddies spent some time waiting for a bus in some quite extreme weather. Given that the site was only a few hundred yards square with few refuges, this joke was a brave move. The Chinook was scheduled to reposition a cabin on the site and we watched as the pilot manoeuvred the huge airframe amongst the tangle of radio masts and portable buildings, at times perilously close to obstructions. In the end it seemed easy as the cabin was dropped into its new location and, after dropping the strop, the helicopter set off for its next destination.

The whole complex consisted of a series of ISO shipping containers welded together which was more robust than it first appeared. With winds approaching storm force at times, light skinned structures could be blown away, literally. A 'tin city' was heavier and more secure. They could not be described as pretty and would easily be targeted from the air but they were surprisingly comfortable inside. The control cabins were similar to many radar control cabins I had seen during my service. Small and cramped, at least the controllers only sat in the cabins during actual missions, although an unfortunate surveillance operator had to monitor the early warning picture at all times.

It was fascinating to watch a pair of Tornados being controlled and to see the story from the controller's perspective. For an intercept mission, the crews would call the controller in advance to discuss their requirements. In the UK that would often include limitations on the available airspace which the controller would have to comply with. These constraints might be caused by another pair of fighters in the area or civilian air traffic passing through the airspace. The pre-brief from the crews, normally decided by the lead navigator, included the intercept geometry, the height profile, the split range and the type of control. For a typical mission this might be 90 to 180 intercepts where the target would cross the fighters track on one of these aspects, low level attack runs below 5,000 feet under 'Delta control' which meant the fighter controller would give only an initial range. After that, it was up to the navigator. Various codes allowed these parameters to be varied in the air. As we watched, the controller showed how he set up the intercepts using various little 'gizmos' on his radar tube. In the UK, his major task might be to deconflict from civilian traffic which was rarely a problem in the free airspace 'Down South'. He or she would give an initial outbound vector to both the fighter and the target to separate them to the opposite ends of the 'play area'. Once the fighters were far enough apart – this was known as the 'split range' – he would turn them towards each other on their appropriate inbound vectors and offer the nominated level of control. The fighter would search for the target and, once detected on radar, would call a range and bearing of the contact. If confirmed, the navigator in the fighter would take control of the intercept by using the code word 'Judy'. From that point a wise controller monitored the run closely as a call of 'more help' at any time meant that the navigator had lost contact and the controller should begin to help the crew to reacquire by calling range and bearings on the contact.

Although the GCI radars provided an excellent two- dimensional picture, the hardest thing for a controller to interpret was height and an intercept was a three-dimensional problem. Dedicated height finding radars would be aimed at the target to give a height read out. These sensors were separate to the huge rotating air defence radars which gave a plan picture of the airspace. Small, elongated dishes, they nodded up and down generating tight 'pencil beams' which determined the actual height of a target. When full-blown day tactics sorties were practised in the Falklands, targets would change their height profile regularly and violently making it hard for crews and controllers alike to keep track of the three- dimensional picture. This was intentional to try to evade being intercepted. For safety reasons when operating live armed aircraft, the most important call of the whole intercept was 'switches safe', made at ten miles. At that point, both target and fighter would ensure that the armament safety interlocks were in place and that it was impossible to inadvertently fire an air-to-air missile. What the controller didn't realise was that my pilot on the occasion of my visit was the very one who had mistakenly fired a Sidewinder missile at a Jaguar bomber in Germany in 1981. On that occasion, the Sidewinder had destroyed the Jaguar which crashed in open fields, although thankfully, the pilot was unhurt. By then the trauma had passed and my pilot had a genuine sense of humour about an incident which had been a dire moment of his career.

Not only was the squadron affected by the transition to exercise flying as I described in the RAF Stanley chapter but there were occasional incidents at the air defence sites. A friend, who was a fighter controller at the time and later became a Tornado F3 navigator, told a story of one night when mayhem reigned briefly. In 1984, tensions were still high and the risk of rogue air attacks real. There were regular visits to the islands by the Combined Services Entertainment Team which provided shows for deployed personnel. The radar unit had been put on minimum manning to allow as many personnel as possible to see the show and only essential personnel were on shift. A Type 42 destroyer was at sea acting as the radar picket ship and was providing inputs to the recognised air picture. Midway through the show starring Bob Carolgees and Spit the Dog, events took a more serious turn. Controllers were suddenly pulled from the show and rushed back to their positions. The Rapier missile engagement zones had been activated and crews deployed with Blowpipe missiles to defend the site. The ship at sea was on high alert and the Quick Reaction Alert Phantoms from RAF Stanley had been scrambled and were vectoring west at high speed. Two fast, low-level tracks had been reported heading for the islands. As he took his position, my friend was mystified at the reports. He knew the radar coverage well and it was unlikely that tracks would be in that particular sector. The air raid warning sirens had already sounded in Stanley and the local people were making for cover fearing a rogue attack by Argentinian warplanes. Everyone was tense and QRA would be authorised to engage if contact was made. There were high value targets which were vulnerable to a pop up attack, not least of which were the radar sites themselves, so time was of the essence. The Phantom crews searched for the intruders but no contact was made and, eventually, tensions relaxed. The true facts were never established and far be it for the Junior Service to suggest that the weapons controllers from the Senior Service may have loaded a training scenario into their radar by accident! My friend, however, took some satisfaction in explaining to Commander British Forces Falkland Islands the following day why the incident may have been a 'figment of the imagination' rather than a true incursion.

One of the highlights of the day for the personnel in these remote locations was the visit by the Tornados after the sortie. Each mission included a 'Measles' exercise to provide targets for the operators of the Javelin high velocity missiles which were deployed on site to protect the installation. These MANPADS were deployed at the sites as 'back stop' protection against air attack but like any complex weapon system, training was vital. I think I can safely say that it was extremely unlikely that the missiles were broken out for every 'Measles' exercise. Despite that, the sound of fast jets passing through the overhead at low level during these exercises was not only a morale booster but a good reminder of why we were all there. At Alice, a 'Measles' pass was particularly dramatic. The rule to which the crews flew envisioned an imaginary 250-foot bubble around the aircraft and providing that the bubble did not encroach on the terrain or an obstruction, everything was legal. Being perched on a hill, the approach to the site was over the low-lying surrounding landscape and inlets and the Tornado would be silhouetted against this backdrop before pulling up for the 'attack'.

Invariably, the quickest way to egress and give the missile operator the hardest target to track was to roll inverted above the radar site before pulling hard back down towards the lee slope. Once back down in the valleys, a roll upright followed by a low level departure at high speed was, without doubt, a dramatic sight. In the case of the Tornado, there was an unmistakable indicator of the speed of the pass. The wings were at 25-degree sweep for a slow pass, 45 degrees for mid range speeds and fully swept for a high-speed pass meaning well over 500 knots. I have to admit that the 'Measles' exercises I saw during my brief stay were somewhat muted but it was only a week after I'd delivered my 'Boss's warning' about flying discipline after the 'Top Gun Moment' during the QRA 'siting board'. Somehow, a young technician suggesting that I should have seen the one last week may have meant the update on the rules had been timely, although I may have been the guilty party myself!

One of the more pleasant aspects of the visit was that the officers of 751 SU were holding a Dining In Night and I was lucky enough to be invited by the Chief Controller at Mount Alice to attend. In the UK, a Dining In Night was a formal event requiring all officers to turn out in No 5 Home Dress which was the formal Air Force dress uniform and the equivalent of civilian 'Black Tie'. A Dining In Night in the Falklands was worlds apart and camouflage greens were the dress code. Even so, it did not prevent the normal format from being followed. Pre-drinks were followed by polite conversation during the meal culminating in the Loyal Toast. At that point, mayhem normally ensued for the speeches, banter was mandatory and this occasion was no exception. A visiting fighter crew was cannon fodder! After-dinner drinks were memorable in that the locals had designed and built a makeshift cannon from old shell cases rescued from the battlefields. Primed with a dubious mildly explosive mixture and stuffed with a projectile made of rolled up 'bodge tape', the homemade device was aimed at a target from across the ante room. Naturally, inter unit rivalry was paramount and reputations were at stake as each shot was meticulously scored. Regrettably, the hospitality was of such a high standard that, not only did the

Looking Northeast from Mount Alice.

A sense of humour was vital to survive.

Right: The 'Air Terminal' at Mount Alice complete with a bus stop.

Below: A captured Argentinian artillery piece at Mount Alice.

1435 Flight crew not perform well, I have little recollection of the result. The one fact that was always guaranteed was the ability of the RAF chefs to produce the most amazing dinner menu, in the most austere conditions, to the highest standards. As always, the meal was outstanding. My sympathies were reserved for the duty staff who were completely sober during the proceedings. Essential tasks never stopped.

CHAPTER 11
The Islands True Inhabitants

The islanders are a sturdy bunch coping amazing well with the harsh climate. The majority are farmers and fishermen with a relatively austere lifestyle but fiercely loyal to the Crown. No one who has visited can ever doubt their desire to remain British and, on most of my visits to the settlements, I was reminded in no uncertain terms. The most recent Falkland Islands Government census in 2012 indicated a resident population of 2,841 of whom 59% consider themselves to be a 'Falkland Islander', 29% British, 9.8% St Helenian and 5.4% Chilean.

There was no one more famous than Sir Rex Hunt, topically, a former RAF Spitfire pilot turned career diplomat, who was Governor of the Islands during the period before and after the conflict. Although born in Redcar in North Yorkshire, he was considered to be an honorary islander after his pivotal role during the conflict. Originally installed to persuade the residents that a transition to Argentinian rule might be in their best interests, he was easily persuaded to the contrary and was accused by the Foreign Office of 'going native'. He was famous for meeting the Argentinian commander after the invasion wearing his full official regalia and insisting that he remove his forces from the islands. His response was to be forcibly expelled to Uruguay where he was unable to assist further during the conflict. Repatriated to London with his family, he sat out the war in the UK returning to Stanley shortly after the Liberation. Sir Rex was granted the Freedom of Stanley in 1985 and was Chairman of the Falkland Islands Association for many years but died on 25 November 2012.

Many of the islanders who suffered the indignities of the conflict are aging rapidly. Those younger than thirty years of age will have no memory of the stresses and disruptions to life during those brief months of occupation. More telling, they will have no recollection of the unspoilt nature of the islands before the arrival of thousands of troops; both invaders and liberators. It will be interesting to see how relationships mature in future. To have a base of 1,200 servicemen and women on short duration detachments in such a closed environment must exert enormous stresses on a small community. Unlike a rural county in the UK where service men and women integrate into the local area, detached personnel are a captive audience with little to occupy their time other than work. Personnel make the most of that occasional free time but can be prone to alcohol induced bravado or high jinks and, in a closed environment, can be difficult to control. Despite the obvious potential for friction, the locals are invariably tolerant. During my two tours of duty I met only genuinely kind people who would offer their last scrap of food and were eternally grateful for their liberty.

Once out in the settlements the scenes are reminiscent of the Scottish Isles, although the stone built crofts are substituted by slightly less substantial houses with tin roofs painted in bright colours. Wood and bricks are at a premium as a building material so the structures have a distinctive style unique to the islands. Life in the rural areas is a total contrast to that in the capital and the community spirit is strong.

There are still many traditional activities which make up island life and one of the claims to fame is that Port Stanley hosts the most southerly golf course in the world. Set just outside of the capital, the clubhouse is the antithesis of the elegant

Stanley Golf Course.

Racing at Stanley Racecourse.]

clubs in the south of England, although, probably, equally revered. Originally established in 1930, the club in its present form dates to 1980. Set back from a rough, albeit paved road, the clubhouse is little more than a Portakabin but it has all the trappings of any local club with its par 67 course. The golfing holes sport evocative names such as 'Shell Holes' and 'Hunt's Home'. The playing conditions certainly hark back to the roots of the game on the links courses of the Scottish Isles. I'm sure many a hardy Scots golfer would feel perfectly at home on the bleak and windswept fairways.

One of the major events of the year is the Race Meeting at Stanley Racecourse just outside the town between Victory Green and The Golf Course. Held during the summer, which falls around Christmas in the southern hemisphere, it brings the islanders together for a great social event. The racecourse offers only a flat course as the terrain is a little inhospitable for full jumps. Even so, it is a hugely popular event and adds to the colour of local life. The grandstand is painted a vivid pink and proudly sports the Islands' flag on its flagpole. With the cluster of race goers lining the rails you could easily be visiting a provincial racecourse in England. After watching a comprehensive race card, I confess to wondering where the horses appeared from as they are seen rarely during visits to the settlements. One significant difference was the cluster of military trucks which appeared complete with furniture borrowed for the day from one of the

A visit to QRA by the local
Boy Scouts.

Messes at MPA. Temporary 'enclosures' were set up complete with Pimms and
refreshments in a scene more reminiscent of a village fête than Ascot.

I was fortunate enough to be able to host a number of visits to RAF Mount
Pleasant, none more pleasurable than seeing the wide eyed faces of the local
Boy Scouts given a chance to get up close to a 1435 Flight Tornado sitting on
Quick Reaction Alert. The questions were typical of any young kid given the first
chance to touch a real fast jet but the use of the term 'our jets' by one young lad
said more than I could ever convey.

The true stars of the Falkland Islands are the numerous species of wildlife.
Although seeing the wildlife up close was one of the high points of a tour
in the region, high performance aircraft and nature, particularly birds, were
uncomfortable neighbours.

One of the main species of birds, and the one which appears on many of the
tourist badges sold on the islands is the Upland Goose which gave its name to
the main hotel in Port Stanley. Over 200,000 pairs are thought to breed on the
Islands. Like many birds, the male and female are quite different. Both about the
same height, about 45cm tall, the male is white but the female is a dowdy brown.
Living on grass and berries the airfield is a perfect feeding ground and they are a

constant worry to the bird control unit on the airfield at Mount Pleasant. Luckily they tend to nest in the longer grass laying their eggs in September so keeping the grass shorter around the operational areas is a good way to separate the 'warring factions'. Goslings appear late in the year and are ready to fly ten weeks after hatching. With up to eight goslings from each pair, early February, which is mid-summer in the South Atlantic, can be a busy time. Not only do they pose a threat to jet engines but the adult males can have quite vicious fights and can be a threat to themselves. Taxiing out for one sortie, we headed towards the runway threshold meeting two Upland geese which were wandering casually along the parallel taxiway. The noise of two approaching RB199 engines, apparently, was of no concern to them and they steadfastly held their ground with just a casual look towards us. Edging the jet closer had no effect and, unlike my car, the Tornado F3 is not fitted with a horn. Eventually a Mexican stand off ensued and the geese remained firmly in control of the centre ground in the middle of the taxiway. It was only by calling air traffic control to ask the bird control unit to assist were we able to use the taxiway for its intended purpose. Even then, it took some persuasion from the BCU before the pair ambled off into the grass.

The danger from birds was often evident. We returned after one training sortie, taxied in normally and shut down before returning to operations. As we signed in the aircraft, I was called down to the 'housey' where our No 2's aircraft had parked. There was no explanation just a, 'Boss, you need to see this'. Fearing the worst I made my way over to be greeted by a crowd clustered around the right wing leading edge.

Unbeknownst to him, our wingman had struck a bird on short finals and the remains were embedded in the airframe. As the aircrew had dismounted using the ladders on the left side of the aircraft, the carnage had been invisible to them but the gruesome sight of the head of a goose wedged in the leading edge slat was a timely reminder of the risks of a bird strike. Where the rest of its carcass had gone would remain a mystery. Had a bird of that size been ingested into an engine or, even worse, struck the canopy, the implications for flight safety were far more sinister. Luckily, no damage had been done to the airframe as major structural repairs could be problematic in the remote location. After a quick clean up, the aircraft was turned around and was back on the flying programme later in the day. Sadly, the same could not be said for the goose.

Wildlife colonies were marked on a chart produced by the Government and, apart from a chicken farm, were the only low flying restrictions. Penguins were dotted all around the islands but the four major breeds lived in distinctly different ways. By far the most widespread, the Gentoos, lived in small colonies normally on, or close to, the beach. Individual nests were grouped in a large circular scrape. Penguins in a colony seemed remarkable unfazed by their human visitors. The headquarters staff briefed us all on the dos and don'ts of viewing the wildlife and most of us were extremely careful to respect the rules and stayed alert to signs of distress. A long lens helped capture the stunning detail but, quite often, it was apparent that the penguins had not listened to the briefing. Their inquisitive nature meant that the more confident birds would approach human visitors to view the strange intruders at closer quarters offering unique photo opportunities. The islanders clearly had not had the brief as they would approach the birds as if meeting old friends.

One of the rather less politically correct stories was of one Phantom crew which in the early days had been tasked to fly a visual combat air patrol just off the northern coastline. Flown in a figure-of-8, the visual pattern only a minute in length, was much shorter than a radar CAP and remained in sight of an observer on the ground. The crew noticed that their presence was of great interest to the penguin colony which was tracking their progress quite closely. Even from the confines of a fast jet cockpit you could tell when the penguins were watching because of their colouring. With bright white breast feathers if they were looking at you, the colony showed bright white. Turn their backs and you would see the darker plumage. The crew noticed that as they turned towards the colony, the penguins tracked their progress as the Phantom flew along the coastline. As the exercise was quiet, they began, as aircrew tend to do, to experiment to fill the time. By easing in towards the colony, the movement of the penguins became more exaggerated. Eventually, they passed almost overhead causing the penguins, in unison, to topple onto their backs.

The stars of the penguin world are the King penguins which live predominantly on a small peninsular at the extreme north eastern corner of East Falkland at Volunteer Point, although there is another colony on Saunders Island. The only way to visit is by taking a long off-road trek by Land Rover across the rugged terrain; undoubtedly one of the highlights of a tour of duty. With a life expectancy of thirty years, there are two million pairs in the world and around 400 breeding pairs in the Falkland Islands. The King is the most striking as well as the largest of the species on the islands. Standing about four feet tall it is the vivid yellows and oranges around its neck which make it stand out from the crowd. A single egg is incubated on the feet of both parents who take turns to keep it warm until the chick is born. Emerging as a strange grey bundle of feathers it is perhaps a classic example of a youngster which eventually grows into its looks. As the grey feathers moult, the 'Ugly Duckling' transforms leaving the sleek white feathers of the adult visible below.

The King penguins were less formal than the Gentoos and their nesting habits seemed less social. Rumour had it that the reason the Kings migrated north was a legacy of the war. Many years ago, a colony was thriving in the Stanley area but the Argentinians sowed minefields around the coastline in an effort to protect against attack from the task force. A number of sheep were killed when they strayed into mine fields as they were heavy enough to detonate the pressure plate triggers. The smaller penguins seemed immune but the Kings seemed to be just large enough to be vulnerable. How true this fact is will only be known to the locals and, certainly, by the time I arrived on the islands, sighting a King penguin around Stanley was rare. I finally visited the King penguin colony on my second detachment. Located on the barren north-eastern coastline of East Falkland it was a long, hard drive across the rugged countryside and a convoy of vehicles was accompanied by a local guide who was familiar with the terrain. Even in a Land Rover, the journey took a couple of hours and proved how versatile the Land Rover could be as a military vehicle. Its ability to cope with an apparently vertical incline was truly impressive. The Kings seemed to group in smaller communities some way back from the beach yet made regular trips to the sea. Like all penguins the transition from land to sea was dramatic. The long trek to the shore took time but the switch from the ungainly Charlie Chaplin style gait to the effortless agility as they launched into the surf was striking. They became different animals. Even though they quickly dropped from sight under the water, their occasional appearance as they broke the surface in graceful arcs, was a treat. Their return to land was often equally ungainly as they were carried on a wave through the breaking surf and deposited unceremoniously on their bellies on the sand. It was fascinating to watch the antics of a colony and I could only guess at the hierarchy. One on occasion, a pair of Kings strutted quite purposefully towards an, apparently, dominant male. After a show of preening and much animated penguin chatter, one of the pair struck the male quite firmly around the head. He offered a return blow before all three decided that discretion may be a wiser option and backed away from a showdown.

The third breed, the Magellan penguins are in decline and are considered to be a threatened species. For protection and shelter, they live in burrows in the tussock grass and use the same burrow each year. Similar in size to the Gentoos, standing about a foot tall, they have a much shorter life than the Kings living for only five years. They lay two eggs in the burrow and the parent birds keep close watch during incubation. Magellans were the most strident when approached, particularly near their burrows and it was readily apparent when to back off so as not to disturb them. A distressed Magellan makes a rhythmic circular rocking motion with its head, often blocking the entrance to its burrow. Given their living habits it was almost impossible to avoid them completely and quite often you would come across a burrow as you walked through the scrubland. Some showed indifference but some were noticeably nervous presumably when the chicks were hatching.

The final major breed was the Rockhopper which was only found in a few locations one of which was on Sea Lion Island. A visit to the remote island was the easiest way to see these birds in their natural environment but it was only accessible by helicopter. It took some negotiating to visit the island as it was a little off the normal route so it was only possible when a helicopter was going to particular sites. The smallest of the four indigenous species, it is true to its name as it lives in the rocky outcrops along the coastline. The nests were dotted among the rocks and watching the little birds offered hours of fun as they jumped around amongst the outcrops and into the sea. The final breed, the Macaroni penguin was less easily spotted and lived among the Rockhopper colonies.

With the advent of the LAN Chile flight and the proliferation of cruises in the South Atlantic, tourists had begun to appear by 1994. One such visit demonstrated, graphically, the gulf between the visitors and the islanders. An American with her small party, visiting the islands for the first time, had been dropped on Saunders Island to walk the coastline. As she passed the settlement she asked for directions to the albatross colony that thrived on the north facing cliffs above the ocean. Our host had pointed along the track, which was the only route to the nesting places, and the tourists set off. Some hours passed and she was becoming worried that the party had not been seen and considered sending out a search party. The tourists eventually returned and she asked if they had enjoyed seeing the albatross. The tourist seemed genuinely disappointed and said that they hadn't been able to find them. Confused, the visitor was quizzed further, finally admitting that all she'd been able to find were some big seagulls. The Falkland Island seagulls apparently had 6-foot wingspans!

Another of the undoubted highlights was a visit to the elephant seal colony on Sea Lion Island. The animals were largely unaffected by human contact as Sea Lion Island is remote and uninhabited lying at the southern extremity of Lafonia. A helicopter was tasked to visit one of the southern drop-off points and, with a little negotiation, we persuaded the pilot to drop us off at the helicopter landing site which lies close to the beach. Careful to confirm the pickup time – there is no way off the island by foot – we set off towards the noise of the surf. It immediately provided one of the scariest moments of my detachment, making turning upside down at 250 feet above the ground in a fast jet seem tame in comparison. The main seal colonies lived on the beaches where they spent hours basking in the weak sun. As we threaded our way through the network of passageways in the shoulder-high scrub grass we turned a corner coming face-to-face with a twelve-foot long elephant seal. I'm not sure who was most surprised but the heavy and, undoubtedly, disgruntled snort from the startled animal convinced both my pilot and myself to retreat as swiftly as possible. Elephant seals can move remarkably fast and it was a relief to find that our unceremonious

The simple memorial to those who were lost
aboard HMS *Sheffield*. It sits on Sea Lion Island
facing out to sea close to where she was hit.

retreat was enough to satisfy the seal that it could continue its morning snooze
unmolested. An alternative route took us to the beautiful sandy beaches where
the massive elephant seals shared the sand with their smaller cousins. The
elephant seal is the largest of the seal species reaching a massive six metres in
length and weighing over three tons. The distinctive feature of adult males is the
inflatable nose giving it its name. The adult bulls arrive in September followed
by the cows and form groups before the pups are born in October. In a strange
cycle, the pup is fed for only twenty-three days during which time mating occurs.
After the pup is weaned the mother leaves and they fend for themselves.

Also present on the island are the Southern Sea Lions which are also in decline
in the Falklands. The total number is thought to be about 3,000 and the Falkland
Islands are an important breeding ground. Eating mostly octopus and squid, only
rogue bulls take penguins.

The list could go on as the region is a haven for seabirds which thrive around
the coastline. The striking fact when watching the wonders of nature is that
reminders of the conflict were never far away. After a day watching Rockhoppers,
I was brought back to reality by finding the memorial to HMS *Sheffield* which
was lost at sea some miles south of Sea Lion Island. It stands as a stark reminder
that military operations are never conducted without sacrifice.

CHAPTER 12
Today

Since XV469 landed at RAF Stanley on 17 October 1982, first 29 (F) Squadron and then 23 (F) Squadron guarded the Falkland Islands from the airstrip outside the capital. The Phantoms moved to RAF Mount Pleasant on 1 May 1986 into their new dispersal until the squadron was downsized. At that time, 1435 Flight reformed in November 1988 operating the Phantom at RAF Mount Pleasant until June 1992 when the Tornado F3 assumed the role, eventually being replaced by the Typhoon in September 2009. The 23 Squadron badge transferred to the E3D Sentry Training Flight at RAF Waddington. Although the routine strength at MPA is, typically, 700 to 1000 RAF personnel, literally tens of thousands have supported operations at some time over the last thirty years.

There were many changes of equipment over the years and, in addition to the fighters, the most significant was the replacement of the two C130K tankers with a single VC10 in 1996 retaining a single C130 for maritime patrol and long range SAR. The rapidly modified Hercules held the tanking role for fourteen years proving to be one of the most cost effective procurement programmes ever. A further change is the VC10 retirement in 2013 replaced by the Airbus A330 Voyager tanker. The helicopter types have remained the same but the numbers have varied and the contract for inter island logistics is re-let every so often. All Rapiers in the Armed Forces are now operated by The Army after the RAF Regiment relinquished the role under one of the many defence reviews.

The most significant change for air defence was the deployment of Typhoon. The arrival, in reality, did little to affect the balance of forces as, by then, the Tornado F3 was a hugely capable aircraft, albeit with an undeservedly poor reputation. The re-equipment of the Argentinian Air Force with the A4AR in the mid 90s was an escalation which the UK made little of at the time, despite the fact that it was a much more capable aircraft than its predecessor. The same cannot be said of Argentina when Typhoon arrived on the islands. There was much political rhetoric which was repeated with the deployment of HMS

Dauntless in 2012. The version of the Tornado which relinquished its duties in 2009 was a quantum improvement over the version I first flew in 1985 and even the upgraded version I flew in 1994. It would have been more than a match for an A4 being equipped with the Advanced Medium Range Air-to-air missile (AMRAAM) and the Advanced Short Range Air-to-air missile (ASRAAM), the Joint Tactical Distribution System (JTIDS) which gave a superb air picture and a chaff and flare defensive system. The Typhoon weapons system is an enormous improvement but not such a massive leap ahead in pure capability, although it is far easier to operate and the Typhoon is simply a much more capable airframe in air combat. Designed as a multinational collaboration between the UK, Germany, Italy and Spain, it was designed from the outset in the air-to-air role. The UK always had a need for a multi role aircraft and the ground attack capability was included as a secondary role even though it was not a design driver. The progress in the man-machine interface meant that a single pilot was able to cope with the cockpit workload which, hitherto, had needed two people. Despite being equipped with radar, a forward looking infra-red sensor, a defensive aids system or DASS, and a multi function information distribution system or MIDS, the level of integration means that the pilot is fed with a situation awareness display from all the sensors combined. Built around three multi function displays in the cockpit, the pilot can display a 'God's eye' view of the battle space, a radar display in both elevation or plan, the defensive systems display or aircraft systems status in any combination he or she chooses.

The major step forward is the provision of a wide angle head up display, or HUD, integrated with a helmet mounted sight. The aircraft sensors display the position of the targets in the HUD and the pilot can designate his selected target using controls on the control column and throttles. Hands-on-throttle-and-stick, or HOTAS as this is known, means that the pilot does not spend any more time than is absolutely necessary looking inside the cockpit. He or she can spend all the effort keeping track of their own formation members and the 'bogies'. Other systems identify the opponent electronically in a far more effective way than in the past. Crucially, the weapons are much improved over past fighters. The long range AMRAAM which eventually equipped the Tornado F3, replaces the semi-active Skyflash of previous generations. This is an active missile which means that, although it receives mid-course guidance from the host Typhoon, it is 'fire and forget'. In other words, once launched, the pilot does not have to track the target all the way to impact leaving much more tactical freedom. Similarly, ASRAAM replaces the older Sidewinder generation giving a much improved short range combat capability. ASRAAM is a high-speed missile, capable of reaching speeds greater than Mach 3 and is highly manoeuvrable. This increases the range over its predecessors yet retains the all aspect performance. Modern technology, known as 'imaging', is used in the seeker head which makes the missile better able to track and discriminate targets. Rather than sensing a 'hot spot' like older seekers, it senses a picture of the overall heat signature of its target. It is also fitted with comprehensive electronic counter-countermeasures to protect against infra-red decoys which combined with the imaging technology makes it hard to defeat electronically. Designated by the helmet mounted sight it can be launched almost anywhere within the pilots field of view. After much political interference a gun was finally fitted after it was found that it would be more expensive to remove the gun from the design than it was to fit it.

The ultimate weapon will be Meteor which is a European missile giving an even longer range and moving into ramjet technology for propulsion. Meteor was always the weapon of choice but it was not available in the timescales which drove the Eurofighter project. Ironically, with Sweden likely to be the lead customer, it will eventually re-equip the aircraft of the Eurofighter consortium much later starting in 2015, politics and finance permitting. An active radar guided, beyond-visual-range, air-to-air missile being developed by MBDA, it will give a much improved multi-shot capability at much greater range than AMRAAM in an electronic countermeasures environment. Crucially, it will not be constrained by any American export restrictions which limit the marketability of Typhoon. An airframe is useless without the missile it carries.

Despite old loyalties, having only a single pilot saves weight and is more efficient in terms of the numbers of expensive aircrew needed on a squadron. The days when electronics were user-intensive are fading so a single operator can now do the job that needed both a pilot and a navigator in the past. Integrated displays and controls and modern processed data flow means it is easy to access essential tactical data which is presented in an integrated and easily assimilated way. This is in no way meant to decry the skills which a Typhoon pilot of the future will need.

Introducing a new fighter into service is always a complex affair and Typhoon was no different to its predecessors. The baseline capability was already more mature than, for example, the Tornado F2 at the equivalent stage when it finally entered service in 2005/2006, yet the design was late, over cost and many systems still do not meet their specification. Despite frustrations over our flawed procurement system, the pilots are genuinely excited about the aerodynamic performance of Typhoon. It is a match for any of the air superiority fighters deployed around the world, with the exception perhaps of the hugely more expensive US F22 stealth fighter. It was designed under a new procurement method known as a 'top down' design whereby the top level functions which were needed were identified at the outset. These requirements fed down to the individual 'black boxes' so that individual modules complete multiple operational tasks. This means that the radar computer can also control the defensive aids functions and so on. The design was driven by the tasks the aircraft had to complete not driven by what the airframe could do. That said, packaging such a complex series of systems in a weight limited airframe was a challenge for the designers.

The Typhoon is undoubtedly a match for anything Argentina could deploy against it. Four aircraft on the islands is not the ideal number and any commander would want more. That said, it is a sound compromise and the numbers would be reinforced rapidly in the event of a significant rise in military tensions. Unlike its predecessor, the secondary ground attack capability gives flexibility and would make it far easier to support a dual role squadron than two dedicated types which would have been needed in the past. The main limitation at present is that Typhoon cannot carry the broad range of ground attack weapons as its role specific counterpart the Tornado GR4.

The Typhoon detachment has already made the news when a formation diverted to Punta Arenas in Chile after fog prevented them landing back on the islands. Reported in the South American press, after negotiating with Commodoro Rivadavia control in Argentina, the VC10 and two Typhoons transited across the narrow straights which border Argentina landing at the Chilean Air Force at Chacabunco where they were hosted by the 4th Air Brigade overnight. They returned the following day having set an interesting precedent. I can only imagine the discussions with London which my successor as OC1435 Flight would have enjoyed during their absence.

I touched on the most brutal legacy of war namely the minefields which blighted the landscape after the war. It is thought that the Argentinians laid as many as 20,000 mines in 120 separate minefields during the conflict. Ironically, it was the UK Government's decision to sign the Ottawa Convention in 1998, which required Nations to remove all landmines on their sovereign territory which was the catalyst for change, although progress was slow. With the establishment of The Falkland Island Demining Programme Office (FIDPO) in Stanley in October 2009, a major step forward was taken. A British company was awarded the contract to rid the island of the scars. The team used metal detectors to locate the unexploded ordnance which was then unearthed using simple tools more akin to gardening than a high tech clearance operation. Once exposed and identified, an explosive charge was placed alongside and each mine was destroyed *in situ*. Reading a narrative of the operation struck a chord as the team leader described the typical frustrations associated with technical operations 'Down South', namely lack of key essentials and his high tech equipment breaking when least expected. Nearly 200 Spanish anti-personnel mines, two BL 755 bomblets and a rifle grenade were cleared from Sapper Hill near Stanley. Surf Bay east of Stanley, which had been an area where the Argentinians had expected a British landing, yielded a staggering 900 Italian anti-vehicle and anti-personnel mines and a further five grenades. It transpired that the records for the minefields close to the capital, contrary to earlier military assessments, were good. It was only as the Argentinian commanders realised that the attack would come from the west that the placement of mines outside the urban boundaries became more haphazard and less well recorded.

After making the capital safe, the team moved on to Goose Green and Fox Bay. It had been hoped to finally complete the clearance in 2010 but work was still going on in mid 2012. Over the years of the operation, approaching two thousand mines were recovered and destroyed by disposal experts making large areas of the islands useable again. The detritus which was destroyed, however, proved that caution had, indeed, been merited. Not surprisingly, the deminers were popular with the islanders and were hugely respected for the work they did.

Politics is a minefield so best avoided in a book concerning military matters. There has been much speculation over the years as to Argentina's future intent. It seems likely that all ideas of a military takeover have now gone replaced by a political campaign backed up by sanctions. It seems ironic that Argentina still presses a claim citing colonialism as the reason for them losing the islands yet the British Government is firm in its view that the islanders must have the right to self determination. The key question is whether the islanders wish to become Argentinian nationals and the referendum in Spring 2013 has registered their view. My litmus test has always been how I have perceived their traits and customs in my numerous contacts with them. Throughout, I felt as though I was talking to a fellow Briton rather than a displaced Argentinian. I was struck by their fierce loyalty to the Crown, sometimes feeling embarrassed at my own failure to match their true patriotism. A good way to answer the question might be to look at the actions of the Military Governor immediately after the occupation in 1982. Insulting Argentinian soldiers was frowned upon, curfews were instituted, driving on the right introduced and he initiated plans to convert the school curriculum into Spanish. As a sweetener, he planned to distribute video recorders to a population who had no TV station and few TV sets. This total lack of awareness of the islanders' needs and values was telling.

The intervention in 2012 by, presumably well-intentioned outsiders and celebrities, seemed designed only to grab headlines. One actor thinks Britain is being 'colonialist, ludicrous and archaic' about the Falkland Islands, and suggests that the islanders should accept some sort of sovereignty sharing agreement with Argentina. His speech was delivered in Buenos Aires to a Hispanic audience without reference or discussion with the real residents. It would be interesting to canvass his views if a similar proposal was made to repatriate California or Texas to Mexico. Presumably the few remaining 'Texicans' would be consulted.

The cynic would say that the discovery of oil in the territorial waters and the mineral rights in Antarctica conferred by the islands may be a factor. Whatever the motivation, significant oil deposits would change the way of life beyond recognition. It would give the islanders a much more powerful voice on the international stage by virtue of income but perhaps make life a little more unstable. I just hope it doesn't change them as a people and that they remain the same genuine characters I met over the years. Whichever way the politics develops it seems certain that the islanders will have the say over any future course.

The military presence will continue for the foreseeable future. Contingency plans are regularly reviewed and the possibility of a series of exercises designed to show commitment to the defence of the islands will undoubtedly follow if the political rhetoric continues. The Royal Navy destroyer remains on station in the South Atlantic, alongside the fisheries patrol ship HMS *Clyde*, a fleet tanker and the ice patrol ship HMS *Protector*. The resident infantry company could be reinforced to full Company strength or more if needed and the four Typhoons could easily be bolstered by returning 1435 Flight to Squadron strength. Analysts watch Argentinian moves carefully and, undoubtedly, certain triggers are set which would guarantee a reinforcement if appropriate. Whilst a repeat of the 1982 invasion seems unlikely, Argentinian stunts cannot be discounted as they seek to justify their sovereignty claim.

From a personal perspective, it was sad news to hear that XV409, the Phantom which had acted as gate guardian outside the Air Terminal at RAF Mount Pleasant, had been broken up. The aircraft was the last of the 1435 Flight airframes which defended the airspace for so many years. The MOD decided that the years sitting at the mercy of the elements had resulted in serious deterioration of the airframe to such an extent that it could not be maintained. Happily the cockpit was saved and will be displayed in a museum on the island as a legacy of the years the aircraft defended the airspace.

For me I had a very personal and pleasant postscript to my duties on the islands. The Commander British Forces Falkland Islands during my final detachment was Major-General Sir Iain Mackay-Dick who led the landing by the Scots Guards at Fitzroy during the war. I had also formed a great working relationship with Sir Alan Massey, then Commander of HMS *Newcastle* and eventually The Second Sea Lord. During my second tour of duty in the Ministry of Defence I received a 'phone call inviting me to a working lunch with the General, who was by then the General Officer Commanding, The Household Division and General Officer Commanding the London District. It gave me a huge insight into the workings of the ceremonial organisation in London and the opportunity to catch up. The invitation was extended to a small group of us who had commanded the individual units under the General's command. Little did I realise that the General's office was on Horse Guards directly above the often-pictured archway with a window which overlooked the famous parade ground. The meeting was slightly surreal as we gazed in awe at the huge portrait of one of Sir Iain's predecessors which hung on the wall; a certain Lord Wellington! The General still used the same desk as his illustrious predecessor so many years before. That memory was to be my last true, albeit tenuous link with the islands as I moved into new military fields shortly afterwards. I can safely say, however, that the Falkland Islands occupies a special place in my affections and is probably one of the highlights of my career which still causes me to reminisce despite the passage of time; or perhaps because of the passage of time.

The defining quote of the campaign is worth repeating:

> *Best pleased to inform Her Majesty that the Union Jack once again flies over Stanley. God Save The Queen.*
> *Major General Jeremy Moore on 14 June 1982*

I will leave the penultimate word to our former Prime Minister Margaret Thatcher, who was so instrumental in returning the islands to the people:

> *The people of the Falkland Islands, like the people of the United Kingdom, are an island race. They are few in number but they have the right to live in peace, to choose their own way of life and to determine their own allegiance. Their way of life is British; their allegiance is to the Crown. It is the wish of the British people and the duty of Her Majesty's Government to do everything that we can to uphold that right.*
> *Margaret Thatcher on 3 April 1982*

Ironically, the islanders had the final say when they answered the question set in a referendum, delivering their verdict on 12 March 2013. In the preamble the islanders were given some facts.

> The current political status of the Falkland Islands is that they are an Overseas Territory of the United Kingdom. The Islands are internally self-governing, with the United Kingdom being responsible for matters including defence and foreign affairs. Under the Falkland Islands Constitution the people of the Falkland Islands have the right to self-determination, which they can exercise at any time. Given that Argentina is calling for negotiations over the sovereignty of the Falkland Islands, this referendum is being undertaken to consult the people regarding their views on the political status of the

Falkland Islands. Should the majority of votes cast be against the current status, the Falkland Islands Government will undertake necessary consultation and preparatory work in order to conduct a further referendum on alternative options.

The question asked simply:

Do you wish the Falkland Islands to retain their current political status as an Overseas Territory of the United Kingdom? YES or NO?

By now their decision is known internationally and it was a resounding 'Yes'. In total, 1,517 votes were cast and only three voters answered 'No'. The turnout was a massive 90% from the 1,672 islanders who were eligible to vote. Such staggering voting figures would be the envy of most British politicians if carried over to a British election. It is also a statistic which the Argentinian Government would do well to heed as nations which have tried to drive out an ethnic population against their will have incurred the displeasure of the international community many times in the recent past. I can only reflect that the quest for territory should never outweigh the rights of a population to determine its own future. Who knows how future Falkland Islanders will feel but, for now, their wishes have been made clear and, given their grit and determination, undoubtedly, they will ride out any obstacles thrown in their way.

'Desire the Right'